# Labour and Living Standards in Pre-Colonial West Africa



Sub-Saharan Africa is presently the poorest region in the world, but has this always been the case? This book explores this question through the study of the material living standards of the population in pre-colonial West Africa, focusing on the Gold Coast.

*Labour and Living Standards in Pre-Colonial West Africa* employs a variety of sources, ranging from travel accounts to economic accounts of European companies established in the region. From these sources, this book gathers evidence on the conditions that common Africans worked under and the economic living standards that could be achieved by the money earned from their labour. Using records from the English Royal African Company, alongside contemporary published accounts, Rönnbäck is able to reconstruct the material wealth and living standards of the population at a time when the Atlantic slave trade brought money and men into the area. He explores the racial bias that permeated the colonists' accounts and how the 'lazy African' stereotype was used to justify slavery.

This volume will enrich the understanding of long-term West African economic development and the issues that still exist today. It is suitable for those who study development economics, economic history and African history.

**Klas Rönnbäck** is an Associate Professor of Economic History at the University of Gothenburg, Sweden.

**Perspectives in Economic and Social History**
Series Editors: Andrew August
Jari Eloranta

*For a complete list of titles in this series, please visit www.routledge.com*

**Titles in this series**

1 **Migrants and Urban Change**
Newcomers to Antwerp, 1760–1860
*Anne Winter*

2 **Female Entrepreneurs in Nineteenth-Century Russia**
*Galina Ulianova*

3 **Barriers to Competition**
The evolution of the debate
*Ana Rosado Cubero*

4 **Rural Unwed Mothers**
An American experience, 1870–1950
*Mazie Hough*

5 **English Catholics and the Education of the Poor, 1847–1902**
*Eric G. Tenbus*

6 **The World of Carolus Clusius**
Natural history in the making, 1550–1610
*Florike Egmond*

7 **The Determinants of Entrepreneurship**
Leadership, culture, institutions
*José L. García-Ruiz and Pier Angelo Toninelli (eds)*

8 **London Clerical Workers, 1880–1914**
Development of the labour market
*Michael Heller*

9 **The Decline of Jute**
Managing industrial change
*Jim Tomlinson, Carlo Morelli and Valerie Wright*

10 **Mining and the state in Brazilian development**
*Gail D. Triner*

11 **Global Trade and Commercial Networks**
Eighteenth-century diamond merchants
*Tijl Vanneste*

12 **The Clothing Trade in Provincial England, 1800–1850**
*Alison Toplis*

13 **Sex in Japan's Globalization, 1870–1930**
Prostitutes, emigration and nation building
*Bill Mihalopoulos*

14 **Financing India's Imperial Railways, 1875–1914**
*Stuart Sweeney*

**15 Energy, Trade and Finance in Asia**
A political and economic analysis
*Justin Dargin and Tai Wei Lim*

**16 Violence and Racism in Football**
Politics and cultural conflict in British society, 1968–1998
*Brett Bebber*

**17 The Economies of Latin America**
New cliometric data
*César Yáñez and Albert Carreras (eds)*

**18 Meat, Commerce and the City**
The London food market, 1800–1855
*Robyn S. Metcalfe*

**19 Merchant Colonies in the Early Modern Period**
*Victor N. Zakharov, Gelina Harlaftis and Olga Katsiardi-Hering (eds)*

**20 Markets and Growth in Early Modern Europe**
*Victoria N. Bateman*

**21 Welfare and Old Age in Europe and North America**
The development of social insurance
*Bernard Harris (ed.)*

**22 Female Economic Strategies in the Modern World**
*Beatrice Moring (ed.)*

**23 Crime and Community in Reformation Scotland**
Negotiating power in a burgh society
*J. R. D. Falconer*

**24 Policing Prostitution, 1856–1886**
Deviance, surveillance and morality
*Catherine Lee*

**25 Narratives of Drunkenness**
Belgium, 1830–1914
*An Vleugels*

**26 Respectability and the London Poor, 1780–1870**
The value of virtue
*Lynn MacKay*

**27 Residential Institutions in Britain, 1725–1970**
Inmates and environments
*Jane Hamlett, Lesley Hoskins and Rebecca Preston (eds)*

**28 Conflict, Commerce and Franco-Scottish Relations, 1560–1713**
*Siobhan Talbott*

**29 Drink in the Eighteenth and Nineteenth Centuries**
*Susanne Schmid and Barbara Schmidt-Haberkamp (eds)*

**30 Merchants and Profit in the Age of Commerce, 1680–1830**
*Pierre Gervais, Yannick Lemarchand and Dominique Margairaz (eds)*

**31 Jewish Immigrants in London, 1880–1939**
*Susan L. Tananbaum*

**32 Commercial Networks and European Cities, 1400–1800**
*Andrea Caracausi and Christof Jeggle (eds)*

**33 A Global Conceptual History of Asia, 1860–1940**
*Hagen Schulz-Forberg (ed.)*

34 **Consuls and the Institutions of Global Capitalism, 1783–1914**
*Ferry de Goey*

35 **Merchant Communities in Asia, 1600–1980**
*Lin Yu-ju and Madeleine Zelin*

36 **Insanity and the Lunatic Asylum in the Nineteenth Century**
*Thomas Knowles and Serena Trowbridge (eds)*

37 **Philanthropy and the Funding of the Church of England, 1856–1914**
*Sarah Flew*

38 **Merchants and Trading in the Sixteenth Century**
The Golden Age of Antwerp
*Jeroen Puttevils*

39 **Early Modern Trading Networks in Europe**
Cooperation and the Case of Simon Ruiz
*Ana Sofia Ribeiro*

40 **Prostitution and Social Control in Eighteenth-Century Ports**
*Marion Pluskota*

41 **Labour and Living Standards in Pre-Colonial West Africa**
The Case of the Gold Coast
*Klas Rönnbäck*

**Forthcoming titles**

**Development Economics in the Twenty-First Century**
*Davide Gualerzi and Claudia Sunna (eds)*

**Sanitation in Urban Britain, 1560–1700**
*Leona Jayne Skelton*

**A History of Drink and the English, 1500–2000**
*Paul Jennings*

**Franco Modigliani and Keynesian Economics**
Theory, facts and policy
*Antonella Rancan*

**Rural–Urban Relationships in the Nineteenth Century**
Uneasy neighbours?
*Mary Hammond and Barry Sloan (eds)*

**Merchants and Trade Networks in the Atlantic and the Mediterranean, 1550–1800**
Connectors of commercial maritime systems
*Manuel Herrero Sánchez and Klemens Kaps (eds)*

**Workers, Unions and Payment in Kind**
The fight for real wages in Britain, 1820–1986
*Christopher Frank*

# Labour and Living Standards in Pre-Colonial West Africa

## The case of the Gold Coast

**Klas Rönnbäck**

Routledge
Taylor & Francis Group
LONDON AND NEW YORK

First published 2016 by Routledge

2 Park Square, Milton Park, Abingdon, Oxfordshire OX14 4RN
52 Vanderbilt Avenue, New York, NY 10017

*Routledge is an imprint of the Taylor & Francis Group, an informa business*

First issued in paperback 2020



*British Library Cataloguing in Publication Data*
A catalogue record for this book is available from the British Library

*Library of Congress Cataloging in Publication Data*
A catalog record for this book has been requested

ISBN: 978-1-84893-578-5 (hbk)
ISBN: 978-0-367-66859-4 (pbk)

Typeset in Times New Roman
by Florence Production Ltd, Stoodleigh, Devon, UK

# Contents

# Figures

# Tables

# Graphs

# Acknowledgements

This book would not have been possible without the invaluable work of many archivists and librarians. I would in particular like to thank the staff at the British National Archives in Kew, England, as well as the staff at the university library at the University of Gothenburg, Sweden.

Many of my colleagues at the University of Gothenburg have been very supportive and provided constructive comments in the process of writing this book. A collective 'thank you' to all my colleagues who have provided thoughts and ideas for this project. A particular thank you to Stefan Öberg for his extremely generous help with everything related to the processing of quantitative data and for being a great support in general as well as being a true friend. I'm also especially grateful to my colleagues Malin Nilsson and Lovisa Broström, for in the dialogue with them, I've constantly been forced to rethink, revise and improve what I've been doing myself.

The research underlying this book has been presented in a number of different international conferences and workshops. The author would like to thank the participants in these conferences for many constructive comments on how to improve the research. The author would in particular like to thank Holger Weiss, Robin Law, Gareth Austin, Anthony G. Hopkins, Adam Jones, Robert Allen, Paul Lovejoy, Rina Cáceres Gómez, Jaime Reis, Deirdre McCloskey, James Fenske, Debin Ma, Pim de Zwart and Angus Dalrymple-Smith for many encouraging and constructive comments on the various aspects of the research presented at these conferences as well as for helping out with everything from references to previous research to useful secondary sources of data.

The research has been supported economically by a generous grant from Jan Wallanders and Tom Hedelius Stiftelse in Sweden, for which I am very grateful.

I would also like to thank my editors at Pickering & Chatto and Routledge for very constructive cooperation in publishing this book.

The greatest thank you is however to Irene Elmerot, for help with assembling parts of the data underlying the book, for help with translating text from languages I knew nothing or all too little of, for help with text-editing the final manuscript, and last – but certainly not least – for the enormous mental support to finalize this project: mɛ ku drɔ lɛ ŋu wo, ne ku drɔ lɛ ŋu nyɛ.

# Acknowledgements

# Abbreviations

| | |
|---|---|
| ECCO | Eighteenth Century Collections Online |
| EEBO | Early English Books Online |
| GCPLD | Gold Coast Pre-Colonial Labour Database |
| GCPPD | Gold Coast Pre-Colonial Price Database |
| HISCLASS | Historical International Social Class Scheme |
| HISCO | Historical International Standard Classifications of Occupations |
| MOMW | The Making of the Modern World Database |
| RAC | Royal African Company |
| TSTD | Trans-Atlantic Slave Trade Database |

# 1 Introduction

## Theory and method

### Historical living standards in global comparison

Why are some nations rich, while others are poor? Why are some people in a country rich, while others are poor? Estimating and explaining historical living standards is doubtless one of the key issues in economic history. There have, therefore, been many attempts at studying historical living standards in various countries, using a number of different methods and source materials. One problem has, for a long time, been to compare living standards between countries. Studies using qualitative sources and methods might in many cases be too vague to allow for any more detailed comparison with studies from other countries. Studies using quantitative sources and methods might, on the other hand, not always be possible to replicate in other countries because of a lack of similar primary sources. This is, not least, a central problem as soon as one wants to study living standards in countries outside Europe.

The issue of historical living standards has received renewed attention in recent years, not least because of the work of Robert Allen, who has pioneered a method called 'welfare ratios' or 'subsistence ratios' that allows for comparing historical living standards in different countries quantitatively, using data quite frequently existing in historical sources. This is a method that will be discussed in some detail later in this book (Chapter 3). A number of studies have appeared, studying the historical living standards of the population in various countries around the world using Allen's method, including a number of countries in early modern Europe (for example England, the Netherlands, Spain, France, Italy, Germany, Austria, Poland, Sweden and Denmark);[1] in Asia (India, China, Japan and Sri Lanka);[2] and the Americas (Mexico, Colombia, Bolivia, and several cities in what later became the United States).[3] In these attempts at writing the global comparative economic history of the living standards of the population, the African continent has, however, largely been left out.

### The neo-institutionalist interpretation of African development

It is not hard to find leading scholars in the field of African history arguing that historically, Africa, in general, was very poor.[4] Estimating the living standards in a country is one thing, explaining them is another. If it is true that Africans were comparatively poor historically, why is that? Has Africa been poor for as long as it is possible to tell, or was modern-day poverty caused by some historical factors? In recent years, leading scholars such as Gareth Austin have argued that a neo-institutionalist theoretical approach is necessary in order to understand African economic history.[5] Institutions, it is also argued, have a very close relationship with various measures of socio-economic development.[6] For anybody interested in living standards and economic development in Africa, the impact of various institutions ought, therefore, to be a key concern.

In liberal economic theory, the lack of economic development is primarily a matter of lagging behind economic leaders, that is, the 'developed' or industrialized, capitalist countries. The neo-institutionalist school was initially pioneered by scholars of Western European economic history, such as Douglass North. North's aim was to explain why it was that some countries, in the first place, became leaders in economic terms.[7] By 'institutions', North meant 'the humanly devised constraints that structure political, economic and social interaction'.[8] On a general theoretical level, the claim that institutions, defined in this very general way, do matter for economic development seems almost tautological, and would only be a relevant critique of some of the most formal, ahistorical economic modelling of interactions between individuals on abstract markets. On a more specific theoretical level, the neo-institutionalist school has not only argued that institutions in general are important, but also that a particular set of institutions have been crucial for historical economic development. Most importantly, the set of institutions generally emphasized include key capitalist institutions such as private property rights, contract law and a functioning market economy (in particular factor markets, i.e. markets for land, labour and capital). In order to arrive at functioning institutions in these areas, many neo-institutionalists argue, a minimal, non-interventionist, but efficient, state might be necessary.[9]

One key claim of the neo-institutionalist theory is therefore that a lack of development in a country or a region, such as Africa, is primarily due to lacking, incomplete or inefficient institutions. In the case of pre-colonial Africa, the absence of private property rights to land could be just such an institution that could contribute to a lack of development. One example would be that this situation could cast property rights in people, that is, slavery, as the only means for accumulation of wealth, thus contributing to the growth of this institution, which might inhibit further economic development.[10] An alternative might be that absence of or insecure private property rights to land might decrease private investments of capital in the land-dependent agricultural sector.[11]

In recent years, there has been a resurgence of work on African economic history based on, or starting out from, a neo-institutionalist analysis of economic development.[12] Some of the recent contributions in the study field of pre-colonial economic development in Africa have in particular emphasized the negative impact of the external slave trade, hypothesizing that the slave trade created insecurities and conflicts within and between increasingly ethnically stratified African societies; that it created long-term mistrust between peoples undermining economic exchange between them; or that it fostered the development of authoritarian governments in Africa. In essence, the slave trade thus undermined what are thought to be key social institutions, which in this analysis has turned out to be highly negative for long-term development in Africa.[13]

## Dependency theory and its critics

By emphasizing the importance of the slave trade for socio-economic development in Africa, this recent research within the neo-institutionalist theoretical framework has reignited a much older controversy on African development and 'underdevelopment'. This controversy was to a large extent initiated by the school of dependency theory.

Dependency theory presented a critique of liberal development theory, where the emergence and development of capitalism was seen as a process involving scientific and technological progress, in tandem with a movement towards more efficient, capitalist market economies, leading to productivity growth. A key cornerstone in dependency theory was instead the idea that economic development in core or metropolitan countries was intimately associated with the underdevelopment of peripheral countries. Underdevelopment is *not* simply being stuck in an original, undeveloped condition, or the effect of some countries lagging behind others. On the contrary, development and underdevelopment are essentially two sides of the same coin: development in one part of the world was claimed to be based on the exploitation (and thus underdevelopment) of other parts of the world. The theories were quite diverse. They did, however, all have in common an idea that an exploitative relationship between a group of core and a group of peripheral countries was crucial for the development/underdevelopment process. The exact mechanisms for how this exploitative relationship created development and underdevelopment, respectively, was, however, not always very clearly elaborated upon.[14]

There has been a lot of justified critique raised against dependency theory. For one thing, the notion of 'dependency' is often quite vaguely defined in much of the literature. Anthony Hopkins has even argued that the 'notion of dependency is used in such a diffuse way as to be tautological', a critique that other scholars have shared.[15] In some of the variations of dependency theory, one can furthermore find many strong assumptions or claims about development and underdevelopment, for example that the 'development of underdevelopment' is inevitable, or that underdevelopment is more or less permanent once it has occurred (unless a socialist revolution occurs). Actual historical development processes – taking place in many 'underdeveloped' countries ever since dependency theory was first sketched out – have certainly shown many such assumptions or claims to be severely flawed.[16] Yet another very important problem in much of the writings on dependency theory, to some extent related to the one discussed previously, is a tendency to portray the relationship between the core and the periphery as the *sole* explanatory factor for processes of development and underdevelopment. Many dependency theorists only (or virtually only) looked at the interests of the agents in core countries to have access to an underdeveloped periphery for access to cheap resources and labour.[17] This can at best provide one part of the story of the underdevelopment of the periphery, since there are many agents in the peripheral countries whose interests may be contradictory to those of agents in core countries. It, therefore, seems more reasonable – as some, but far from all, dependency theorists have done – to emphasize the *interplay* between internal and external structures in order to arrive at an understanding of 'concrete situations of dependency'.[18]

## The underdevelopment of Africa

Many dependency theorists have given very little attention to African history. The continent only figured very briefly in the works of some leading dependency theorists such as André Gunder Frank or Immanuel Wallerstein, and was then only described as a slave-exporting continent, with virtually no attention given to domestic factors influencing development in Africa.[19] The slave trade, it was further argued in this literature, wreaked havoc on many African societies, and thereby 'served as the cutting edge of the peripheralization of Africa', as Wallerstein once put it.[20] The dependency theorist most concerned with the African continent was, without a doubt, Walter Rodney, author of the book *How Europe Underdeveloped Africa*.[21] The main thrust of his book is already evident in the title: the blame for African underdevelopment was put on the European nations. Africa's capacity for domestic development was undermined by European intervention in and exploitation of Africa, Rodney argued. One key aspect of this exploitation was, according to Rodney, the transatlantic slave trade.[22] Domestic institutions and structures in Africa were experiencing a slow evolution, and many societies in Africa were already undergoing a long period of transition, including social stratification and state formation, at the time of European contact.[23] The slave trade, however, led to a drastic, and very negative, transformation of African societies, Rodney argued. The trade decreased population growth (and thereby also reduced a pressure for advancement), especially draining the continent of its young labour force. In the wake of the slave trade, wars on the African continent, which often were fought specifically in order to acquire further slaves, also followed. Once this trade, and the ensuing conflicts, had started in certain parts of Africa, it gave rise to a dialectic process: aggression among neighbouring countries or societies soon led to an ever greater militarization of the African continent. Individuals or specific societies had by this time little choice to opt out of the process, even if they had wanted to. The increasing violence associated with the slave trade in turn undermined productive economic activities on the African continent. The transatlantic slave trade was therefore, according to Rodney, a 'basic factor' for African underdevelopment.[24] Underdevelopment in pre-colonial times furthermore laid a foundation for European colonialism in Africa during the nineteenth century, which, according to Rodney, led to even further underdevelopment of the continent.[25]

As will be elaborated upon further in Chapter 2, many of Walter Rodney's claims have been hotly contested by other scholars. One way of dealing with the dependency school's quite one-sided emphasis upon external factors behind underdevelopment was the theorizing over a so-called 'African mode of production'. By the concept 'mode of production', Karl Marx essentially meant a 'system of forces of production and social relations that organizes and directs the forces of production'.[26] In Marx's early writings, he described the modes of production as a set sequence, or a set of stages of development, including slavery, feudalism and capitalism.[27] The sequence was based primarily on Marx's reading of the history of Western societies, and it has not always been possible to fit non-European societies into Marx's general stage-theory of development. Paul Lovejoy has for example argued that many African societies never were ruled by a slavery mode of production.[28] Marx himself added the caveat that there existed a specific 'Asiatic mode of production', which on many accounts differed from the modes of production associated with Western societies, being instead based on communal village life and a strong, centralized tributary state. In the spirit of this claim, some Marxist scholars have theorized about a specific 'African mode of production'. Catherine Coquery-Vidrovitch has provided a synthetic overview of much research on this topic, and then suggested that many African societies were not ruled by despotism to the same extent as Asian societies generally were at this time, and further emphasized the importance of long-distance trade for the generation of a surplus for African elites.[29]

More recently, John Thornton has in his well-cited book *Africa and Africans in the Making of the Atlantic World, 1400–1800* put forth many theoretical objections to Rodney's variant of dependency theory. In his book, Thornton has argued that while many African historians researched 'African initiative, skills and progress', dependency theorists 'clung to and developed the idea of ultimate African weakness', where the peoples of Africa had played a passive role in the development of the early modern Atlantic world.[30] Obviously, Africans had a will and preferences of their own, and the capacity to take their own initiatives. As Frederick Cooper once put it: 'that Africans had their own points of view and their own history was revealing only to people who had believed they did not'.[31] That there was African 'agency', therefore, seems obvious. An important question is, however, how large an influence various agents had over the historical development processes in Africa: were these processes mainly influenced and/or determined by domestic or by external agents? Thornton suggested an interpretation of African history where many Africans were active participants in the trade and had considerably more influence over the process of development (or underdevelopment) than what Rodney and other dependency theorists allowed for.[32] The transatlantic slave trade, Thornton argued, was not necessarily forced upon African societies. On the contrary, he argued, the external slave trade 'grew out of and was rationalized by the African societies who participated in it and had complete control over it until the slaves were loaded onto European ships'.[33] At the same time, he contested the claims about any increasing social disruptions in the wake of the external slave trade. Instead, Thornton provided an institutional explanation of internal slavery in Africa: slavery was the main means to the accumulation of private wealth in Africa, in the absence of private property rights in land. This in turn provided an economic logic for local elites to undertake slave raids within Africa, regardless of whether there existed any external demand from European buyers or not. It is therefore not certain, Thornton argued, that the transatlantic slave trade in any way contributed to an *increase* in violence and social disruption in Africa, compared to the incentives already created by domestic institutions.[34] In essence, Thornton therefore argued, 'African participation in the slave trade was voluntary and under the control of African decision makers. [. . .] The willingness of Africa's commercial and political elite to supply slaves should be sought in their own internal dynamics and history'.[35]

The debate between dependency theorists and their critics has remained quite controversial among scholars of African history. Joseph Inikori has, for example, for many years continued to argue in line with many of the key claims of dependency theory about the important role that the slave trade, in particular, played for African underdevelopment.[36] The idea that African participation in the slave trade was voluntary has also continued to be a very controversial issue. While most scholars certainly agree that local elites in many African societies did participate in the trade, the people who did participate did not represent the majority of the population on the African continent. It might therefore seem problematic to talk in general terms about 'African participation' in the slave trade without giving this aspect more recognition. Hilary Beckles has for example argued that Africans across the continent in general resisted slavery and enslavement, and that those who participated in the trade only constituted a small group of 'client political collaborators'.[37] The collaborators, such a formulation suggests, possibly had quite little influence over the historical development processes in the region, but would primarily have tried to profit themselves from a process that was out of their control, thus perhaps saving their own skins by ruining people's lives. Some scholars have even questioned how voluntary the participation was among the elites. Even if the elites in a single polity would have wanted to stay out of the external slave trade, and attempted to do so, they could be dragged into this cycle involuntarily. That no African had virtually any influence whatsoever over the processes taking place at this time has been argued most bluntly by J.F. Ade-Ajayi, when he wrote that 'even the slave trading chiefs were themselves virtually as much victims of the slave trade as the slaves who were sold away', since the slave trade 'armed your neighbours and compelled you to be perpetually at war with them'.[38] Many scholars thus seemingly still believe in Rodney's general argument that the 'African participation' in the external slave trade often was far from voluntary.

The controversy between dependency theorists on the one hand, and critics such as Thornton on the other hand, has thus been concerned with two core issues. First, the extent to which the socio-economic development (or underdevelopment) in African societies was the result of internal dynamics or external factors. Second, if there was any decisive impact from the (external) slave trade upon African societies, and if so, what the exact nature of this impact was. This book will return primarily to the second controversy in Chapter 2, reviewing the previous research in the field of African economic history more in depth.

## African labour history

The agency and strategies of various historical African agents, or groups of agents, have been studied in many previous academic works. As for the pre-colonial economic history of Africa, most attention has perhaps been given to more privileged groups, such as affluent merchants and traders involved in the external trade.[39] Kwame Daaku suitably called many of them 'merchant princes'.[40] The attention given to this group of people is motivated on the one hand by the crucial role they supposedly played for the development of the external trade in the pre-colonial era, and the debate on how voluntary African elites' participation in the slave trade was. On the other hand, much research has focused on this group simply because of the availability of sources. The merchants and traders do not only figure quite regularly in the European sources from this period (since they constituted the group that the Europeans most often came into contact with), but would also occasionally themselves produce sources that have been preserved for modern-day scholars to study. But while studying this particular social group might be important for determining certain historical issues, the merchants only formed a minor stratum of pre-colonial African society.

In this book, I am instead particularly interested in the life and social conditions of the common population, the working classes, including their agency and the strategies employed by them in order to improve upon their lot. The book could therefore be considered as a contribution to the field of African labour history. The terms 'labour' and 'working-class' must however not be interpreted too narrowly. As Marcel van der Linden has put it:

> Labor and working-class history were for a long time understood as 'the history of wage earners' – workers who, as free individuals, can dispose of their labor power as their own commodity and who have no other commodity for sale. [. . .] This narrow conceptualization is called in question by the 'globalization' of the research terrain.[41]

Karin Hofmeester and co-authors have on a similar note argued that this very distinct, a-priori determined separation between free proletarians on the one hand and slaves on the other, has created a problematic chasm in African studies: 'the history of wage workers and of slaves in Africa and elsewhere are often seen as two different histories rather than two parts of one single, local, regional and global history of work'.[42] Marcel van der Linden therefore suggests a reconceptualization of the working class, based on what united all subaltern workers: the commodification of their labour power, and thereby, their associated economic exploitation by employers.[43] This is a conceptualization that will be adhered to in this book. The term 'labourer' (nor 'labour' per se) will thus not be assumed from the outset to be associated with any particular legal status (i.e. slave or free), but might be applied to labourers regardless of their legal status.

Nonetheless, for the analysis in many cases, it will be of utmost importance to distinguish between the free and slave labourers. There has been a lot of theorizing as to the rationale behind the institution of slavery. One of the key theories in this regard is the so-called Nieboer–Domar hypothesis. The hypothesis was pioneered by H.J. Nieboer by the year 1900. Studying the existence of slavery in various societies around the world, Nieboer came to the conclusion that slavery most frequently (albeit not exclusively) existed in societies with 'open resources' (such as easy access to fertile land), as opposed to those with 'closed resources'.[44] In an article published many decades later, Evsey Domar reformulated the hypothesis more generally into a relationship between population density and the existence of slavery, so that slavery was associated with land-abundance, or a high land/labour ratio. The reason for this, Domar hypothesized, was that in a context of land-abundance, people had little incentive to work for others, since they easily could move elsewhere in search of land to work for their own benefit, rather than work for somebody else's profit. Assuming quite homogeneous land productivity and negligible economies of scale in agriculture, landowners would therefore be unable to find a labour force to work the land at a wage where the landowner could make a profit from employing them. In such a context, it would be very tempting for a landowner to try to coerce people to work the land for them, rather than allow the labour force to leave or to pay the labourers a wage that would have been competitive to what they could have earned from being self-employed. There might even be no wage rate at all, which would be mutually acceptable for both the potential labourer and the landowner. With land-scarcity (a low land/labour ratio), on the other hand, people without access to land would have considerably fewer options in order to make a living, and might be forced by sheer necessity to accept to work for someone else, even if on highly exploitative terms. Land-scarcity would therefore reduce the reservation wage (i.e. the wage that a labourer would require in order to work voluntarily for an employer in the first place), thus making it quite unnecessary for the landholders to coerce the labour force any further. According to this Nieboer–Domar hypothesis, there would thus be a positive correlation between land-abundance and slavery, or other forms of coercive labour practices such as feudalism.[45] Anthony Hopkins modified the Nieboer–Domar hypothesis slightly when applied to West Africa, arguing that the use of slaves was 'a matter of deliberate choice on the part of the African employers', and was preferred 'because the costs of acquiring and maintaining them were less than the cost of hiring labour'.[46] Coercion of labour not only reduced the reservation wage. Stanley Engerman has argued that it also meant 'that desired labour force participation, work vs leisure, preferred type of establishment to work in, and the location of residence could all be determined by the owner and not by the worker'.[47] Slavery thus implied a degree of power and control over the labour force that was impossible over a free labour force. Slaves, however, never did accept their fate passively. On the contrary, just like slaves have done in most societies throughout history, Africans often tried to resist being enslaved in the first place, and tried to resist their subaltern status if reduced to the status of slave.[48]

Not everyone agreed with such an economistic interpretation of the institution of slavery, where the slaves are understood primarily as units of labour to be economically exploited by a slaveholder. Most famously, Suzanne Miers and Igor

Kopytoff have argued that a shortage of labour is 'but one kind of shortage of personnel that people may seek to remedy'. There also existed a number of non-productive and non-economic factors contributing to the existence of slavery, including the social and political roles of slaves.[49]

In the literature on historical labour relations in Africa, slavery thus plays a key role. There has on the other hand been a long discussion in the field about to what extent there was any free labour (in the sense of people whose labour-power could be hired by an employer, rather than purchased as slaves) at all in pre-colonial Africa. That no such free labour existed is an idea that seems to have originated in the writings of some of the European travellers in pre-colonial Africa. By the late eighteenth century, the English explorer Mungo Park for example argued that 'hired servants, by which I mean persons of free condition, voluntarily working for pay, are unknown in Africa'.[50] The scholar J.D. Fage would interpret such evidence as showing that the continent was completely dominated by slave labour well into the modern era: 'the development of [a system of wage-earning] could only be gradual. The more immediate recourse was to a slave economy'.[51]

In his, by now classic, study of the economic history of West Africa, Anthony Hopkins argued that factor markets for land, labour and capital only developed in cases where the resource in question was scarce. Labour was in Hopkins' view certainly a scarce resource in pre-colonial Africa. Most labour was used for subsistence production.[52] Additional labour, to complement the labour available within the extended family, could be found if a landowner so wished. The labour market was however primarily a market in slaves, rather than a market for hiring voluntary labour.[53] John Iliffe on the other hand found that hired labourers actually were employed for certain tasks in pre-colonial Africa, for example as porters or in craft industries, but were very rare in agriculture. Wage labour could however exist 'where other modes of production are dominant', and then in antagonism to the dominant mode of production.[54] Gareth Austin has more recently developed Hopkins' argument further, concurring with Iliffe in that waged work was not completely unknown to the African continent. It was however in Austin's view 'vanishingly rare', and mainly concentrated in the European enclaves. In many societies, Austin furthermore argued, it was not possible for a free labour market to exist at all, since no wage rate would have been mutually acceptable to both parties, given the high living standards that a person could earn by working for him- or herself.[55] Humphrey Fisher has, on the other hand, suggested that previous scholars' emphasis on slavery as the key, or even sole, institution for mobilizing labour in pre-colonial Africa might reflect a bias in the scholarly research, rather than reflect what the African societies really looked like:

> there were, nearly always, and nearly everywhere in black Africa, alternative [to slavery, that is], non-violent, 'effective means of mobilizing labour'. So fascinated, so obsessed even, has modern scholarship become with slavery studies, that we often miss the wider scenario of demographic mobility, including more-or-less voluntary, even fully voluntary, movement.[56]

Much of the analysis of African factor markets for labour was directly or indirectly influenced by the analysis of economic development implied in much of the Marxist literature on the different modes of production, discussed above. In this literature, free labourers were argued to exist only, or at least primarily, in a more developed capitalist stage, compared to a more primitive stage of a slave-based mode of production. Tom Brass has instead suggested an alternative approach, where the institutions governing markets for labour are the subject of continuous class struggles between various classes. Most importantly, the process is not unidirectional, from a slave-based mode of production to a mode of production based on proletarians (i.e. legally free but also propertyless labourers). In various case studies from around the world, Brass has instead provided evidence of the reverse process, deproletarianization, when this has been in the interest of landlords or capitalists, and when they have been successful enough in the class struggle to impose their interest upon the working classes.[57]

## The aim of this book

The aim of this book is to contribute to our knowledge on the living standards in pre-colonial Africa, particularly the living standards of the working classes. Living standards should here be interpreted broadly to include not only the purchasing power enabled by an income or the local consumption of various goods but also issues such as the terms and conditions of work for the working classes, including, not least, the issue of the status of the workers. The book will also try to deal with the particular issue of the impact of the transatlantic slave trade upon living standards in Africa. The agency behind, and the cultural and socio-economic impact of, the transatlantic slave trade is a topic that so far has generated a considerable amount of theoretical controversy – ranging from dependency to neo-institutionalist theory – as has been described in this chapter. While there has been much justified critique raised against the school of dependency theory, it at least provided an important input about the potentially destructive impact that the external slave trade could have for many African societies. Empirical studies of the topic have so far been focused on some particular aspects of this impact, including demography and the incidence of conflicts (see more on this in Chapter 2), whereas other issues – such as the living standards of the population – have largely been left un-researched.

## A historical case study of the Gold Coast

African societies varied considerably on many accounts, for example, in the geographical, cultural, social, political and institutional conditions. The present study will not attempt to conduct a survey of living standards throughout pre-colonial Africa, but will instead study in-depth the historical case of the Gold Coast, in West Africa, in the pre-colonial period. The region that was then called the Gold Coast, today forms the southern part of Ghana in West Africa, as is illustrated in Figure 1.1.

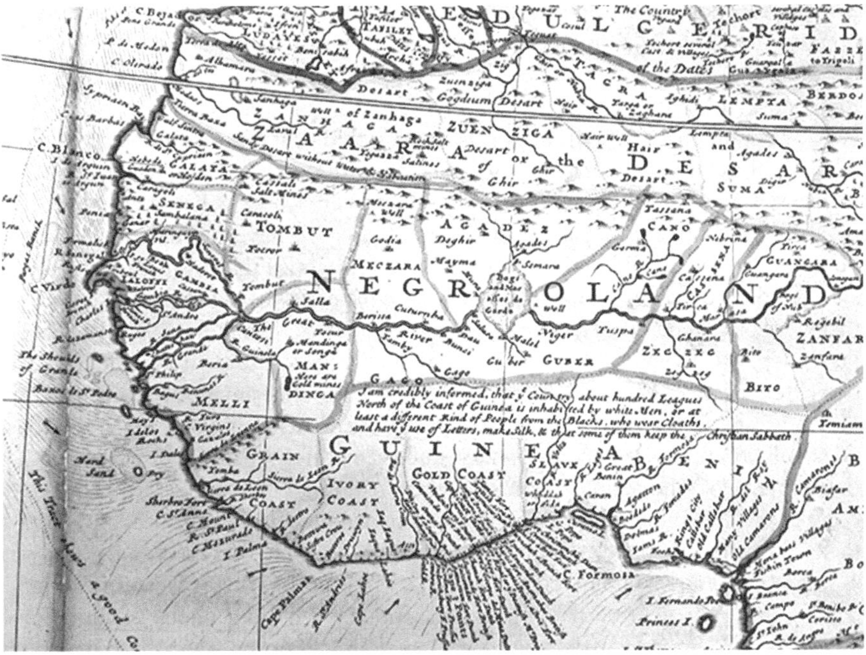


*Figure 1.1* Map depicting West Africa, from 'Atlas of the world on 27 sheets', by Herman Moll, c.1719.

Source: British National Archives WO 78/419. Reproduction by the author.

It is not possible to generalize about African societies based on a single historical case study such as this. As Robert Yin has argued, however, the point of a case study is not to generalize about populations or societies, in the sense that the case studied is to be considered a representative sample of population or societies on the continent. The point is, instead, to attempt to study the case in relation to more general theoretical propositions.[58] In the particular case studied in this book, these include the theories discussed previously in this chapter.

Studying pre-colonial African history is highly problematic due to a lack of primary sources. The Gold Coast is particularly well-suited for a study of the topic in focus in this book. As the European name of the region implies, the Gold Coast was for a long time trading primarily in gold rather than slaves. The slave trade only took off in this region by the late seventeenth century, at a time when Europeans already had been present on this part of the coast for around two centuries. There is, therefore, quite a large amount of sources that can provide both qualitative and quantitative evidence about labour and living standards on the Gold Coast starting well before the time when the external slave trade accelerated in this region. The available primary sources are thus in this particular case perhaps uniquely rich, compared to the sources that are available regarding many other African societies. The choice of case to study could therefore be considered to be what

Robert Yin has called a 'revelatory case', which is a case where there is an opportunity to study an issue that, perhaps, is impossible to study in other cases. As such, the case can by itself contribute important new knowledge on the issues to be studied.[59]

At the same time, it is of interest to know whether the case is to be considered what Yin has labelled 'common' or 'unusual' cases, respectively, when compared to other societies on the continent.[60] Albert van Dantzig has suggested that, regarding the impact of the external slave trade, we have to make a distinction between three categories of African societies: societies that were the 'objects of slave-raids', societies that engaged in the practice of enslaving others, and societies that were engaged in the trade in slaves. Any negative impact from the slave trade, he argues, was most urgently felt by the first category of societies, while the other two categories might be in a better position to experience any positive effects from the trade, and fewer of the negative effects.[61] The many polities on the Gold Coast do not always fit neatly into any of these three categories, as will be discussed further in Chapter 2, so the people in these societies could include both victims of slave-raids or the enslaving of prisoners of war, and agents enslaving others and trading in slaves from other societies. It is furthermore possible that the Gold Coast was rather unusual when compared to many other polities in West Africa, for example, due to the high degree of commercial, non-slave-trading contacts with Europeans already from an early stage mentioned above, or through a high degree of commercialization of the economy in general (see more on this in Chapter 2).

In an attempt to determine the common or the unusual, the case is compared to other West African societies; the book will, where it is possible, compare the evidence from the Gold Coast with evidence from a somewhat wider geographic area along the West African coast. This will enable some discussion on the extent to which the particular case of the Gold Coast was common or unusual at least when compared to other coastal societies in West Africa.

The 'pre-colonial' period in African history is of course not an obvious chronological delimitation; it could, if interpreted literally, be interpreted as stretching back in history through the millennia, all the way to the birth of human societies. This is not how the term should be interpreted in this study. Prior to when Europeans arrived on the West African coast, the region that later came to be called the 'Gold Coast' was made up of a number of different polities, shifting over time.[62] As a result of the regional specializations in the external trade, the Europeans came to give the name of the 'Gold Coast' to this particular part of the West African coast.[63] Chronologically, the current book will deal with this period of the history of the pre-colonial Gold Coast: from around the time that the Gold Coast experienced contact with the Europeans in the fifteenth century, to the early nineteenth century. In reality, most of the emphasis will be upon an even shorter period of time: the seventeenth and eighteenth centuries in particular. This was the time when the transatlantic slave trade expanded drastically from this part of the African coast.

The book, finally, will be delimited to contributing to the *economic* history of the Gold Coast. Other aspects, such as the cultural, political or religious history of the region, have been dealt with in much previous research. These aspects of Gold Coast history will only be touched upon in the present book when deemed necessary in order to interpret the region's economic history. Since the book will thus focus specifically on the case of the Gold Coast, Chapter 2 will, therefore, turn to a more detailed overview of the previous research on the economic history of the Gold Coast. The reader already familiar with this literature can easily move directly to Chapter 3, describing the sources used for the research in this particular book.

## Notes

1 Allen, R., 'The Great Divergence in European Wages and Prices from the Middle Ages to the First World War', *Explorations in Economic History*, 38 (2001), pp. 411–47; Allen, R., *The British Industrial Revolution in Global Perspective* (Cambridge: Cambridge University Press, 2009); Rönnbäck, K., 'An Early Modern Consumer Revolution in the Baltic?' *Scandinavian Journal of History*, 35(2) (2010), pp. 177–97.

2 Allen, R., 'India in the Great Divergence', in T. Hatton, K. O'Rourke and A. Taylor (eds), *The New Comparative Economic History: Essays in Honor of Jeffrey G. Williamson* (Cambridge: MIT Press, 2007), pp. 9–32; Allen, R., Bassino, J.-P., Ma, D., Moll-Murata, C. and van Zanden, J.L., 'Wages, Prices, and Living Standards in China, 1738–1925: In Comparison with Europe, Japan and India', *Economic History Review*, 64 (2011), pp. 8–38; De Zwart, P., 'Population, Labour and Living Standards in Early Modern Ceylon: An Empirical Contribution to the Convergence Debate', *Indian Economic Social History Review*, 49 (2012), pp. 365–98.

3 Allen, R., Murphy, T. and Schneider, E., 'The Colonial Origins of the Divergence in the Americas: A Labour Market Approach', *Journal of Economic History*, 72 (2012), pp. 863–94.

4 See for example Acemoglu, D. and Robinson, J., 'Why is Africa Poor?', *Economic History of Developing Regions*, 25(1) (2010), pp. 21–50, especially p. 22.

5 Austin, G., *Labour, Land and Capital in Ghana: From Slavery to Free Labour in Asante, 1807–1956* (Rochester: University of Rochester Press, 2005), pp. 27–33; Acemoglu and Robinson, 'Why is Africa poor?' pp. 21–2.

6 Fenske, J., 'The Causal History of Africa: A Response to Hopkins', *Economic History of Developing Regions*, 25(2) (2010), pp. 177–212, quote on p. 188.

7 North, D., *Institutions, Institutional Change and Economic Performance* (Cambridge: Cambridge University Press, 1990); North, D., 'Institutions', *Journal of Economic Perspectives*, 5(1) (1991), pp. 97–112.

8 North, 'Institutions', p. 97.

9 See for example North, 'Institutions'.

10 As suggested for example by Thornton, J., *Africa and Africans in the Making of the Atlantic World, 1400–1800* (Cambridge: Cambridge University Press, 1998), chapter 3.

11 See for example Firmin-Sellers, K., *The Transformation of Property Rights in the Gold Coast* (Cambridge: Cambridge University Press, 1996).

12 For an overview of and controversy over much of this literature see Hopkins, A., 'The New Economic History of Africa', *Journal of African History*, 50 (2009), pp. 155–77; Fenske, 'The Causal History'.

13 See for example Nunn, N., 'The Long-Term Effects of Africa's Slave Trades'. *Quarterly Journal of Economics*, 123 (2008), pp. 139–76; Acemoglu and Robinson, 'Why is Africa Poor?'; Nunn, N. and Wantchekon, L., 'The Slave Trade and the Origins of Mistrust in Africa', *American Economic Review*, 101 (2011), pp. 3221–52; Whatley,

W. and Gillezeau, R., 'The Impact of the Transatlantic Slave Trade on Ethnic Stratification in Africa', *American Economic Review*, 101 (2011), pp. 571–6; Whatley, W., 'The Transatlantic Slave Trade and the Evolution of Political Authority in West Africa', in E. Akyeampong, R.H. Bates, N. Nunn and J.A. Robinson (eds), *Africa's Development in Historical Perspective* (Cambridge: Cambridge University Press, 2014), pp. 460–88.

14 Peet, R. and Hartwick, E., *Theories of Development: Contentions, Arguments, Alternatives* (New York: Guilford Press, 2009), pp. 166–71.

15 Hopkins, A., 'On Importing André Gunder Frank into Africa', *African Economic History Review*, 2(1) (1975), pp. 13–21, quote on p. 16. See also Warren, B., *Imperialism: Pioneer of Capitalism* (London: Verso, 1980).

16 Warren, *Imperialism: Pioneer of Capitalism*; Peet and Hartwick, *Theories of Development*, pp. 181–2; Palma, J.G., 'Dependency', in S. Durlauf and L. Blume (eds), *The New Palgrave Dictionary of Economics*, 2nd edn (Palgrave Macmillan 2008), at www.dictionaryofeconomics.com [accessed 30 July 2014].

17 Peet and Hartwick, *Theories of Development*, p. 172; Palma, 'Dependency'.

18 Palma, 'Dependency'.

19 Frank, A.G., *World Accumulation 1492–1789* (London: Macmillan, 1978), pp. 129–34; Amin, S., *Unequal Development: An Essay on the Social Formations of Peripheral Capitalism* (Hassocks: Harvester Press, 1976), p. 320; Wallerstein, I., *The Modern World-System III: The Second Era of Great Expansion of the Capitalist World-Economy, 1730–1840s* (San Diego: Academic Press, 1989), pp. 142–3; see also critique by Hopkins, 'On Importing', p. 18.

20 Wallerstein, I., 'The Three Stages of African Involvement in the World Economy', in P. Gutkind and I. Wallerstein (eds), *The Political Economy of Contemporary Africa* (Beverly Hills: Sage Publications, 1976), pp. 30–57, quote on p. 40.

21 Rodney, W., *How Europe Underdeveloped Africa* (Washington DC: Howard University Press, 1982 [1972]).

22 Rodney, *How Europe Underdeveloped*, pp. 77–8.

23 Rodney, *How Europe Underdeveloped*, chapter 2.

24 Rodney, *How Europe Underdeveloped*, chapter 4.

25 Rodney, *How Europe Underdeveloped*, pp. 135–45; see also Howard, R., *Colonialism and Underdevelopment in Ghana* (London: Croom Helm, 1978).

26 Peet and Hartwick, *Theories of Development*, p. 156.

27 Peet and Hartwick, *Theories of Development*, pp. 158–9.

28 Lovejoy, P., *Transformations in Slavery: A History of Slavery in Africa*, 2nd edn (Cambridge: Cambridge University Press, 2000), pp. 276–80.

29 Coquery-Vidrovitch, C., 'Research on an African Mode of Production', in R.R. Grinker, S. Lubkemann and C. Steiner (eds), *Perspectives on Africa: A Reader in Culture, History and Representation* (Malden: Wiley-Blackwell, 2010 [1969]), pp. 139–50; see also Seddon, D. (ed.), *Relations of Production. Marxist Approaches to Economic Anthropology* (London: Frank Cass, 1978); Stewart, C.C., 'Emergent Classes and the Early State: The Southern Sahara', in D. Crummey and C.C. Stewart (eds), *Modes of Production in Africa – The Precolonial Era* (Beverly Hills: Sage Publications, 1981), pp. 69–92; Walker Kilkenny, R., 'The Slave Mode of Production: Precolonial Dahomey', in D. Crummey and C.C. Stewart (eds), *Modes of Production in Africa – The Precolonial Era* (Beverly Hills: Sage Publications, 1981), pp. 157–74; Amin, *Unequal Development*, p. 17.

30 Thornton, *Africa and Africans*, p. 5.

31 Cooper, F., 'Africa and the World Economy', *African Studies Review*, 24(2/3) (1981), pp. 1–86, quote on p. 1.

32 Thornton, *Africa and Africans*, pp. 6–7.

33 Thornton, *Africa and Africans*, p. 74.

34 Thornton, *Africa and Africans*, chapters 3–4.
35 Thornton, *Africa and Africans*, p. 125.
36 See for example Inikori, J., 'Africa in World History: The Export Slave Trade from Africa and the Emergence of the Atlantic Economic Order', in B.A. Ogot (ed.), *General History of Africa V: Africa from the Sixteenth to the Eighteenth Century* (Paris: UNESCO, 1999), pp. 39–55.
37 Beckles, H.M, 'African Resistance to the Transatlantic Slave Trade', in J.K. Anquandah (ed.), *The Transatlantic Slave Trade: Landmarks, Legacies, Expectations* (Accra: Sub-Saharan, 2007), pp. 81–91, quote on p. 83; see also Lamousé-Smith, W.B., 'African Resistance to Slavery and Myths for Diasporan Disunity', in J.K. Anquandah (ed.), *The Transatlantic Slave Trade: Landmarks, Legacies, Expectations* (Accra: Sub-Saharan, 2007) pp. 225–40; Diouf, S. (ed.), *Fighting the Slave Trade – West African Strategies* (Athens: Ohio University Press, 2003).
38 Ade-Ajayi, J.F., 'Remembering the Slave Trade', in J.K. Anquandah (ed.), *The Transatlantic Slave Trade: Landmarks, Legacies, Expectations* (Accra: Sub-, 2007), pp. 365–70, quote on p. 366.
39 See for example Priestley, M., *West African Trade and Coast Society: A Family Study* (London: Oxford University Press, 1969); Daaku, K., *Trade and Politics on the Gold Coast 1600–1720: A Study of the African Reaction to European Trade* (Oxford: Clarendon Press, 1970); Daaku, K., 'Trade and Trading Patterns of the Akan in the Seventeenth and Eighteenth Centuries', in C. Meillassoux (ed.), *The Development of Indigenous Trade and Markets in West Africa* (Oxford: Oxford University Press, 1971), pp. 168–81; Dumett, R., 'African Merchants of the Gold Coast, 1860–1905 – Dynamics of Indigenous Entrepreneurship', *Comparative Studies in Society and History*, 25(4) (1983), pp. 661–93; Sparks, R., 'Two Princes of Calabar: An Atlantic Odyssey from Slavery to Freedom', *William and Mary Quarterly*, 59(3) (2002), pp. 555–84; Sparks, R., *Two Princes of Calabar* (Cambridge: Harvard University Press, 2004); Behrendt, S., Latham, A.J.H. and Northrup, D., *The Diary of Antera Duk, an Eighteenth-Century African Slave Trader* (New York: Oxford University Press, 2012); Kea, R., *A Cultural and Social History of Ghana from the Seventeenth to the Nineteenth Century*, 2 vols. (Lewiston: Edwin Mellen Press, 2012), chapter 1.
40 Daaku, *Trade and Politics*, p. 107.
41 Van der Linden, M., 'The Promise and Challenge of Global Labor History', *International Labor and Working-Class History*, 82 (2012), pp. 57–76, quote on p. 63.
42 Hofmeester, K., Lucassen, J. and Ribeiro da Silva, F., 'No Global Labor History without Africa: Reciprocal Comparison and Beyond', *History in Africa*, 41 (2014), pp. 249–76, quote on p. 259.
43 Van der Linden, 'The Promise and Challenge', p. 67.
44 Nieboer, H.J., *Slavery as an Industrial System*, 2nd rev. edn (Den Haag: Nijhoff, 1910).
45 Domar, E., 'The Causes of Slavery and Serfdom: A Hypothesis', *Journal of Economic History*, 30(1) (1970), pp. 18–32.
46 Hopkins, A., *An Economic History of West Africa* (London: Longman, 1973), p. 25.
47 Engerman, S., 'Some Considerations relating to Property Rights in Man', *Journal of Economic History*, 33(1) (1973), pp. 43–65, quote on p. 49.
48 See for example Rathbone, R., 'Some Thoughts on Resistance to Enslavement in West Africa', *Slavery & Abolition*, 6(3) (1985), pp. 11–22; McGowan, W., 'African Resistance to the Atlantic Slave Trade in West Africa', *Slavery & Abolition*, 11(1) (1990), pp. 5–29; Rashid, I., 'Escape, Revolt, and Marronage in Eighteenth and Nineteenth Century Sierra Leone Hinterland', *Canadian Journal of African Studies*, 34(3) (2000), pp. 656–83; Rashid, I., "Do Dady Nor Lef Me Make Dem Carry Me": Slave Resistance and Emancipation in Sierra Leone, 1894–1928', *Slavery & Abolition*, 19(2) (1998), pp. 208–31; Diouf, *Fighting the Slave Trade*.

49 Kopytoff, I. and Miers, S., 'African "Slavery" as an Institution of Marginality', in S. Miers and I. Kopytoff (eds), *Slavery in Africa: Historical and Anthropological Perspectives* (Madison: University of Wisconsin Press, 1977), pp. 3–81, quote on p. 69. See also Stilwell, S., *Slavery and Slaving in African History* (Cambridge: Cambridge University Press, 2014).
50 Quoted in Austin, G., 'Factor Markets in Nieboer Conditions: Pre-Colonial West Africa, c.1500–c.1900', *Continuity and Change*, 24 (2009), pp. 23–53, quote on p. 38.
51 Fage, J.D., *A History of West Africa*, 4th edn (Cambridge: Cambridge University Press, 1969), p. 94; see also Fage, J.D., 'Slavery and the Slave Trade in the Context of West African History', *Journal of African History*, 10(3) (1969), pp. 393–404. Similar generalizations can also be found from other leading Africanist scholars as well, see for example Wilks, I., 'The State of the Akan and the Akan States: A Discursion', *Cahiers d'Études Africaines*, 22(87/88) (1982), pp. 231–49; Berry, S., *No Condition is Permanent: The Social Dynamics of Agrarian Change in Sub-Saharan Africa* (Madison: University of Wisconsin Press, 1993), chapter 6.
52 Hopkins, *An Economic History*, p. 23.
53 Hopkins, *An Economic History*, pp. 23–5.
54 Iliffe, J., *The Emergence of African Capitalism* (London: Macmillan, 1983), pp. 4–8.
55 Austin, 'Factor Markets', pp. 38–42; Austin, 'Factor Markets', p. 38; Austin, G., 'Coercion and Markets: Integrating Economic and Social Explanations of Slavery in Precolonial West Africa, c1450–c1900' (paper presented at the Historical Economics Workshop in Paris, 2009), p. 11.
56 Fisher, H., *Slavery in the History of Muslim Black Africa* (London: Hurst & Company, 2001), p. 2.
57 See for example Brass, T., *Towards a Comparative Political Economy of Unfree Labour: Case Studies and Debates* (London: Routledge, 1999).
58 Yin, R.K., *Case Study Research – Design and Methods* (Los Angeles: Sage, 2014), p. 21.
59 Yin, *Case Study Research*, p. 52.
60 Yin, *Case Study Research*, p. 52.
61 Van Dantzig, A., 'Effects of the Atlantic Slave Trade on some West African Societies', *Revue Francaise d'Histoire d'Outre-Mer*, 62 (226/227) (1975), pp. 252–69.
62 For overviews over the older history of the region, see for example Andah, B.W. and Anquandah, J.R., 'The Guinean Belt: The Peoples between Mount Cameroon and Côte d'Ivoire', in I. Hrbek (ed.), *General History of Africa, vol. III: Africa from the Seventh to the Eleventh Century* (Paris: UNESCO, 1992), pp. 240–57; Kipre, P., 'From the Ivory Coast Lagoons to the Volta', in D.T. Niane (ed.), *General History of Africa, vol. IV: Africa from the Twelfth to the Sixteenth Century* (1984), pp. 324–38; Boahen, A., 'The States and Cultures of the Lower Guinean Coast', in B.A. Ogot (ed.), *General History of Africa, vol. V: Africa from the Sixteenth to the Eighteenth Century* (Paris: UNESCO, 1999), pp. 204–20.
63 Boahen, 'The States and Cultures', p. 208.

# 2 Previous research

## The Gold Coast in African economic history

### Introduction

As was noted in Chapter 1, pre-colonial Africa has for a long time been, and is still in many recent publications, portrayed as having been a very poor continent.[1] This idea of African poverty is, no doubt, to a large degree inspired by the many European travellers to pre-colonial Africa, who wrote about the great poverty of the common population in the societies that they encountered.[2] All scholars, however, do not agree that Africa really was especially poor historically. John Thornton has, for example, argued that the external trade provided Africa with nothing that Africans did not already produce themselves in pre-colonial times, and that the domestic manufacturing in Africa could provide for all that was needed on the continent.[3] In order to understand this controversy more in-depth, we need to explore several aspects of African economic history. This chapter will attempt to summarize the main results of previous research on the economic history of West Africa, focusing in particular upon the case of the Gold Coast.

### Agriculture – the primary sector

The Gold Coast was situated in West Africa, on the part of the coast stretching from the river Volta in the east to around the river Ankobra, beyond Cape Three Points, in the west – that is, roughly the southern part of current-day Ghana. The climate of much of this region is tropical, with an average temperature around 25°C–30°C throughout the year. Geographically, the region is dominated by two different sorts of ecosystems: coastal savannah (primarily in the eastern part of the Gold Coast) and tropical forest (dominating much of the western part of the region, as well as the zone north of the coastal savannah). Further north, in what is current-day northern Ghana, is a zone of interior savannah.[4]

The various ecosystems in the region enabled a variety in crop production. One core foodstuff produced in much of West Africa was what in the sources was called *millie* or 'corn'. These terms are quite ambiguous, and could denominate either 'Indian corn' (i.e. maize) or 'Guinea corn' (i.e. sorghum or millet). Other staple crops included cassava, yams, plantain, beans and palm oil. Many of the crops grown were indigenous to the region.[5] One very important exception was 'Indian corn', maize, which might have been introduced into West Africa already in the sixteenth century.[6] The palm tree was indigenous to the tropical forest zone. In pre-colonial times, it could therefore easily be grown in the forest zone just north of the coast, and could provide both palm oil and palm wine. Other staple crops, such as yams, sorghum and millet, were instead most easily grown on the savannah. Maize, on the other hand, was quite adaptable to various conditions, and could easily be grown both in the coastal thicket, forest and savannah zones. Much of the maize supplied in the markets on the Gold Coast in pre-colonial times, therefore, presumably originated in areas quite close to the coast. Many of these crops can also be found depicted in contemporary travel accounts, as Figure 2.1 gives an example of.

A common idea is that productivity in African agriculture probably was low compared to that of agriculture in other parts of the world. Gareth Austin has, for example, argued that the fertility of the land generally was quite low, especially during the dry season of the year. Animal-drawn ploughs were impossible to use in many regions because of the high prevalence of the tsetse fly-borne disease, trypanosomiasis, reducing the use of domesticated animals. Thin soils were furthermore easily eroded once any protective forest cover had been cleared.[7] One important development was therefore the introduction of new crops, such as maize, which often gave higher yields than most domestic alternatives, and that at several times per year.[8] John Thornton has however argued that land productivity possibly was much higher than this received wisdom would have it, and has even put forth

*Figure 2.1* The agriculture on the Gold Coast – including maize, millet, palm oil and rice.

Source: Illustration from the manuscripts of Jean Barbot, 1688. British National Archives ADM 7/830B. Reproduction by the author.

the (rather contested) claim that the productivity might have been higher in Africa than in many other parts of the world, based on some anecdotal evidence from European travel accounts.[9]

## Demography

Due to the low land productivity, pre-colonial Africa is generally assumed to have had very low population densities (or, put in another way, a comparatively high land/labour ratio). The Gold Coast might have been among the most densely populated regions of both Africa in general, and West Africa in particular. Even so, population densities on the Gold Coast were still probably very low in global comparison.[10] Estimating the historical populations of pre-colonial African states is however fraught with problems, mainly because of a lack of primary sources to use for any such estimate.

Ray Kea has attempted to arrive at estimates of the size of the population on the Gold Coast based on what information there is from European travelogues from the region. Some of the European authors of these accounts provide observations, for example, about the number of huts or fishing canoes in a village. The numbers can often be quite crude guesses or estimates. To make use of such observations in order to arrive at a population estimate, it is furthermore necessary to make a number of assumptions, such as how many people lived in a hut or how many people a fishing canoe could provide for. The population estimates therefore differ widely: Kea's population estimates for the polity of Fante in the seventeenth century, for example, range from 64,000 to 432,000.[11] To some extent, the size of the population might have varied between the different times of observation. Since the differences between the estimates are so large, however, it seems more reasonable to assume that estimates based on such crude measures are highly unreliable.

Another attempt to estimate the population in the area comes from attempts to backcast population censuses from the twentieth century, under a set of assumptions about how large the population growth might have been at various times and in specific regions. Backcasting is highly problematic not only because of the many assumptions required about the historic levels of population growth but also because the benchmark level backcasted from becomes extremely important. In the case of African societies, many of the early censuses available are known to be quite unreliable.[12] One attempt at such backcasting was nonetheless undertaken by Patrick Manning, backcasting population figures for Africa to 1850 to begin with. In his model, he assumed a stylized population growth for Africa, and then modified it for each region and time-period depending on a set of historical factors. He then arrived at a population estimate for the Akan-speaking parts of the Gold Coast in 1850 of 1.8 to 2.2 million people.[13] In more recent research, this data has been extrapolated even further backwards in African history. Manning then assumed a quite substantial depopulation in the wake of the growing slave trade, and therefore arrived at an estimated population on the Gold Coast by the early eighteenth century of perhaps around 2.9 million people, thus considerably larger than what it might have been 150 years later.[14] Manning has since received criticism from Ewout Frankema and Morten Jerven. They argued that the assumed baseline figure for the population growth that Manning uses in his models is too low. He, therefore, arrived at much too high a figure in his 1850 population estimates (and, consequently, also for the earlier benchmark estimates as well). If one were to use their assumptions, the population on the Gold Coast in 1850 would instead have been around 1.3 million people.[15]

## Political fragmentation

The size and density of the population are key aspects for the emergence and strength of states. One of the most striking features of pre-colonial Africa was the large number of different polities on the continent. Much of the West African coast was dominated by tiny states.[16] This is also true for the Gold Coast in particular. The Gold Coast was primarily occupied by people of Akan ethnic origin, along with smaller regions populated by the Ga-Adangme and the Ewe. These peoples, including the Akan, were split into a large number of different polities. On a map from 1629 it is possible to find almost forty separate polities mentioned, in an area that might have been smaller than the Netherlands (judging from the fact that it covers a stretch of the coast from Cape Three Points to around Accra, perhaps some 20,000–30,000 km$^2$).[17]

One of the most important developments on the Gold Coast during the period under study in this book was therefore, as Adu Boahen has argued, a process of state-centralization and the emergence of increasingly larger polities in the region.[18] This was a development that had started already prior to direct contact with the Europeans in the fifteenth century. When the Portuguese arrived on the coast, they found a number of smaller coastal states, such as Efutu, Agona and Accra, on the Gold Coast. During the sixteenth century, a number of different states started to develop, but the process was accelerated in the last decades of this century. The seventeenth century therefore saw the drastic growth of a couple of polities on the Gold Coast, particularly three growing empires: Denkyira and Akwamu in the interior rainforest zone of the Gold Coast, and Accra on the actual coast. With the growth of these states also followed the growth of an administrative apparatus that controlled the state. The expansion of these states often led to conflicts and outright wars with the neighbouring states, in which many older polities were conquered by the three growing empires. The power of these empires peaked during the middle of seventeenth century. In the early eighteenth century, a new power emerged on the Gold Coast: the Asante. In a few decades' time, the Asante had conquered the old Denkyira Empire, followed by their conquering many of Denkyira's previous vassal states in the region. At about the same time, the Akwamu Empire was defeated by a number of different states – including the Accra – who had allied together. This alliance was soon, in turn, conquered by the growing Asante Empire.[19]

By the middle of the eighteenth century, the only independent competitor to the Asante remaining on the Gold Coast was Fante on the very coast. Fante had entered an expansionist phase itself at around the same time as the Asante started to emerge as a powerful empire further north. For the Fante, this included conquering the Fetu (the polity where the Cape Coast Castle was situated) in 1711, as well as several other neighbouring polities. The competition and repeated direct conflicts between the Fante and the Asante would then impact the development on the Gold Coast throughout the eighteenth century. This was largely a result of commercial rivalry where many nations – both African and European – wanted to influence the patterns of trade, and steer it to favour their own interests.[20]

In this context of highly fragmented polities, European companies often attempted to influence local politics. On the Gold Coast, the Europeans often tried to exploit rivalries between local polities in order to favour their own interests – making alliances, or supporting one side in a particular conflict in order to get them to fight a proxy war, instead of having to get directly involved in a conflict. Kwame Daaku has argued that European guns became one important factor in the emergence of some of the new empires during the seventeenth century, including Denkyira and Akwamu.[21] James Sanders has furthermore argued that the English generally supported the expansionist policies of the Fante, by providing them with arms and ammunition, since they found that this favoured their own economic interests, given that most English forts on the Gold Coast were located in Fante territory.[22] On some other occasions, if the outcomes of a rivalry were too uncertain, Europeans chose not to get involved in local politics. This was the case in the power struggles between the Denkyira and the emerging Asante Empire by the late seventeenth and early eighteenth centuries. In this conflict, the Dutch – who previously often had supported the Denkyira Empire – consciously chose to remain neutral, since they did not want to ruin their chances to continue trading after the conflict, should the Asante Empire win.[23]

## Systems of land tenure

Anthony Hopkins famously argued that there existed a very limited factor market in land not because of African backwardness, but because 'land was not scarce enough to acquire a market value'.[24] Gareth Austin has more recently added the caveat that a general abundance of land does not 'preclude scarcities of particularly fertile land with relatively cheap access to markets'.[25] The physical availability of land per capita, that is, the land/labour ratio, is but one aspect to the equation determining access to land. Another important aspect is the institutional one, that is, systems of land tenure. A key question is who could get access to land, and under what conditions. Stephen Hymer claimed that there was easy access to land for virtually anybody in pre-colonial Ghana.[26] Kwame Daaku went further, to claim that the system of land tenure in pre-colonial Akan society (in current-day Ghana) was highly egalitarian.[27] Unfortunately, neither of these two authors provides much empirical evidence in favour of these respective claims.

Asante, one of the major Akan-speaking nations on the Gold Coast, has been the focus of comparatively much research on the pre-colonial forms of land tenure. Some older scholars have then argued that land ownership in pre-colonial

Asante in practice was limited to a restricted circle of people, and that most people had to pay rents to the landlords to be allowed to cultivate a plot of land, quite similar to feudalism in Europe.[28] On the other hand, Gareth Austin has more recently argued that these rents were low, and that land usually was available 'for token payment or none at all'.[29] In essence, therefore, 'over most of Asante the right to cultivate land was essentially a free good': a factor market in land was absent because there was no scarcity of the resource, as Hopkins suggested.[30] This also gave immigrants quite a bit of bargaining power, when trying to get access to land to settle on.[31] As a further consequence, Gareth Austin has argued, chiefs and heads of villages often welcomed strangers to settle and become subjects.[32]

In the coastal polities on the Gold Coast, Ray Kea has on the other hand claimed that quite substantial land rents probably were extracted from the peasant population. Exactly how high the rents really were is however never reported.[33] Kea has furthermore suggested that the appropriation of land rents changed over time, so that land rents, initially paid in the form of money, were replaced by land rents paid in kind. This, he then inferred, furthermore changed the geographical distribution of the population on the Gold Coast, since such a change reduced the need for the peasants to live close to towns and their markets.[34] Ray Kea also found anecdotal evidence suggesting that the rents charged on the Gold Coast were so high that some peasants became indebted to the landowners, or to urban creditors. This indebtedness was furthermore argued to have caused peasant migration to the towns.[35]

The previous literature is thus divided on the issue. This might at least partly be the result of scholars studying different geographical areas, and that the systems of land tenure might have differed geographically. The issue will be discussed further in the present study.

## Labour regimes: slaves, pawns and free labourers

As was noted already in Chapter 1, many scholars argue that there existed little or even no free wage labour in pre-colonial sub-Saharan Africa, largely because of the high land/labour ratio, as predicted by the Nieboer–Domar hypothesis. This applies also to research on the Gold Coast and its surroundings. J.D. Fage argued, seemingly based on a single quote from a European travel account, that it was 'difficult' to hire free labour on the pre-colonial Gold Coast.[36] Gareth Austin has more recently claimed that he could find no indication of the existence of wage labour or long-term hiring of labour in Asante prior to the 1890s.[37] The reason for this, he believes, was economic: the reservation wage of free labourers (had they existed) ought to have been too high. This conclusion is based on estimates of what a free, self-employed miner supposedly could earn at the time.[38] Austin's estimates shows that while free labour might have been 'an alternative possibility in cultural terms, it was *not* feasible economically', at least in Asante by the late nineteenth and early twentieth century.[39] Many other scholars have agreed that free wage labour was completely or virtually non-existent on the pre-colonial Gold Coast.[40] Gareth Austin has added the caveat that the scarcity of labour was highly seasonal: labour could actually be underemployed in agriculture in the dry season of the year. Labour could therefore be abundant for other employers during certain periods of the year, and this seasonal reserve army of labour could potentially be a source of wage labourers.[41]

One quite common institution in many parts of West Africa was pawnship. A human pawn was held as collateral for debt, but the pawn's labour power could also be exploited by the lender as a form of interest for the loan. Paul Lovejoy has suggested that the institution had little connection to the trade in slaves in much of Atlantic Africa, in contrast to West Central Africa, where the connection was much closer between the two institutions.[42] On the Gold Coast, gold and jewellery were commonly pawned as collateral for debt until well into the seventeenth century. In the eighteenth century, human pawnship did however become more common on the Gold Coast as well.[43]

The relationship between different labour regimes changed over time. While slavery was abolished in the British Crown colonies in the 1830s, the Gold Coast had by this time not been formally incorporated into the British Empire as such a colony. It would take a long time before slavery actually was abolished on the Gold Coast, even in the areas controlled by Britain.[44] By the late nineteenth century, Akosua Perbi has argued, European observers believed that domestic slavery was still ubiquitous throughout the Gold Coast. At the same time, they also argued that 'hired labour was rarely procurable'.[45]

We will return to the issue of labour in the European enclaves below. But what about the labour regimes outside enclaves such as the European settlements on the Gold Coast? On the one hand, the importance of slavery in Africa might in some cases be exaggerated. Joseph Inikori has, for example, argued that some of the institutions in Africa that came to be classified as slavery, in actual fact resembled serfdom more closely.[46] On the other hand, an absence of evidence of wage labour (outside European enclaves) is not necessarily strong proof that no such wage labour existed. There are relatively few sources that can shed light on pre-colonial African history outside the European enclaves in the first place, and what sources there are (including oral tradition) might furthermore have a selective bias in that they might take little interest in such an issue as the possibility of employing hired labour. In essence, we ought to expect to find little evidence of the existence of wage labour in pre-colonial Africa, regardless of whether it did exist or not. Previous scholars have, however, found several examples of European explorers and travellers who actually came across the hiring of free labour, or even hired labour themselves, quite far from the European enclaves.[47]

## Labour in the European enclaves on the Gold Coast

The Portuguese were the first Europeans to explore the West African coast. The reason why they established a castle at Elmina on the Gold Coast by the late fifteenth century was initially primarily to trade in gold from the Gold Coast. One early source talks about the existence of a 'large settlement' on the site even before the fort was built, but is unfortunately not clear on whether it was an African or

European settlement.[48] Starting in the early sixteenth century, other European nations – France, England, the Netherlands, Sweden, Denmark and Brandenburg – all started to take an interest in trading in Africa as well. The European nations generally came to use chartered companies, that is, legal monopolies, for trading on the coast.[49] One such company was the English Royal African Company, established in 1672 as the successor of some previous attempts to trade in Africa. By 1698, the company lost its monopoly rights to English trade in Africa, and saw the trade opened up for any English subject on payment of a 10 per cent export duty on the goods traded.[50]

In contrast to most trade elsewhere along the African coast, the trade on the Gold Coast was conducted with several castles and forts as a base. The Europeans generally built these forts with permission from the local authorities, and had to pay rent for the land they used for any construction.[51] Even though many of the forts and castles had a garden where vegetables and fruits were grown, they were never self-sufficient. Instead, they had to rely on the local economy for the provisioning of enough foodstuffs to supply not only the staff at the forts, but also the ships arriving at the forts to trade. Three major castles (the Portuguese, later Dutch, Elmina; the British Cape Coast Castle; and the Danish Christiansborg) and dozens of smaller forts and factories dotted the coastline of the Gold Coast. The African headquarters of the English Royal African Company came to be the Cape Coast Castle, on the Gold Coast. The early history of the town of Cape Coast is uncertain, but oral tradition has it that the town of Amanforo (later to be renamed Cabo Corso, and then Cape Coast, by the Europeans) was founded by the Afutu prior to when Europeans arrived on the coast.[52] A castle was initially built at the Cape Coast by the slave-trading Swedish Africa Company (*Svenska Afrikakompaniet*) in the 1650s, but had been taken over by the British following a series of conflicts over the control of the castle.[53] Conflicts between the European nations continued, and quite soon, the two main competitors remaining to trade on the coast were the English and the Dutch, with a minor stake kept by the Danish company.[54]

Many scholars have noted that contact with Europeans set in motion many new processes along the African coast. One such process was, according to Kwame Daaku, the development of a new socio-economic class of salaried labourers.[55] In order to run these castles and forts, the European companies in charge of them also had to garrison them with a permanent staff. This staff came to be of both European and African origin, and of both free and slave status. In the beginning, most of the employed staff was of European origin. As time went by, the European companies started to employ an increasing number of Africans, as well as increasing the number of castle slaves owned by the companies.[56]

There has therefore been some research into the free labourers living in such European enclaves, most particularly on the Gold Coast.[57] Some of the most important people that the European companies employed were perhaps the African interpreters, without whom little or no trade could have been conducted. These people provided not only interpretation services, but in many cases also held key social positions in African societies. In many pre-colonial societies on the Gold

Coast, for example, the chiefs and kings only communicated to their subordinates through a special spokesperson, an 'interpreter' or 'linguist'.[58] Such an interpreter could therefore, if employed by the Company, also help the Europeans with getting important access to local networks.

Another key group of labourers were the African canoemen employed at the forts and castles. Since the Gold Coast exhibited few natural harbours, goods generally had to be transported to and from visiting ships on smaller vessels, most importantly canoes manoeuvred by local canoemen. The European companies could therefore employ quite large numbers of canoemen, either per journey to/from a ship, for the whole stay of a specific ship, or for even longer periods of time. Canoemen were also used for other tasks than that of transporting goods to and from ocean-going ships. Examples include carrying correspondence or supplies between the forts along the coast. While it is clear that many of these canoemen were hired, and worked voluntarily for the European companies, their exact relationship to any means of production is unclear. Some scholars have noted that the canoemen employed by the Europeans often were or had been local fishermen.[59] On the other hand, it remains uncertain if they were truly proletarianized, only working for wages, or whether they still had access to some means of production of their own. These canoemen on the Gold Coast nonetheless seem to have developed a particularly high degree of consciousness and collective organization, on some occasions refusing to work under what they found to be unacceptable conditions.[60] The canoemen were probably all men. The Company occasionally also employed female labourers, for construction work. The female workers were then paid a lower wage than the male workers.[61]

Aside from employing a number of free labourers for wages, the European companies also came to own and exploit a number of slaves to run the daily business in the forts and castles. These 'castle slaves' were kept and treated separately from the 'trade slaves' that the European companies were in the business of trading. Castle slaves came into more frequent use particularly from the early eighteenth century. This was to a large extent a reflection of an attempt to exchange or complement free labourers with slaves, possibly in order to reduce the cost of labour. Free canoemen in particular objected to the use of castle slaves in their trade, and refused to cooperate with slave canoemen.[62]

The slaves were used for a whole host of different tasks, ranging from very unskilled manual labour, to quite highly skilled craftsmanship. Many of these skilled slaves had been trained at the forts. The division of labour was highly gendered, with most of the skilled craftwork done by male slaves.[63] Female castle slaves were instead set to do much of the domestic and reproductive work, including raising child slaves. These children were not always the biological offspring of the women themselves, but some female slaves could be set to care for not just their biological children, but also those of other women, including the children of 'trade slaves' sold off the coast, in cases where the buyer was uninterested in purchasing the children too.[64] Just as would be expected from a system of slavery, punishments were not uncommon, and could in many cases be very brutal.[65] Many slaves did therefore try to run away, something that was made easier by the fact that many of the castle slaves were allowed to live in the town outside the castle walls, rather than within the castle walls.[66]

In some parts of the world, slaves could occasionally be paid for 'overwork' or given rewards if they had been particularly industrious and loyal.[67] The castle slaves on the Gold Coast were also paid for their labour. In the previous literature these payments are simply described as 'subsistence wages'.[68] It has however never been estimated how high the wages really were in comparison to the cost of living on the coast. Anecdotal evidence suggests that in dear times (for example in years of drought), the wages paid might not have been enough to feed the slaves, so extra allowances could at least in some cases be made under such circumstances.[69] The wages were furthermore differentiated between the slaves. Per Hernæs, studying the wages paid to Danish castle slaves, argued that the wages reflected the slaves' 'personal commitment and – personal need'.[70] The slaves could furthermore earn extra money in the form of occasional bonuses or 'dashes' (gifts) or through 'overwork', that is, work beyond the customary hours per day. The wages thus operated as 'sweeteners within the system', as Per Hernæs put it.[71] The wages thereby became an important aspect of the labour regime in the European enclaves on the Gold Coast.

## The mobility of labour

A key issue for the relationship between the European enclaves and the surrounding societies is the mobility of the population. Whether Europeans were able to hire any wage labourers depended on the willingness of people living not just in the coastal towns per se to work for wages, but also that of the population in the surrounding hinterland. The extent to which any wages paid to workers at the forts and castles reflect the living standards in the region more broadly depends upon the mobility of labour.

Much of the literature touching upon the issue of historical mobility in pre-colonial Africa has assumed or claimed that the mobility of the population might have been quite high – particularly along the coasts – but there are few in-depth studies of the topic.[72] Temporary labour migration among the Kru – a nation that was famous for its high labour mobility, originating in current-day Sierra Leone – has been studied by both George Brooks and Diane Frost. Many of the Kru were recruited to work on the ships trading along the West African coast in the eighteenth century.[73] Francois Manchuelle has argued that a similar pattern can be found among the Soninke of Senegambia around the same time, where they were recruited to work as seamen for French fleets working on the Senegal River. Yet another form of mobility in that region was a rather common form of trade-migration: at least from the late eighteenth century, young men moved from inland regions of West Africa to the coast of Senegambia, looking for a way to make a living there for a while, in order to earn enough to purchase European goods that could be sold at a profit inland.[74] As for the Gold Coast, Ray Kea has argued that canoemen, fishermen and the propertyless day-labourers exhibited a particularly high degree of mobility, moving from one port to another along the coast.[75]

Harvey Feinberg has at the same time suggested that migration to urban areas on the Gold Coast (such as Elmina, which is the focus of his study) was quite common, 'since refuge was apparently readily given'.[76] The issue will be discussed further in the course of this book.

## The 'othering' of the African labourer

Several previous scholars have shown how the European writings about Africa were permeated with negative stereotypes and racial prejudice about the African population. In general, Europeans described the Africans as lazy, savage and uncivilized.[77] One key explanation to the particular stereotype of idleness, according to many of these previous scholars, was that the Europeans thought that a 'tropical exuberance' induced the idleness: nature was so bountiful and provided everything one needed so easily that there was little reason to work hard. An implicit assumption behind this idea is, of course, that the people were satisfied with just the basic necessities provided by nature, not valuing material luxuries very highly.[78] In his classic study of West African economic history, Anthony Hopkins instead proposed another explanation to the stereotype:

> Where there *was* underemployment in Africa [. . .], it was due to lack of opportunities rather than to a culture-bound leisure preference, for the preference implies choice, and choice was often absent. The 'lazy' African is in reality usually either debilitated or without a market for his labour – or both.[79]

According to Hopkins, the stereotypical description of Africans as lazy had nothing to do with preferences, but was simply the result of a market failure: a failure to create an effective demand for the goods that the commoners could produce (or a failure to demand their labour services), and a failure of the markets to supply goods that the common population was interested in consuming in exchange for their labour services. Yet another explanation for the stereotype put forth by some scholars was that feigned idleness was a conscious strategy of resistance by the workers against exploitation by the European employers.[80]

Ester Boserup has on the other hand suggested that one key factor behind the stereotype of the 'lazy African' simply was the gendered division of labour in Africa. Boserup claimed, based on modern-day anthropological studies, that in Africa, much of the agricultural work was undertaken by women. This had an impact upon the 'othering' of Africans:

> The Europeans, accustomed to the male farming systems of their home countries, looked with little sympathy on this unfamiliar distribution of the work load between the sexes and understandably, the concept of the 'lazy African men' was firmly fixed in the minds of settlers and administrators.[81]

Scholars writing about the stereotypical 'othering' of Africans have rarely connected this discussion with Boserup's hypothesis. Much scholarly research on the historical gendered division of labour in pre-colonial Africa has however supported Boserup's claim that African women were responsible for a very large share of all work undertaken in African societies, including much work that was in the male domain in Europe. Many studies have found that women often were in charge of both domestic and agricultural work in Africa, including everyday production and processing of food.[82] Gareth Austin has suggested the generalization that the gendered division of labour in Africa historically was largely along subsistence lines: female tasks included reproduction in the broadest sense, including subsistence production and farming, while male tasks primarily included extra-subsistence production (various forms of money-making activities, such as mining, long-distance trading, metal working, wood carving or hunting).[83] In some societies, not the least on the Gold Coast, women also worked as traders, even if their involvement primarily might have been on the markets for local goods.[84]

Africans were by no means the only people to have been stereotypically described as 'lazy' or 'indolent'. The stereotype was also used by Europeans in Southeast Asia, argued Syed Hussein Alatas, when they would not accept to work for the Europeans voluntarily.[85] It was also often used by many early modern European authors when describing the working class in their own home-nation.[86] Regardless of the origins of the stereotype of the 'lazy African (man)', it was frequently used as justification for a coercive labour regime. As Ania Loomba has put it, the stereotypes were not just reflections of the economic and material realities of colonialism, but were involved in a dialectical process 'with racial assumptions both arising out of and structuring economic exploitation'.[87] In his classic, powerful attack on colonialism, Alberto Memmi discussed how such 'othering' of the colonized served a socio-economic purpose under colonialism, exemplifying in particular with the stereotype of laziness, which could be used as justification for paying the colonized low wages.[88] In the case of African history, it has also been argued that this particular form of 'othering' of Africans was developed particularly as a justification for the transatlantic slave trade.[89]

## The living standards of the working classes

In an often-cited book, *The African Poor: A History*, John Iliffe argued that there has been a 'widespread belief that until recently, there were no poor in Africa, because economic differentiation was slight, resources were freely available, and the "extended family" supported its less fortunate members'.[90] This, Iliffe argues, is largely a myth. He instead argued for a distinction between conjunctural and structural poverty. Conjunctural poverty was caused by temporary crises. The chief form of conjunctural poverty was, according to Iliffe, induced by famine. Famines could be caused by political insecurity and social disruptions, most importantly wars, but also by natural events such as droughts, floods or locusts.[91] Structural poverty, on the other hand, was determined by the social relations in a society. Iliffe famously argued that in general structural poverty in Africa for a long time was limited to individuals who for some reason were unable to work to support themselves – the sick, disabled or the elderly – but that widespread structural poverty was a relatively recent phenomenon. In particular, Iliffe argued that the high land/labour ratio in Africa was of key importance to the low level of structural poverty, since 'structural poverty resulting from land scarcity appeared only slowly in Africa'.[92]

Iliffe argued that the Gold Coast might have been an exception to the general conclusion about little structural poverty in pre-colonial Africa: drawing on research by Ray Kea, Iliffe noted that many of the Europeans describing poverty in this region often attributed it to a lack of access to any means of production, rather than to particular, incapacitated individuals only.[93] The issue of living standards on the Gold Coast in particular was thus discussed in Ray Kea's work on the Gold Coast in the seventeenth century. Kea then showed that there was an advanced social stratification in Gold Coast societies. From the European accounts describing this stratification, it is often not possible to get a more nuanced picture than that there existed at least two social classes or estates: one class of relatively more affluent people – often described collectively in terms of nobility – and one class of poor(er) people. Many of these commoners were literally being referred to as 'the poor' (or various synonyms on this topic, in different European languages).[94] Taxes on the common population could be quite high, and Ray Kea believed that the taxes on the Gold Coast also increased during the seventeenth century. Fishermen, for example, initially paid a tenth of their production by the early part of the century, but this supposedly increased to a third of their production by the end of the century.[95] How poor the common people on the Gold Coast in reality were, compared to commoners in Africa or elsewhere in the world, remains unclear. Ray Kea reported nominal wages for Africans employed by the Dutch company trading on the coast in the middle of the seventeenth century, and gave examples of what purchasing power such a nominal wage could mean in the form of specific goods: for example, how many yams, sheep or mirrors could be bought from the wages earned.[96] Kea did, however, not try to use this data for any systematic analysis of the living standards in the region.

There have been a few other studies that have attempted to estimate quantitatively the real wages elsewhere in pre-colonial Africa. Some studies exist that deal with living standards as measured by the real wages earned in early modern South Africa. These studies have, however, been limited to studying the living standards of the white settler population, not being able to capture the living standards of the native population.[97] Another way of quantitatively measuring living standards of the African population is to look at anthropometric data, particularly the stature of the population. It is well-known that there is a relationship between the nutritional intake during childhood and stature as an adult. A tall population is therefore an indication that the people have had good access to the necessary nutrition during childhood and youth. In the case of pre-colonial Africa, two such studies have been undertaken, studying the stature among people in northern Ghana and Burkina Faso in one study and the Yorubas, in the other. Both studies deal with the early nineteenth century, and both find that living standards (as measured by human stature) in pre-colonial West Africa at this time might have been on roughly the same level as those found in many other parts of the world around the same time.[98]

A potential, complementary qualitative indicator of material living standards of a region could be the material culture of the population. Many studies from early modern Europe have attempted to study this issue, using for example probate inventories from samples of the population as source material.[99] Such sources are unfortunately generally unavailable in the case of pre-colonial West Africa. What evidence there is about the material culture of the population therefore only comes from travel accounts of Europeans describing life in the region. The issue has so far not received much specific research, but is touched upon in some studies focusing on other research questions. Art historians have for example studied how Africans were depicted in travel accounts, showing how Europeans perceived the material standards evidenced by the style and quality of the clothing used in the pictures.[100] Housing standards have also received some attention in previous research. Christopher DeCorse has then shown how some of the housing in Elmina on the Gold Coast changed from traditional wattle-and-daub to stone housing after contact with the Europeans began.[101] The spread of architectural practices has also been studied in a couple of other places along the West African coast.[102] One limitation of archaeological research, which is what many studies of housing standards are based on, is that it might be biased towards more durable objects and structures, such as more persistent types of houses. Evidence of non-durable objects and structures – ranging from the consumption of foodstuffs to the building of less durable types of housing – is considerably harder to gather from archaeological excavations alone, even if they might have been of great importance at the time.[103] Adam Jones has in this context argued that some scholars who have written about material culture in pre-colonial Africa 'simply have not done enough homework', when not using evidence available in European travel accounts exhaustively.[104] Using such sources, the social stratification of, for example, housing can also be studied. Houses of stone or adobe were a sign of wealth, primarily owned by affluent groups of Africans involved in trade with the Europeans, as Ray Kea has argued was the case on the Gold Coast or as Robin Law has argued in the case of the Slave Coast.[105] In general, traditional housing of the common population was in contrast often described as quite simple huts, mostly made of wattle-and-daub.[106]

There is thus, in essence, not much in-depth research into the living standards of the common population on the Gold Coast in the pre-colonial period, particularly not from any comparative perspective. This will be a key concern for this book.

## Domestic and external trade

In his work *An Economic History of West Africa*, published in 1973, Anthony Hopkins argued that market principles were considerably more widespread in West Africa than what many previous scholars by then had allowed for.[107] While this claim might have been controversial when Hopkins' book was first published, it is much less controversial today – so uncontroversial, in fact, that Gareth Austin has declared that there now exists a consensus that 'the extent of market orientation in pre-colonial economies, at least by the nineteenth century, was remarkably high' given the circumstances they operated under.[108]

Austin has at the same time noted that very little is known in detail about the dynamics of these markets.[109] In general, African markets were periodical ones, held less than daily. Daily markets could be held only in large centres of population.[110] Many factors have been argued to have influenced the prices on the local markets. In two often-cited articles, Robin Law showed that prices on the markets in Dahomey (east of the Gold Coast along the African coast) were set by the interplay between supply and demand, and were the object of both long- and short-term variations in prices, most importantly long-term inflation.[111] Another important factor influencing prices was certainly climate-induced shifts in agricultural yields. Droughts could most importantly increase the price of a crop substantially, which many European travel accounts provide ample evidence of, as could the affliction of locusts.[112] Yet another important factor was the prevalence of wars. These could many times destroy production as well as the supply of foodstuffs to the urban areas.[113] There might also have existed a seasonal variation in prices, with prices falling in the period immediately after a major harvest.[114]

As for the Gold Coast in particular, it is often argued in the previous research that it was among the most advanced economies on the West African Coast. European observers, such as merchants trading in the area, often described this region as having large markets, with many goods for sale. There was also considerable regional specialization and trade in gold, kola, foodstuffs, cloths and forest products.[115]

Aside from markets for commodities, a limited and highly imperfect factor market for capital had emerged in pre-colonial West Africa. Gareth Austin, studying Asante, has shown that the interest rates there were extremely high in international comparison, amounting to the equivalent of several hundred per cent interest per annum.[116]

In some parts of West Africa, cowries were the dominant means of exchange.[117] On the Gold Coast, cowries were virtually only used in the eastern parts of the region, from Accra and further east. Along the western stretch of the Gold Coast, including the major trading ports of Cape Coast and Elmina, the means of exchange was gold. This was in use as a currency already by the time of the first European contacts.[118]

With the arrival of Europeans on the coast came new opportunities to trade. West Africa's external trade expanded substantially particularly during the late seventeenth and early eighteenth century. The value of African exports to the Americas and Europe increased five-fold over the eighteenth century, and the value of imports more than ten-fold.[119] Imports into West Africa included more than 150 different commodities. The mark-up on these imports could be quite high – in some cases upwards of 100 per cent relative to the cost for the European traders.[120] One of the most important imports to West Africa was textiles of various sorts. Eltis and Jennings have estimated that in the seventeenth and eighteenth centuries, textiles made up roughly half of all the imports to West Africa (in terms of value). Firearms also became an increasingly important product imported into

West Africa during the seventeenth and eighteenth centuries, an issue we will return to below.[121] Other key imports were tobacco and alcohol as well as a host of other miscellaneous products. Alcohol was at this time closely related to traditional religion on the Gold Coast, and consumption was a guarded privilege for a small elite of male elders. Alcohol in general, and imported alcohol in particular, could therefore be a way of transforming material wealth into social status.[122]

Even though the value of the imports was increasing, the absolute volumes were quite small during the period studied: Eltis and Jennings estimated that all the textiles imported to West Africa in the year 1780 at most enabled an average consumption of less than one yard per person per year, and the figures were much lower a century earlier. Much of the consumption was therefore most probably concentrated to a small elite, which had the purchasing power to buy imported textiles.[123] Unequal purchasing power of the population was further reinforced in some societies such as Asante by sumptuary laws, restricting access to more luxurious consumer goods to more privileged groups in society.[124]

As was argued in Chapter 1, there has been a long debate among theoreticians as to what effect this external trade had upon African societies: dependency theorists such as Walter Rodney argued that the trade was largely determined by European interests, whereas critics, such as John Thornton, have emphasized Africans' own agency in the process. According to Kwame Daaku, trade on the Gold Coast, at least, was largely determined by African interests and demand.[125] Even though the Europeans tried, Daaku argued, they could never replace the African middlemen necessary for the trade, for the simple reason that the Europeans never went inland to the areas where local production was sited. The Europeans furthermore certainly sold adulterated goods – but so did many of their African counterparts, as well. Attempts to get the African agents to cease trading with European interlopers also failed miserably in general.[126] Further, the description Daaku provided of some of the new 'merchant princes' did not indicate that they were mere puppets to European interests, but that their agency and interests played an important role for development on the Gold Coast.[127]

According to the dependency school of thought, furthermore, deteriorating terms of trade can drain a country of its riches and undermine the possibilities for further development. Evidence provided by Gemery, Hogendorn and Johnson showed on the other hand that the terms of trade most probably improved for African exports, at least during the eighteenth century and in their trade with England. On the one hand, this was due to increasing prices for the main African export at the time, slaves. On the other hand, falling prices for many English exports also contributed to improving the African terms of trade.[128] The fall in real prices for the imported goods also contributed to a change in demand from African consumers, as a growing number of consumers were able to purchase increasingly cheaper imports.[129]

## The impact of the transatlantic slave trade

There has been a great amount of research into the transatlantic slave trade, ranging from the number of people trafficked, to a host of different issues related to the slave trade.[130] Today, there is a consensus that slavery certainly existed in Africa long before the Europeans started to find their way along the West African coast.[131] This was also true in the particular case of the Gold Coast.[132] Domestic slaves were a means for many African elites to enrich themselves without undermining the traditional kinship structures of African societies.[133] At the same time, many scholars also adhere to Paul Lovejoy's argument that even though slavery and slave trade might have existed in Africa prior to contact with the Europeans, the external slave trades *transformed* slavery in African societies substantially:

> Firstly, slavery became more common over an increasingly greater geographical area, spreading outward from those places that participated directly in the external slave trade. Secondly, the role of slaves in the economy and society became more important, resulting in the transformation of the social, economic, and political order.[134]

The size of the trade westwards across the Atlantic is quite well-established by now, following the publication of the Transatlantic Slave Trade Database. The estimates from the database suggest that, in total for the whole period from the fifteenth to the nineteenth century, approximately 12.5 million people were forced to leave the African continent.[135] On average, around 10 to 15 per cent of those shipped across the Atlantic died before they reached the Americas. How many people died while resisting being enslaved, while being marched to the coast, or while waiting to leave the coast, is largely unknown, but it does not seem unreasonable to assume that it might have added up to several million people more.[136]

It is well-known from previous research that the Gold Coast largely was spared from the transatlantic slave trade until the late seventeenth century, in contrast to many other parts of the West African coast. European states were initially instead primarily purchasing gold from the Gold Coast, in barter for the European goods exported there. This picture changed by the late seventeenth and early eighteenth centuries, when slaves started to become a major export from the region.[137] Once the slave trade had taken off from the Gold Coast, it expanded rapidly in volume. This is shown in Graph 2.1, using data from the Transatlantic Slave Trade Database. Studies of the ethnic origin of slaves on American plantations suggest that people of Akan ethnic origin made up a comparatively small share of the slaves in the Americas, indicating that much of the slave trade from the Gold Coast region might have been in people of ethnic origin other than the Akan.[138]

What impact did the slave trade then have upon African societies? The previous published literature has largely been concerned with two potential aspects of the impact: the demographic impact and the impact on the level of warfare within and between African societies. As was noted in the previous chapter, Walter Rodney argued that one of the key impacts of the transatlantic slave trade was to decrease population growth in the impacted parts of the continent (see Chapter 1). J.D. Fage was one of the first to criticize Rodney's claims about the demographic effects of

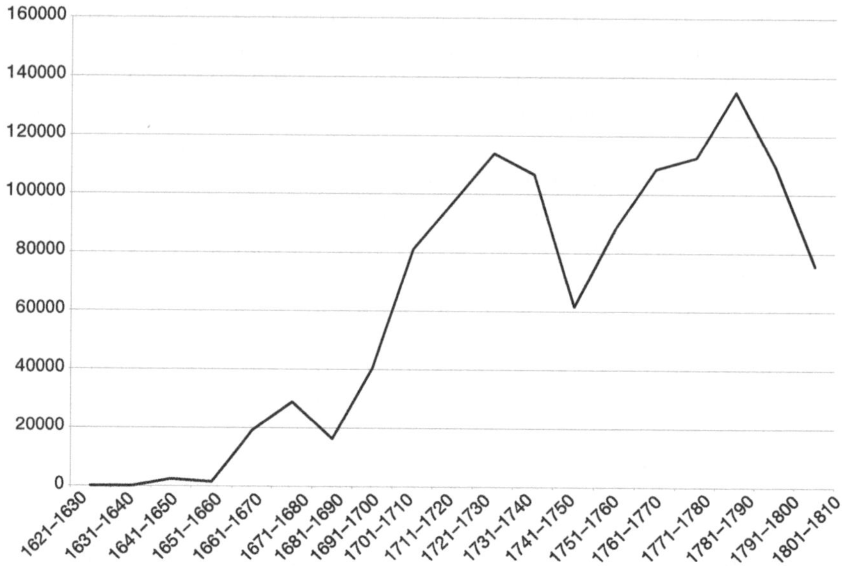


*Graph 2.1* Number of slaves exported from the Gold Coast, by decade, 1621 to 1810.
Source: TSTD2.

the slave trade. Fage instead argued that the demographic effect probably was quite limited, at most decreasing the rate of population growth marginally.[139] Many scholars nowadays seem to agree with Rodney in that the external slave trade probably had a negative demographic effect on many African societies. The trade was not evenly spread out across the continent, but impacted societies within a limited distance from the coast most severely.[140] Since many European buyers primarily demanded male slaves, possibly in combination with a domestic demand in favour of female slaves, this created certain gender imbalances in many African societies.[141] The slave trade furthermore led to migratory movements within Africa, when people fled from areas affected by slave catchers to areas where they hoped to find refuge. In that way, the slave trade shifted the population density within Africa.[142]

On the other hand, more controversial, as was seen in Chapter 1, is the claim that the external slave trade intensified the level of militarization and warfare on the African continent. Paul Lovejoy has for his part argued that while slave raiding by local warlords certainly was of old historical origin in Africa, the massive growth of the export market during the early modern period 'could not have taken place without [. . .] an intensification of political violence'.[143] John Thornton has, on the other hand, doubted whether the external slave trade really had any decisive impact upon African polities, arguing that there is no persuasive evidence showing that the level of violence actually increased in the wake of the slave trade. Thornton instead argued that slave raiding probably was endemic in Africa, since property rights in people was a substitute for private property rights to land as a means to the accumulation of wealth.[144] The issue is still highly controversial. Many Africanist scholars have in particular adhered to the so-called 'guns-for-slaves' hypothesis.[145] According to this hypothesis, guns became an important commodity in the trade on Africa at least from the eighteenth century onwards. Firearms also started to spread deeper into the African continent at this time, beyond the polities on the coast trading directly with the Europeans.[146] These guns, it is argued, were to a very large extent bartered for slaves.[147] There is however rather little direct evidence in support of this hypothesis. David Northrup has therefore argued that even though there might exist a superficial correlation between slaves exported from, and firearms imported to, some parts of Western Africa, this is not sufficient evidence to say that there was actual, systematic relationship between the two. Northrup has instead suggested that the majority of the arms 'must have gone into the hands of common people, who used them for hunting, for self-defence, and for firing at funerals and other ceremonial occasions, rather than for war'.[148] In a couple of recent contributions, Warren Whatley and Rob Gillezeau have, however, argued that the relationship between gun imports and slave exports indeed was not spurious, applying statistical methods to aggregate trade data to prove their point.[149] The issue is thus far from settled, and will be discussed further in the present book.

Just as there has been an academic debate about violence associated with the transatlantic slave trade on a continent-wide level, there has been a controversy about the relationship between the slave trade and regional warfare on the Gold Coast in particular.[150] Kwame Daaku has noted that there certainly seems to exist a correlation between the growth of the slave trade from the region, during the late seventeenth century, and the growth of empires in the region at the same time (Denkyira, Akwamu, and later also the Asante). Daaku suggests – citing a couple of African rulers' testimonies – that the seeming correlation between the growth of empires and external slave trade was simply spurious, and that in many cases, the 'wars were more political than economic, with the slaves as the incidental products of the wars'.[151]

A third potential aspect, which so far has received considerably less attention in the literature, is whether the slave trade had any impact upon the social stratification in African societies. According to Lovejoy, the expansion of slavery certainly had this effect: older, kinship-based modes of production gave way to new stratifications, where warlords and merchants became major slave-owners and slave-traders. Slaves were also put to use in an increasing number of economic activities, including plantations in Asante.[152] Much research has also shown that there were some groups of or individual Africans, particularly from the commercial and political elites in African societies, which could profit from the slave trade.[153] Local elites, such as the Asantehene of the Asante, are considered to have made considerable profits from the slave trade, even though it might be impossible to ever quantify the level of these profits.[154]

Other scholars have argued that the slave trade could be beneficial not just for a small elite in, but for quite broad segments of, certain African societies. George Metcalf has claimed that while the slave trade enriched the wealthy elites on the Gold Coast, 'it does not appear to have rendered the poor any poorer'.[155] Unfortunately, it is very unclear what Metcalf based this claim on. Harvey Feinberg has made an even stronger claim based on his study of Elmina on the Gold Coast, arguing that the slave trade created a demand not just for slaves but also for other goods and services:

> In sum, the internal economy of the Gold Coast received a boost from the Europeans residing along the coast. Practically anything required by the Europeans from free Africans brought the latter an income [. . .]. A broad segment of the African population, in addition to the overseas traders, profited from the European presence.[156]

Most important was the demand for food to provision both the forts and castles, and the ships involved in the slave trade.[157] The argument has more recently been raised again by other scholars, most importantly by David Eltis, who has argued that the value of the trade in provisions was substantial compared to the value of the trade in slaves, and that this demand laid the foundation for 'a commercial agriculture that would not have existed without the slave trade'.[158] Joseph Inikori has on the contrary argued that the negative impacts of the slave trade retarded a long-term process of development of market economies that had been taking place in many parts of Africa. Population growth and inter-continental trade had started to commercialize West African societies already by the late centuries of the first millennium, Inikori argues, a process that continued until the seventeenth century. This was perhaps most marked in the case of the Gold Coast, 'a major point in the evolving inter-regional specialization'.[159] But while there had been an evolution of market economies prior to the growth of the external slave trade, Inikori argued, the growth of this trade stopped any further development of the market economies on the continent. This was due to the two primary aspects of the impact of the slave trade emphasized previously: on the one hand, to the stagnation or even decline of the population growth in West Africa, and on the other hand the 'generalized violence' associated with the slave trade.[160] The present book will attempt to contribute to this discussion.

Yet another aspect of the slave trade was its impact upon institutional development. Daron Acemoglu and James Robinson have argued that the slave trade 'created a very perverse institutional dynamic which further precluded many societies in West and Central Africa from taking advantage of all the innovations in economic institutions and technology then taking place'.[161] The authors are unfortunately vague as to exactly which institutions were 'perverted', or how this came about.

Proving causality is highly problematic when discussing the impact of the slave trade. One problem is related to the fact emphasized by Paul Lovejoy, that the external slave trade only was one of many factors contributing to the transformation of African societies at the time.[162] Isolating the impact of the slave trade in particular can therefore become highly problematic, especially if one is looking at a specific polity or region only. Another problem is the potential for mistaking the direction of causality. A number of contributions have, with this in mind, attempted to study the causal impact that the slave trade had upon African economies, using various sets of data and advanced statistical methods.[163] Instead of measuring the contemporary impact of the slave trade, these studies have all been attempting to measure the long-term legacy of the slave trade, in the form of the statistical relationship between the size of specific flows of the historical external slave trades from Africa, and modern-day economic development. The authors argue that a substantial negative relationship exists, explaining it by the increasing levels of conflict that the slave trades contributed to, and the mistrust that followed in its wake. Gareth Austin has certainly criticized such attempts for 'compressing history', that is, ignoring all historical events and processes between the slave trade and the modern-day stages of development of the African societies studied.[164]

## The contribution of this book to the economic history of the Gold Coast

There are, thus, many issues of African economic history in general, and the economic history of the Gold Coast, which still are largely unresolved. This is not least the case when it comes to the issue of living standards in pre-colonial Africa, which is going to be the main issue discussed in this book. The aim is to study this topic in depth in the particular case of the Gold Coast, but to do so from a global, comparative perspective, including both qualitative and quantitative methods. In order to do so, it is necessary to analyse the terms that the working classes were working under including, most importantly, the institutional arrangements governing the markets for labour, free and enslaved. One of the issues to be dealt with is furthermore the impact of the transatlantic slave trade. Whereas there is a vast literature dealing with the transatlantic slave trade per se, the impact that the slave trade had upon living standards in African societies has so far not received nearly as much attention. The aim of this book is thus to contribute to this field of research.

Chapter 3 will discuss the sources used for the study, and the problems they suffer from. Chapter 4 studies the issue of how European sources described the division of labour on the Gold Coast, as well as the ideas that Europeans had about the local population's work ethic. Chapter 5 will then study in depth the labour regime in the European enclaves on the Gold Coast, particularly focusing upon free and enslaved labourers at the Cape Coast Castle. Chapter 6 will turn to a quantitative and qualitative study of the local markets for commodities on the Gold Coast, and how they reacted to various changes, in order to determine the cost of living in the region. Chapter 7 studies qualitatively how Europeans described the material wealth, including the housing standards and various other aspects of the population on the Gold Coast. Chapter 8 estimates the living standards on the Gold Coast quantitatively, using a methodology that allows for a globally comparative perspective. The chapter also studies how the living standards developed over time, as the slave trade expanded from the region. Chapter 9, finally, summarizes the key findings of the research, and how the evidence from this case study contributes to the present state of knowledge in the field.

## Notes

1 See for example Lovejoy, P., 'The Impact of the Atlantic Slave Trade on Africa: A Review of the Literature', *Journal of African History*, 30(3) (1989), pp. 365–94, quote on p. 387; Acemoglu and Robinson, 'Why is Africa Poor?', p. 22.

2 George, K., 'The Civilized West Looks at Primitive Africa: 1400–1800. A Study in Ethnocentrism', *Isis*, 49(1) (1958), pp. 62–72; Iliffe, J., *The African Poor: A History* (Cambridge: Cambridge University Press, 1987), p. 49.

3 Thornton, *Africa and Africans*, p. 44; Thornton, J., 'Precolonial African Industry and the Atlantic Trade, 1500–1800', *African Economic History*, 19 (1990/91), p. 19. See also Freund, B., *The African Worker* (Cambridge: Cambridge University Press, 1988), pp. 1–2.

4 Wills, J.B. (ed.), *Agriculture and Land Use in Ghana* (London: Oxford University Press, 1962), chapter 20.

5 Dickson, K., *A Historical Geography of Ghana* (Cambridge: Cambridge University Press, 1971); Lewicki, T., *West African Food in the Middle Ages according to Arabic Sources* (Cambridge: Cambridge University Press, 1974); Ruskin, F.R., *Lost Crops of Africa, Volume I: Grains* (Washington: National Academy Press, 1996); La Fleur, J.D., *Fusion Foodways of Africa's Gold Coast in the Atlantic Era* (Leiden: Brill, 2012).

6 Miracle, M., 'The Introduction and Spread of Maize in Africa', *Journal of African History*, 6(1) (1965), pp. 39–55; Alpern, S., 'The European Introduction of Crops into West Africa in Precolonial Times', *History in Africa*, 19 (1992), pp. 13–43; McCann, J., *Maize and Grace: Africa's Encounter with a New World Crop, 1500–2000* (Cambridge: Harvard University Press, 2005), chapter 2; La Fleur, *Fusion Foodways*, pp. 90–5.

7 Austin, G., 'Resources, Techniques, and Strategies South of the Sahara: Revisiting the Factor Endowments Perspective on African Economic Development, 1500–2000', *Economic History Review*, 61(3) (2008), pp. 587–624; see also Hopkins, *An Economic History*, p. 37; Austen, R. and Headrick, D., 'The Role of Technology in the African Past', *African Studies Review*, 26(3/4) (1983), pp. 163–84; Austen, R., *African Economic History: Internal Development and External Dependency* (Oxford: James Currey, 1987), p. 18; Manning, P. *Slavery and African Life: Occidental, Oriental, and African Slave Trades*, (Cambridge: Cambridge University Press, 1990), p. 33; Law, R., "There's Nothing Grows in the West Indies but Will Grow Here": Dutch and English Projects of Plantation Agriculture on the Gold Coast, 1650s–1780s' in R. Law, S. Schwarz and S. Strickrodt (eds), *Commercial Agriculture, the Slave Trade and Slavery in Atlantic Africa* (Woodbridge: James Currey, 2013), pp. 116–37.

8 Austin, 'Resources, Techniques, and Strategies', p. 607.

9 Thornton, 'Precolonial African Industry', pp. 6–7. For a critique of this particular claim, see Hogendorn, J.S. and Gemery, H.A., 'Assessing Productivity in Precolonial African Agriculture and Industry 1500–1800', *African Economic History*, 19 (1990/91), pp. 31–5; McDougall, E.A., 'Production in Precolonial Africa', *African Economic History*, 19 (1990/91), pp. 37–43.

10 Hopkins, *An Economic History*, p. 15; Wilks, I., *Asante in the Nineteenth Century. The Structure and Evolution of a Political Order* (Cambridge: Cambridge University Press, 1975), pp. 87–93; Latorre, J., 'Wealth Surpasses Everything: An Economic History of Asante, 1750–1874' (PhD dissertation, Berkeley: University of California, 1978), pp. 133–4; Sanders, J., 'The Political Development of the Fante in the Eighteenth and Nineteenth Centuries: A Study of a West African Merchant Society'

(PhD dissertation, Evanston: Northwestern University, 1980), p. 53; Austin, G., *Labour, Land and Capital*, p. 57; Austin, 'Resources, Techniques, and Strategies', pp. 590–1; Austin, 'Factor Markets', pp. 29–30. See however Thornton, 'Precolonial African Industry' for a dissenting view.

11 Kea, R., *Settlements, Trade, and Polities in the Seventeenth-Century Gold Coast* (Baltimore: Johns Hopkins University Press, 1982). Population estimates on pp. 35 and 138.

12 Fetter, B., 'Decoding and Interpreting African Census Data: Vital Evidence from an Unsavory Witness', *Cahiers d'études africaines*, 27 (105–6) (1987), pp. 83–105; Clarence-Smith, W., 'The Dynamics of the African Slave Trade', *Africa*, 64(2) (1994), pp. 275–86.

13 Manning, P., 'Replication Data for African Population Estimates, 1850–1960' (2009), at *World-Historical Dataverse, Catalog #2*, http://hdl.handle.net/1902.1/15281 [accessed on 19 June 2014].

14 Manning, P., 'African Population, 1650–1950: Methods for New Estimates by Region' (paper presented at *African Economic History Conference*, Vancouver, 2013); Manning, P., 'African Population, 1650–2000: Comparisons and Implications of New Estimates' in E. Akyeampong *et al.* (eds), *Africa's Development in Historical Perspective* (Cambridge: Cambridge University Press, 2014), pp. 131–50.

15 Frankema, E. and Jerven, M., 'Writing History Backwards or Sideways: Towards a Consensus on African Population, 1850–2010', *Economic History Review*, 67(4) (2014), pp. 907–31.

16 Thornton, *Africa and Africans*, p. 104.

17 See Fynn, J.K., *Asante and its Neighbours 1700–1807* (Evanston: Northwestern University Press, 1971), p. 3.

18 Boahen, 'The States and Cultures', pp. 204–20.

19 Fynn, *Asante and its Neighbours*; Feinberg, H., 'Africans and Europeans in West Africa: Elminans and Dutchmen on the Gold Coast during the Eighteenth Century', *Transactions of the American Philosophical Society*, 79 (7) (1989), pp. 10–1; Boahen, 'The States and Cultures'; Rodney, W., 'Gold and Slaves on the Gold Coast', *Transactions of the Historical Society of Ghana*, 10 (1969), pp. 13–28.

20 Fynn, *Asante and its Neighbours*; Boahen, A., 'Fante Diplomacy in the Eighteenth Century' (paper published in the *Proceedings of the Twenty-Fifth Symposium of the Colston Research Society*, London, 1973); Sanders, J., 'The Expansion of the Fante and the Emergence of Asante in the Eighteenth Century', *Journal of African History*, 20(3) (1979), pp. 349–64; Sanders, J., 'The Political Development'; Boahen, 'The States and Cultures'; Shumway, R., *The Fante and the Transatlantic Slave Trade* (Rochester: University of Rochester Press, 2011).

21 Daaku, *Trade and Politics*, p. 5.

22 Sanders, 'The Expansion of the Fante'.

23 Daaku, *Trade and Politics*, p. 165.

24 Hopkins, *An Economic History*, p. 39.

25 Austin, 'Factor Markets', p. 30. See also Austin, 'Resources, Techniques, and Strategies', pp. 591–2.

26 Hymer, S., 'Economic Forms in Pre-Colonial Ghana', *Journal of Economic History*, 30(1) (1970), pp. 33–50.

27 Daaku, K., 'Aspects of Precolonial Akan Economy', *International Journal of African Historical Studies*, 5(2) (1972), pp. 235–47.

28 Goody, J., 'Feudalism in Africa', *Journal of African History*, 4(1) (1963), pp. 1–18; Diagne, P., 'African Political, Economic and Social Structures during this Period' in B.A. Ogot (ed.), *General History of Africa V: Africa from the Sixteenth to the Eighteenth Century* (Paris: UNESCO, 1992), pp. 23–45; Wilks, I., *Forests of Gold: Essays on the Akan and the Kingdom of Asante* (Athens: Ohio University Press, 1993), p. 99.

29 Austin, G., 'Labour and Land in Ghana, 1874–1939: A Shifting Ratio and an Institutional Revolution', *Australian Economic History Review,* 47 (2007), pp. 95–120, quote on p. 97. See also Berry, S., *Chiefs Know their Boundaries: Essays on Property, Power and the Past in Asante, 1896–1996* (Oxford: James Currey, 2001), p. 145; Berry, *No Condition is Permanent*, chapter 5; Daaku, *Trade and Politics*, pp. 50–1.
30 Austin, *Labour, Land and Capital*, p. 104.
31 Austin, *Labour, Land and Capital*, pp. 102–5. See also Austin, G., 'Sub-Saharan Africa: Land Rights and Ethno-National Consciousness in Historically Land-Abundant Economies', in S. Engerman and J. Metzer (eds), *Land Rights, Ethno-Nationality, and Sovereignty in History* (London: Routledge, 2004), pp. 276–93; Austin, G., 'The Political Economy of the Natural Environment in West African History: Asante and its Savanna Neighbors in the Nineteenth and Twentieth Centuries' in R. Kuba and C. Lentz (eds), *Land and the Politics of Belonging in West Africa* (Leiden: Brill, 2006), pp. 187–212.
32 Austin, 'Factor Markets', p. 33; see also Latorre, 'Wealth Surpasses Everything', p. 145; Sanders, 'The Political Development', pp. 36–7; Arhin, K., 'Peasants in Nineteenth Century Asante', *Current Anthropology*, 24 (1983), pp. 471–80.
33 Kea, *Settlements, Trade, and Polities*, p. 108.
34 Kea, *Settlements, Trade, and Polities*, p. 165.
35 Kea, *Settlements, Trade, and Polities*, p. 19.
36 Fage, J.D., 'Slaves and Society in Western Africa, c. 1445–c. 1700', *Journal of African History*, 21(3) (1980), pp. 289–310, see p. 305 in particular.
37 Austin, *Labour, Land and Capital*, p. 113; Austin, 'Factor Markets', p. 38; Austin, 'Coercion and Markets', p. 9.
38 Austin, *Labour, Land and Capital*, p. 162.
39 Austin, *Labour, Land and Capital*, p. 170.
40 See for example Fage, *A History of West Africa*, p. 94; Wilks, 'The State of the Akan and the Akan States', p. 237; Iliffe, *The Emergence of African Capitalism*, pp. 13–15; Dumett, R., 'Traditional Slavery in the Akan Region in the Nineteenth Century: Sources, Issues and Interpretations' in D. Henige and T.C. McCaskie (eds), *West African Economic and Social History: Studies in Memory of Marion Johnson* (Madison: University of Wisconsin, 1990), pp. 7–22; Berry, *No Condition is Permanent*, chapter 6.
41 Austin, 'Resources, Techniques, and Strategies', p. 597; Austin, 'Factor Markets', p. 30; see also Wilks, *Forests of Gold*, pp. 60–1.
42 Lovejoy, P., 'Pawnship, Debt, and "Freedom" in Atlantic Africa during the Era of the Slave Trade: A Reassessment', *Journal of African History*, 55(1) (2014), pp. 55–78.
43 Lovejoy, 'Pawnship, Debt', p. 70; Spicksley, J., 'Pawns on the Gold Coast: The Rise of Asante and Shifts in Security for Debt, 1680–1750', *Journal of African History*, 54(2) (2013), pp. 147–75; see also Austin, G., 'Human Pawning in Asante, 1820–1950: Markets and Coercion, Gender and Cocoa' in P. Lovejoy and T. Falola (eds), *Pawnship, Slavery, and Colonialism in Africa* (Trenton: Africa World Press, 2003), pp. 187–224.
44 Getz, T., *Slavery and Reform in West Africa: Toward Emancipation in Nineteenth-Century Senegal and the Gold Coast* (Athens, OH: Ohio University Press, 2004), chapters 3 and 6.
45 Perbi, A., 'The Relationship between the Domestic Slave Trade and the External Slave Trade in Pre-Colonial Ghana', *Research Review (NS)*, 8(1/2) (1992), pp. 64–75, quote on p. 67. See also Dumett, R., 'The Work of Slaves in the Akan and Adangme Regions of Ghana in the Nineteenth Century', in S. Beswick and J. Spaulding (eds). *African Systems of Slavery* (Trenton: Africa World Press, 2010), pp. 67–104.
46 Inikori, J. 'Slaves or Serfs? A Comparative Study of Slavery and Serfdom in Europe and Africa', in I. Okpewho, C.B. Davies and A. Mazrui (eds), *The African Diaspora:*

*African Origins and New World Identities* (Bloomington: Indiana University Press, 1999), pp. 49–75.

47 Fisher, *Slavery in the History*, pp. 208–31; Iliffe, *The Emergence of African Capitalism*, pp. 6–15; Mandala, E., 'The Making of Wage Laborers in Nineteenth Century Southern Africa: Magololo Porters and David Livingstone, 1853–1861', *International Labor and Working-Class History*, 86 (2014), pp. 15–35.

48 Feinberg, 'Africans and Europeans', p. 27.

49 Davies, K.G., *The Royal African Company* (New York: Octagon Books, 1975), pp. 16–24; Daaku, *Trade and Politics*, pp. 7–9.

50 Davies, *The Royal African Company*, pp. 44–6.

51 St Clair, W., *The Door of No Return: The History of Cape Coast Castle and the Atlantic Slave Trade* (New York: Bluebridge, 2007), pp. 39–40.

52 Meyerowitz, E., *The Early History of the Akan States of Ghana* (London: Red Candle Press, 1975), p. 82.

53 Nováky, G., *Handelskompanier och Kompanihandel. Svenska Afrikakompaniet 1649–1663. En studie i feodal handel* [Trading Companies and Company Trading. The Swedish Africa Company 1649–1663. A Study In Feudal Trade] (Uppsala: Acta Universitatis Upsaliensis, 1990), pp. 98–108.

54 See for example Lawrence, A.W., *Trade Castles and Forts of West Africa* (London: Jonathan Cape, 1963).

55 Daaku, *Trade and Politics*, p. 103; see also Daaku, 'Trade and Trading Patterns', p. 169.

56 Davies, *The Royal African Company*, pp. 240–50; Feinberg, 'Africans and Europeans', p. 35.

57 Gutkind, P., 'Trade and Labor in Early Precolonial African History: The Canoemen of Southern Ghana', in C. Coquery-Vidrovitch and P. Lovejoy (eds), *The Workers of African Trade* (Beverly Hills: Sage Publications, 1985), pp. 25–50; Gutkind, P., 'The Canoemen of the Gold Coast (Ghana): A Survey and an Exploration in Precolonial African Labour History', *Cahiers d'Études Africaines*, 29(115/116) (1989), pp. 339–76; Reese, T., 'The Drudgery of the Slave Trade: Labor at Cape Coast Castle, 1750–1790', in P.A. Coclanis (ed.), *The Atlantic Economy during the Seventeenth and Eighteenth Century: Organization, Operation, Practice, and Personnel* (Columbia: University of South Carolina Press, 2005), pp. 277–96; Reese, T., 'Facilitating the Slave Trade: Company Slaves at Cape Coast Castle, 1750–1807', *Slavery & Abolition*, 31 (2010), pp. 363–77.

58 Yankah, K., *Speaking for the Chief: Kyeame and the Politics of Akan Royal Oratory* (Bloomington: Indiana University Press, 1995).

59 Gutkind, 'The Canoemen', p. 358; Feinberg, 'Africans and Europeans', p. 69; Hernæs, P., ' "Fort Slavery" at Christiansborg on the Gold Coast: Wage Labour in the Making?' in P. Hernæs and T. Iversen (eds), *Slavery across Time and Space: Studies in Slavery in Medieval Europe and Africa* (Trondheim: Norwegian University of Science and Technology, Department of History, 2002), pp. 197–230; Reese, 'The Drudgery', p. 281; Reese, 'Facilitating the Slave Trade', p. 368.

60 Priestley, M., 'An Early Strike in Ghana', *Ghana Notes and Queries*, 7 (1965), p. 25; Gutkind, 'Trade and Labor', pp. 27–8; Gutkind, 'The Canoemen', p. 348; Reese, 'The Drudgery', p. 281; Reese, 'Facilitating the Slave Trade', p. 109.

61 Reese, T., 'Wives, Brokers, and Laborers: Women at Cape Coats, 1750–1807', in D. Catterall and J. Campbell (eds), *Women in Port: Gendering Communities, Economies, and Social Networks in Atlantic Port Cities, 1500–1800* (Leiden: Brill, 2012), pp. 291–314.

62 Hernæs, 'Fort Slavery', p. 204; Kea, *Cultural and Social History*, pp. 139–40; Shumway, *The Fante*, pp. 84–98; Gutkind, 'The Canoemen', p. 357.

63 Davies, *The Royal African Company*, p. 242; Reese, 'Facilitating the Slave Trade', pp. 366–8.
64 Shumway, 'Castle Slaves'.
65 Reese, 'Facilitating the Slave Trade', p. 373; Kea, *Cultural and Social History*, pp. 140–1.
66 St Clair, *The Door of No Return*, p. 133; Reese, 'Facilitating the Slave Trade', p. 364; Shumway, 'Castle Slaves'.
67 Bolland, O.N., 'Proto-Proletarians? Slaves Wages in the Americas: Between Slave Labour and Free Labour', in M. Turner (ed.), *From Chattel Slaves to Wage Slaves: The Dynamics of Labour Bargaining in the Americas* (Kingston: Ian Randle, 1995), pp. 123–47.
68 Hernæs, 'Fort Slavery', p. 207; Reese, 'Facilitating the Slave Trade', p. 364; Reese, 'Wives, Brokers, and Laborers', p. 309; Shumway, 'Castle Slaves'.
69 Hernæs, 'Fort Slavery', p. 212; Reese, 'Facilitating the Slave Trade', p. 372.
70 Hernæs, 'Fort Slavery', p. 206; see also Kea, *Cultural and Social History*, pp. 139–40.
71 Hernæs, 'Fort Slavery', p. 220.
72 Fynn, *Asante and its Neighbours*, p. 24; Hopkins, *An Economic History*, pp. 20–5; Smith, R., 'The Canoe in West African History', *Journal of African History*, 11 (1970), pp. 515–33; Freund, B., 'Labor and Labor History in Africa: A Review of the Literature', *African Studies Review*, 27(2) (1984), p. 20; Manchuelle, F., 'Slavery, Emancipation and Labour Migration in West Africa: The Case of the Soninke', *Journal of African History*, 30 (1989), pp. 89–106.; Kriger, C., Looking for Labor and Markets in the Past. *African Economic History*, 32 (2004), pp. 89–102; Shea, P., 'Big is Sometimes Best: The Sokoto Caliphate and Economic Advantage of Size in the Textile Industry', *African Economic History*, 34 (2006), pp. 5–21; Shumway, *The Fante*, p. 148; Frost, D., *Work and Community among West African Migrant Workers since the Nineteenth Century* (Liverpool: Liverpool University Press, 1999); Vansina, J., 'Population Movements and Emergence of New Socio-Political Forms in Africa', in B.A. Ogot (ed.), *General History of Africa V: Africa from the Sixteenth to the Eighteenth Century* (Paris: UNESCO, 1992), pp. 46–73.
73 Brooks, G., *The Kru Mariner in the Nineteenth Century: A Historical Compendium* (Newark: Liberian Studies Association in America, 1972); Frost, *Work and Community*.
74 Manchuelle, 'Slavery, Emancipation'.
75 Kea, *Settlements, Trade, and Polities*, p. 40.
76 Feinberg, 'Africans and Europeans', pp. 13 and 82.
77 See for example Curtin, P., *The Image of Africa: British Ideas and Action, 1780–1850* (Madison: University of Wisconsin Press, 1973); Barker, A., *The African Link: British Attitudes to the Negro in the Era of the Atlantic Slave Trade, 1550–1807* (London: Frank Cass, 1978); Cohen, W., *The French Encounter with Africans: White Response to Blacks, 1530–1880* (Bloomington: Indiana University Press, 1980) for some broad reviews of European 'othering' of Africans in general. A number of authors have touched upon the stereotype of laziness in particular, including Coetzee, J.M., 'Idleness in South Africa', *Social Dynamics: A Journal of African Studies*, 8(1) (1982), pp. 1–13; Atkins, K., *The Moon is Dead! Give us our Money! The Cultural Origins of an African Work Ethic, Natal, South Africa, 1843–1900* (Portsmouth: Heinemann, 1993); Doty, R.L., *Imperial Encounters: The Politics of Representation in North-South Relations* (Minneapolis: University of Minnesota Press, 1996), chapter 3; Whitehead, A., ' "Lazy men", Time-Use, and Rural Development in Zambia', *Gender & Development*, 7(3) (1999), pp. 49–61; Whitehead, A., 'Continuities and Discontinuities in Political Constructions of the Working Man in Rural Sub-Saharan Africa: The "Lazy Man" in African Agriculture', *European Journal of Development Research*, 12 (2000), pp. 23–52; Magubane, Z., 'Labor Laws and Stereotypes: Images of the Khoikhoi in

the Cape in the Age of Abolition', in M. Palmberg (ed.), *Encounter Images in the Meetings between Africa and Europe* (Uppsala, Nordic Africa Institute, 2001), pp. 76–95. Fall, B., *Social History in French West Africa: Forced Labour, Labour Market, Women and Politics* (Amsterdam: Sephis, 2002), p. 7; Okia, O., *Communal Labor in Colonial Kenya: The Legitimization of Coercion, 1912–1930* (New York: Palgrave Macmillan, 2012).

78 Miracle, M. and Fetter, B., 'Backward-Sloping Labor-Supply Functions and African Economic Behavior', *Economic Development and Cultural Change*, 18(2) (1970), pp. 240–51.

79 Hopkins, *An Economic History*, p. 18.

80 See Rönnbäck, K., 'The Men Seldom Suffer a Woman to Sit Down: The Historical Development of the Stereotype of the "Lazy African"', *African Studies*, 73(2) (2014), pp. 211–27.

81 Boserup, E., *Woman's Role in Economic Development* (London: Allen & Unwin, 1970), p. 19.

82 Boserup, *Woman's Role*; Freund, B., 'Labor and Labor History', pp. 1–58; Bryceson, D.F. (ed.), *Women Wielding the Hoe: Lessons from Rural Africa for Feminist Theory and Development Practice* (Oxford: Berg, 1995); Greene, S., *Gender, Ethnicity, and Social Change on the Upper Slave Coast: A History of the Anlo-Ewe* (London: James Currey, 1996), pp. 4–5; Coquery-Vidrovitch, C., *African Women: A Modern History* (Boulder: Westview Press, 1997), pp. 11–12; Maier, D., 'Precolonial Palm Oil Production and Gender Division of Labor in Nineteenth-Century Gold Coast and Togoland', *African Economic History*, 37 (2009), pp. 1–32; Saidi, C., *Women's Authority and Society in Early East-Central Africa* (Rochester: University of Rochester Press, 2010), p. 15; Falola, T. and Amponsah, N.A., *Women's Roles in Sub-Saharan African (Women's Roles Through History)* (Santa Barbara: Greenwood, 2012), p. 99.

83 Austin, *Labour, Land and Capital*, p. 108.

84 Robertson, C., *Sharing the Same Bowl: A Socioeconomic History of Women and Class in Accra, Ghana* (Bloomington: Indiana University Press, 1984), pp. 75–6; Coquery-Vidrovitch, *African Women*, pp. 30–2; Berger, I. and White, F., *Women in Sub-Saharan Africa: Restoring Women to History* (Bloomington: Indiana University Press, 1999), pp. 68–70.

85 Alatas, S.H., *The Myth of the Lazy Native. A Study of the Image of the Malays, Filipinos and Javanese from the Sixteenth to the Twentieth Century and its Function in the Ideology of Colonial Capitalism* (London: Frank Cass, 1977).

86 See for example Tarasov, A., 'The Religious Aspect of Labour Ethics in Medieval and Early Modern Russia', *International Review of Social History*, 56, Special Issue (2011), pp. 125–40; Jordan, S., *The Anxieties of Idleness: Idleness in Eighteenth-Century British Literature and Culture* (Lewisburg: Bucknell University Press, 2003); Mackay, R., *'Lazy, Improvident People': Myth and Reality in the Writing of Spanish History* (Ithaca: Cornell University Press, 2006), chapter 4; Schmidt, A., 'Labour Ideologies and Women in Northern Netherlands, c. 1500–1800', *International Review of Social History*, 56, Special Issue (2011), pp. 45–67; Kolchin, P., 'In Defense of Servitude: American Proslavery and Russian Proserfdom Arguments, 1760–1860', *American Historical Review*, 85 (1980), pp. 809–27; Glickstein, J, 'Pressures from Below: Pauperism, Chattel Slavery, and the Ideological Construction of Free Market Labor Incentives in Antebellum America', *Radical History Review*, 69 (1997), pp. 114–59. Tarasov (2011); Jordan (2003); Mackay (2006); Schmidt (2011); Blackburn (1997: 357); Kolchin (1980); Glickstein (1997).

87 Loomba, A., *Colonialism/Postcolonialism* (London: Routledge, 1998), p. 113.

88 Memmi, A., *The Colonizer and the Colonized* (London: Earthscan, 2003 [1965]), p. 125.

89 Daykin, J., '"They Themselves Contribute to their Misery by their Sloth": The Justification of Slavery in Eighteenth-Century French Travel Narratives', *European Legacy*, 11 (2006), pp. 623–32.
90 Iliffe, *The African Poor*, p. 3.
91 Iliffe, *The African Poor*, pp. 35–6.
92 Iliffe, *The African Poor*, p. 6.
93 Iliffe, *The African Poor*, pp. 51–2.
94 Kea, *Settlements, Trade, and Polities*, pp. 98–108.
95 Kea, *Settlements, Trade, and Polities*, p. 312.
96 Kea, *Settlements, Trade, and Polities*, tables 8.2–8.3.
97 De Zwart, P., 'Real Wages at the Cape of Good Hope: A Long-Term Perspective, 1652–1912', *Low Countries Journal of Social and Economic History*, 10 (2013), pp. 28–58; Du Plessis, S. and Du Plessis, S. 'Happy in the Service of the Company: The Purchasing Power of VOC Salaries at the Cape in the 18th Century', *Economic History of Developing Regions*, 27(1) (2012), pp. 125–49.
98 Austin, G., Baten, J. and Van Leeuwen, B., 'The Biological Standard of Living in Early Nineteenth Century West Africa: New Anthropometric Evidence for Northern Ghana and Burkina Faso', *Economic History Review*, 64 (2011), pp. 1–23; Eltis, D., 'Welfare Trends among the Yoruba in the Early Nineteenth Century: The Anthropometric Evidence'. *Journal of Economic History*, 50 (1990), pp. 521–40.
99 See for example De Vries, J., *The Industrious Revolution: Consumer Behavior and the Household Economy, 1650 to the Present* (Cambridge: Cambridge University Press, 2008), pp. 123–6; Fourie, J., 'The Remarkable Wealth of the Dutch Cape Colony: Measurements from Eighteenth-Century Probate Inventories', *Economic History Review*, 66(2) (2013), pp. 419–48.
100 Massing, J.M., *The Image of the Black in Western Art. Vol. III, Part 2: From the 'Age of Discovery' to the Age of Abolition. Europe and the World Beyond* (Cambridge: Belknap Press, 2011), chapter 5.
101 DeCorse, C., 'Culture Contact, Continuity, and Change on the Gold Coast, AD 1400–1900', *African Archaeological Review*, 10 (1992), pp. 163–96; DeCorse, C., *An Archaeology of Elmina: Africans and Europeans on the Gold Coast, 1400–1900* (Washington: Smithsonian Institution Press, 2001), pp. 62–6; DeCorse, C. (ed.), *West Africa during the Atlantic Slave Trade – Archaeological Perspectives* (London: Leicester University Press, 2001).
102 Mark, P., 'Constructing Identity: Sixteenth- and Seventeenth-Century Architecture in the Gambia-Geba Region and the Articulation of Luso-African Ethnicity', *History in Africa*, 22 (1995), pp. 307–27; Mark, P., *Portuguese Style and Luso-African Identity* (Bloomington: Indiana University Press, 2002); Feinberg, 'Africans and Europeans', pp. 80–1; Hinchmann, M., 'House and Household on Gorée, Senegal, 1758–1837', *Journal of the Society of Architectural Historians*, 65(2) (2006), pp. 166–87; Freund, B., *The African City: A History* (Cambridge: Cambridge University Press, 2007), pp. 54–5; Thiaw, I., 'Slaves Without Shackles: An Archaeology of Everyday Life on Gorée Island, Senegal', in P. Lane and K. Macdonald (eds), *Slavery in Africa: Archaeology and Memory* (Oxford: Oxford University Press, 2011), pp. 147–66; Farrar, T., *Building Technology and Settlement Planning in a West African Civilization: Precolonial Akan Cities and Towns* (Lewiston: Mellen University Press, 1996).
103 See for example McIntosh, R., 'Archaeology and Mud Wall Decay in a West African Village', *World Archaeology*, 6(2) (1974), pp. 154–71.
104 Jones, A., 'Written Sources for the Material Culture of the Gold Coast before 1800: A Provisional Checklist', *Journal des Africanistes*, 75(2) (2005), p. 26.
105 Kea, *Settlements, Trade, and Polities*, p. 318; Law, R., *Ouidah: The Social History of a West African Slaving 'Port' 1727–1892* (Athens: Ohio University Press, 2004), p. 78.

106 Prussin, L., 'An Introduction to Indigenous African Architecture', *Journal of the Society of Architectural Historians*, 33(3) (1974), pp. 182–205; Hull, R., *African Cities and Towns before the European Conquest* (New York: W.W. Norton, 1976), p. 51; Mark, *Portuguese Style*, p. 10; Hinchmann, 'House and Household', p. 179.
107 Hopkins, *An Economic History*.
108 Austin, G., 'Reconsidering Markets in Precolonial West Africa, c1450–c1890: Structure, Function and Process' (paper presented at the African Economic History Workshop, LSE, London, 2009), forthcoming as a chapter in the book *Markets, Slaves and States in West Africa*, p. 15. See also Inikori, J., 'Changing Commodity Composition of Imports into West Africa, 1650–1850: A Window into the Impact of the Transatlantic Slave Trade on African Societies', in J.K. Anquandah (ed.), *The Transatlantic Slave Trade: Landmarks, Legacies, Expectations*, (Accra: Sub-Saharan, 2007), pp. 57–80.
109 Austin, 'Reconsidering Markets', pp. 2–6.
110 Hill, P., 'Notes on Traditional Market Authority and Market Periodicity in West Africa', *Journal of African History*, 7(2) (1966), pp. 295–311.
111 Law, R., 'Computing Domestic Prices in Precolonial West Africa: A Methodological Exercise from the Slave Coast', *History in Africa*, 18 (1991), pp. 239–57; Law, R., 'Posthumous Questions for Karl Polanyi: Price Inflation in Pre-Colonial Dahomey', *Journal of African History*, 33 (1992), pp. 387–420.
112 Lovejoy, P. and Baier, S., 'The Desert-Side Economy of the Central Sudan', *International Journal of African Historical Studies*, 8 (1975), pp. 551–81; Brooks, G., *Landlords and Strangers: Ecology, Society, and Trade in Western Africa, 1000–1630* (Boulder: Westview Press, 1993), p. 40.
113 See for example Shumway, *The Fante*, pp. 56–61.
114 Law, 'Posthumous Questions', p. 400; Behrendt, S., 'Markets, Transaction Cycles, and Profits: Merchant Decision Making in the British Slave Trade', *William and Mary Quarterly*, 58 (2001), pp. 171–204, especially pp. 182–6.
115 Daaku, 'Aspects of Precolonial Akan Economy'. See however Reynolds, E., *Trade and Economic Change on the Gold Coast, 1807–1874* (New York: Longman, 1974), p. 30 for a dissenting view, seemingly based on a reading of Rattray's classic studies of Asante.
116 Austin, *Labour, Land and Capital*, p. 138; Austin, 'Factor Markets', p. 35; Lovejoy, P. and Richardson, D., 'The Business of Slaving: Pawnship in Western Africa, c. 1600–1810', *Journal of African History*, 42(1) (2001), pp. 67–89.
117 Hogendorn, J. and Johnson, M., *The Shell Money of the Slave Trade* (Cambridge: Cambridge University Press, 1986); Law, R., *The Slave Coast of West Africa 1550–1750: The Impact of the Atlantic Slave Trade on an African Society* (Oxford: Clarendon Press, 1991).
118 Daaku, *Trade and Politics*, p. 35; Kea, *Settlements, Trade, and Polities*, pp. 186–92.
119 Eltis, D. and Jennings, L., 'Trade between Western Africa and the Atlantic World in the Pre-Colonial Era', *American Historical Review*, 93(4) (1988), pp. 936–59.
120 Davies, *The Royal African Company*, p. 234; Feinberg, 'Africans and Europeans', pp. 49–52.
121 Eltis and Jennings, 'Trade between Western Africa', table 2.
122 See for example Dumett, R., 'The Social Impact of the European Liquor Trade on the Akan of Ghana (Gold Coast and Asante), 1875–1910', *Journal of Interdisciplinary History*, 5(1) (1974), pp. 69–101; Akyeampong, E., 'Alcoholism in Ghana – A Socio-Cultural Exploration', *Culture, Medicine and Psychiatry*, 19 (1995), pp. 261–80; Akyeampong, E., *Drink, Power, and Cultural Change: A Social History of Alcohol in Ghana, c. 1800 to Recent Times* (Oxford: James Currey, 1996).
123 Eltis and Jennings, 'Trade between Western Africa', pp. 952–3.

124 Austin, G., ' "No Elders Were Present": Commoners and Private Ownership in Asante, 1807–96', *Journal of African History,* 37(1) (1996), pp. 1–30.
125 Daaku, *Trade and Politics*, p. 24.
126 Daaku, *Trade and Politics*, pp. 40–1.
127 Daaku, *Trade and Politics*, chapter 6.
128 Gemery, H.A., Hogendorn, J. and Johnson, M., 'Evidence on English/African Terms of Trade in the Eighteenth Century', *Explorations in Economic History*, 27 (1990), pp. 157–77.
129 Austin, 'Reconsidering Markets', p. 8.
130 See for example Rawley, J., *The Transatlantic Slave Trade – A History*, rev. edn (Lincoln: University of Nebraska Press, 2005); Klein, H., *The Atlantic Slave Trade*, 2nd edn (Cambridge: Cambridge University Press, 2010).
131 Thornton, *Africa and Africans*, chapter 3; Stilwell, *Slavery and Slaving.*
132 Anquandah, J.K., 'Researching the Historic Slave Trade in Ghana – An Overview', in J.K. Anquandah (ed.), *The Transatlantic Slave Trade: Landmarks, Legacies, Expectations* (Accra: Sub-Saharan, 2007), pp. 23–56; Perbi, 'The Relationship between the Domestic Slave Trade and the External Slave Trade'; Perbi, A., *A History of Indigenous Slavery in Ghana: From the 15th to the Nineteenth Century* (Accra: Sub-Saharan, 2004).
133 Cooper, F., 'The Problem of Slavery in African Studies', *Journal of African History*, 20(1) (1979), pp. 103–25. See also Stilwell, *Slavery and Slaving*, chapter 3.
134 Lovejoy, *Transformations in Slavery*, p. 1; see also Lovejoy, 'The Impact of the Atlantic', pp. 365–94; Stilwell, *Slavery and Slaving*, chapters 4–5.
135 TSTD2 (2010). *Transatlantic Slave Trade Database*, 2010 version, Estimates Spreadsheet, at www.slavevoyages.org/tast [accessed 11 January 2012].
136 See for example estimates in the case of Angola in Miller, J., *Way of Death: Merchant Capitalism and the Angolan Slave Trade 1730–1830* (Madison: University of Wisconsin Press, 1988), pp. 380–7.
137 Rodney, 'Gold and Slaves'; Lovejoy, *Transformations in Slavery*, pp. 57–8; Smallwood, S., *Saltwater Slavery: A Middle Passage from Africa to American Diaspora* (Cambridge: Harvard University Press, 2007).
138 Lovejoy, 'The Impact', table 2.
139 Fage, *A History of West Africa*, p. 86.
140 Austen, *African Economic History*, p. 96; Manning, *Slavery and African Life*; Inikori, 'Africa in World History'; Lovejoy, *Transformations in Slavery*, pp. 62–7; for a dissenting view, see Clarence-Smith, 'Dynamics of the African Slave Trade'.
141 Lovejoy, *Transformations in Slavery*, p. 65; Nwokeji, G.U., 'African Conceptions of Gender and the Slave Traffic', *William and Mary Quarterly*, 58(1) (2001), pp. 47–68.
142 Van Dantzig, 'Effects of the Atlantic', p. 266; Diagne, 'African Political, Economic', p. 38.
143 Lovejoy, *Transformations in Slavery*, p. 68; see also Olaniyan, B., *Economic History of West Africa* (Ibadan: Educational Research Institute, 1971), pp. 44–7; Inikori, 'Africa in World History', pp. 106–7.
144 Thornton, *Africa and Africans*, chapter 4.
145 Rodney, 'Gold and Slaves'; Davidson, B., 'Slaves or Captives? Some Notes on Fantasy and Fact', in Nathan Huggins, Martin Kilson and Daniel Fox (eds), *Key Issues in the Afro-American Experience* (New York: Harcourt Brace Jovanovich, 1971), pp. 54–73.
146 Kea, R., 'Firearms and Warfare on the Gold and Slave Coasts from the Sixteenth to the Nineteenth Centuries', *Journal of African History*, 12(2) (1971), pp. 185–213.
147 Inikori, J., 'The Import of Firearms into West Africa 1750–1807: A Quantitative Analysis', *Journal of African History*, 18(3) (1977), pp. 339–68. See also

Richards, W.A., 'The Import of Firearms into West Africa in the Eighteenth Century', *Journal of African History*, 21(1) (1980), pp. 43–59.

148 Northrup, D., *Africa's Discovery of Europe 1450–1850* (Oxford: Oxford University Press, 2009), p. 104. See also White, G., 'Firearms in Africa: An Introduction', *Journal of African History*, 12(2) (1971), pp. 173–84; Thornton, *Africa and Africans*, pp. 112–16; Curtin, P., *Economic Change in Precolonial Africa: Senegambia in the Era of the Slave Trade* (Madison: University of Wisconsin Press, 1975), p. 325.

149 Whatley, W., *The Gun-Slave Cycle in the 18th Century British Slave Trade in Africa* (Working paper, University of Michigan, 2012); Whatley, W. and Gillezeau, R., 'The Impact of the Transatlantic Slave Trade on Ethnic Stratification in Africa', *American Economic Review*, 101 (2011), pp. 571–6.

150 Rodney, 'Gold and Slaves'; Boahen, 'The States and Cultures'; Anquandah, 'Researching the Historic', pp. 30–1. For an alternative interpretation, see Perbi, *A History of Indigenous*, pp. 63–5.

151 Daaku, *Trade and Politics*, p. 32.

152 Lovejoy, *Transformations in Slavery*, pp. 114–27.

153 Evans, E.W. and Richardson, D., 'Hunting for Rents: The Economics of Slaving in Pre-Colonial Africa', *Economic History Review*, 48(4) (1995), pp. 665–86.

154 Perbi, *A History of Indigenous*, p. 67.

155 Metcalf, G., 'A Microcosm of Why Africans Sold Slaves: Akan Consumption Patterns in the 1770s', *Journal of African History*, 28(3) (1987), pp. 377–94, quote on p. 393.

156 Feinberg, 'Africans and Europeans', p. 71.

157 See also Fage, *A History of West Africa*, p. 81; Austen, *African Economic History*, p. 97; Law, *The Slave Coast*, p. 220; Hernæs, P., 'Afro-Danish Trade on the 18th-Century Gold Coast. A Quantitative Assessment', in P. Hernæs, *The Danish Slave Trade from West Africa and Afro-Danish Relations on the 18th-Century Gold Coast* (Trondheim, 1992), chapter 4, p. 38.

158 Eltis, D., 'The Slave Trade and Commercial Agriculture in an African Context', in R. Law, S. Schwarz and S. Strickrodt (eds), *Commercial Agriculture, The Slave Trade and Slavery in Atlantic Africa* (Woodbridge: James Currey, 2013), pp. 28–53, quote on p. 37; see also Green, T., 'The Export of Rice and Millet from Upper Guinea into the Sixteenth-Century Atlantic Trade', in R. Law, S. Schwarz and S. Strickrodt (eds), *Commercial Agriculture, the Slave Trade and Slavery in Atlantic Africa* (Woodbridge: James Currey, 2013), pp. 79–97.

159 Inikori, J., 'The Development of Commercial Agriculture in Pre-Colonial West Africa', *African Economic History Network Working Paper no. 9/2013* (2013), p. 16.

160 Inikori, 'Changing Commodity Composition of Imports into West Africa, 1650–1850'; Inikori, 'The Development of Commercial', p. 26.

161 Acemoglu and Robinson, 'Why is Africa Poor?', pp. 23 and 30.

162 Lovejoy, 'The Impact of the Atlantic', p. 365.

163 Nunn, 'The Long-Term Effects'; Nunn and Wantchekon, 'The Slave Trade'; Whatley and Gillezeau, 'The Impact of the Transatlantic'; Obikili, N., 'The Trans-Atlantic Slave Trade and Local Political Fragmentation in Africa', *Economic Research Southern Africa Working Paper 406*, (2014).

164 Austin, G., 'The "Reversal of Fortune" Thesis and the Compression of History: Perspectives from African and Comparative Economic History', *Journal of International Development*, 20 (2008), pp. 996–1027.

# 3 Sources and source criticism

## Introduction

This chapter discusses the sources and methods that will be used in the book. It is well known that there is a great dearth of written primary source materials when it comes to African pre-colonial history. Further, what sources there are, are to a very large extent the product of non-African agents – along the West African coast primarily written by Europeans but for other parts of Africa, by Arabs. The book will be based on triangulation of both sources and methods, combining qualitative and quantitative methods, to make as much use as possible of what evidence there is in the scarce primary sources.

## Written sources on African history

Because of the great dearth of source materials from many parts of Africa, as well as the problem of negative stereotypes influencing many Europeans' observations and testimonies, many scholars have argued that historians must use a variety of methods.[1] There are, in many cases, not a lot of written sources to use for a historical study of pre-colonial Africa. In particular, there exist very few accounts written by Africans themselves. What written sources there are, are instead mainly written by external observers, such as European travellers' accounts from the continent. In African historiography, oral tradition has therefore come to play a comparatively important role. Oral tradition is, however, fraught with a number of limitations. One such limitation is the challenge of establishing a chronology to the oral tradition, since the dating of orally transmitted events can be highly imprecise. Another limitation is the lack of independence from other sources (e.g. evidence from written records whose contents have later entered into the oral tradition). A third and, for this book, the most important limitation, is the selectivity of oral tradition.[2] As Jan Vansina has put it: 'Some topics are worthwhile, others are not. Certain individuals or groups of people are interesting, others are not'.[3] It is not uncommon that oral tradition is heavily focused on the matters of state and the lives of the elite, and often includes little or no evidence at all on the topics that this book will deal with, that is, the socio-economic conditions of the common population.

The contribution of this book will be based on empirical evidence gathered from written sources produced in the pre-colonial period, both published and unpublished. The written sources used for this book will broadly be of two kinds: on the one hand published travelogues by European authors, used for qualitative text analyses, and on the other hand unpublished archival materials primarily including the correspondence and economic accounts of European companies trading on the African coast during the period, the latter used primarily for quantitative analyses. The different types of source materials will be used in order to triangulate the evidence from the various sources.[4] These sources might suffer from biases arising from the fact that external observers might have had an agenda with what they observed and wrote down, and that their observations might have been distorted by severe prejudices. Not the least, it is well-known that racism permeated much of European thinking about Africa for a very long time. This might have influenced how many individual Europeans wrote about the continent. This is important to keep in mind when interpreting the evidence found in the sources.

## Qualitative analysis

### *Narrative travel accounts*

The book will to a large extent make use of qualitative text analysis of narratives to be found in written sources – both published and unpublished – to African history. There are hundreds of travel accounts from Africa produced during the pre-colonial era, in a number of European languages. Most accounts were written by authors from the major European nations involved in trading on Africa – Portugal, England, the Netherlands and France – but there are also a fair number of publications in other languages (for example Latin, Italian, German, Danish or Swedish). Adam Jones has noted that these travel accounts deal with issues concerning material culture only to a very limited extent.[5] The same can no doubt be said for other issues related to the living standards on the African coast, in particular, then, the living standards of the common population. Finding information related to living standards and material culture in this type of primary source, therefore, requires searching through large amounts of text, often finding little more than very limited amounts of information on specific issues. Further, what information there is can often be quite vague, which often makes it very hard to try to discern any changes over time from this type of source material, even in cases when separate authors are discussing the same issues.

For this study, the primary sources used have primarily been identified using existing guides to the published sources on African history.[6] Many of these sources were then accessed using a couple of digital databases – most importantly The Making of the Modern World (MOMW), Early English Books Online (EEBO), Eighteenth Century Collections Online (ECCO), and Gallica.[7] The primary sources in their original language have been preferably consulted whenever this has been possible. Due to the author's limited language skills, it has been necessary to consult some translations into English instead of material in the original language. This concerns sources originally published in German, Dutch, Portuguese, Italian or Latin. Admittedly, the use of translations is potentially problematic for analysis. Nuances that could be important might be lost in translation, even if the translator is both skilled and faithful to the original. Bad translations might even introduce errors that were not present in the original documents or publications.[8] It has however been considered better to include these sources, even if only through a translation, than to leave them out because of a lack of language skills, since what they might have to contribute might enrich the analysis.

### *Tendencies in the travel accounts*

There has been much scholarly effort put into trying to tease out what – if any – use European travel literature can be when attempting to write about African history. This is not unique for the travel literature regarding Africa, but a general problem for many historians studying early modern travel literature. There were many factors influencing the genre of travel literature, including political and economic interests, as well as cultural and religious ideas.[9] What is certain is that these European sources all represent an 'alter-perspective' of the societies that they provide evidence of: they are not produced by Africans themselves, but by 'outsiders' observing African societies.[10] Because of their position as outsiders, the European observers might not always understand or grasp the socio-cultural context that they write about, and their observations might be distorted by racial prejudices. The problem of potential racism is certainly particularly problematic in the case of Europeans observing African societies, because of the large amount of stereotypes about Africans that existed. Many Europeans thought of Africans as simply poor, primitive and savage. Such 'othering' of African cultures permeated much of European thinking at the time.[11] This must be kept in mind when analysing the evidence in the European travelogues. The problem is most certainly acute when it comes to some types of observations, such as the character traits of the population. In this case, the racist stereotypes of the 'lazy African' possibly permeated the thoughts of all too many observers to such an extent as to render their testimonies too unreliable to be used as objective evidence of any real behavioural patterns or ethics, as will be discussed in Chapter 4. In other cases, such as when the authors wrote about material possessions or construction techniques, the observations might be more straightforward, and less coloured by any prejudices and stereotypes. They can, therefore, possibly help us understand some aspects of African societies more in depth.

European 'othering' of Africans is not the only problem one has to be aware of when using these sources for a study of the common population. Herbert Applebaum has put the problem of studying the historical work ethic of a population quite succinctly:

> People who work are mostly humble, with no voice in the recorded pages from which histories are written. It is mostly the leisured or the recipients of

> the state's or a patron's largesse who have the time, energy, and training to produce written works. [. . .] while we may see these ideas as representing the values of a culture, we must recognize the class origin of such ideas.[12]

Applebaum's argument is concerned with the issue of studying the work ethic of a population, but the problem is the same when studying many other aspects of social life, not least when it comes to the issue of material welfare: many of the (European) statements about the material welfare of the (African) populations might be coloured not only by European 'othering', but also by a class bias.

It is also important to keep in mind that who the observers were, and what they were doing in Africa, might have influenced what they wrote in their travelogues. Some travel accounts might contain a problematic bias for personal, political or ideological reasons. Examples include the writings of William Snelgrave, Robert Norris and Archibald Dalzel, who all have been argued to have been particularly biased in defence of the slave trade.[13] Since one justification of the slave trade put forth by pro-slavery authors was that the living conditions of Africans generally were primitive and poor (something which the slave trade, according to these authors, relieved them from by transporting them to the much richer Americas), one might expect these authors to have a (negative) bias when discussing any topic that will touch upon living standards in Africa. Other writers, including Anthony Benezet and Charles Bernhard Wadström, were on the other hand all outspoken pro-abolitionist authors.[14] Pro-abolitionist writers might be biased, too, emphasizing instead the high economic development of Africa (real or potential, had it not been for the slave trade). Sources such as these will therefore only play a minor role in the analysis. Many more sources might also be biased for similar reasons, even though the bias might be more subtle than in these discussed examples. Many of the writers on pre-colonial West Africa were directly or indirectly involved in the transatlantic slave trade, as employees of one or another of the European slave-trading companies, and might for that reason be biased towards a pro-slavery position, and therefore portray living standards in Africa in a less favourable light than what might have been justified. This must be kept in mind when analysing the empirical evidence from these sources.

### *Forged travel accounts*

It is possible that some supposed primary sources are simply forgeries, perhaps written in order to earn the author an income from the sales of the publication, or just to enhance the glory and status of the adventurous author. Some travel accounts purportedly reporting about West Africa might indeed be completely spurious. One example is perhaps a publication by Richard Drake, which reports about a visit Drake supposedly made to the kingdom Asante in the early nineteenth century. T.C. McCaskie has questioned whether Drake ever made this journey, after finding that many of the statements made by Drake corroborating it were most certainly borrowed from previous authors.[15] Such accounts have, naturally, not been used as a source in this book. This does in general seem to be a minor problem compared to another one: that of authors borrowing from previous authors – with or without any references to where they got their information.

### *Independence of travel accounts*

One key problem when using travel accounts as a source for African history is undoubtedly the dependence or independence of the observations. A core principle in historical investigation is that a factual statement is considered more credible if it can be corroborated by several independent observations in different primary sources. This is highly problematic in the case of travel accounts from Africa. It is well-known that many of the purported primary sources are, in fact, not primary sources at all. Instead, many of the early modern authors read previously published works. In many cases, this also influenced how they themselves understood or wrote about the African societies. This influence is not always easy to trace. In some cases, it might be quite apparent. In many other cases, the influence from previous authors might on the other hand be very subtle. Much work has therefore gone into decompiling travel accounts, in order to tease out what unique contribution the individual account might have made, that is, separating what might be considered primary source information from secondary or even tertiary source information.[16]

Of all the travel accounts used as primary sources for this particular study, a handful play a considerably more important role than the others. The travel accounts frequently cited in this study include, in particular, the accounts of Pieter de Marees, Nicolas Villault de Bellefond, Wilhelm Müller, Willem Bosman, Jean Barbot, Ludewig Ferdinand Rømer, Paul Erdmann Isert, Henry Meredith and William Hutton. Because of the importance of these particular authors, it is worthwhile to discuss their respective value as a source somewhat at length. Other travel accounts will be treated more briefly here.

#### *Early Portuguese sources*

Many of the early Portuguese sources are considered both quite reliable and independent of each other. An early example is the account of Gomes Eanes de Zurara, a court chronicler whose account of Africa was explicitly based on the earlier writing of Afonso Cerveira.[17] Several accounts were published in the fifteenth and sixteenth centuries by Portuguese explorers who had participated in the Portuguese discoveries of the African coast. As far as historians have been able to tell, they seem to have written their accounts primarily based on their own experiences. Examples include Diogo Gomes, Duarte Pacheco Pereira and Alvise Cadamosto.[18] While these sources provide much evidence on the Portuguese explorations, and the contact with local peoples in West Africa, less information is provided about material culture and living standards in the region.

*Pieter de Marees*

Pieter de Marees was a Dutch merchant and explorer who travelled to the Gold Coast some time in the late sixteenth or early seventeenth century. His account of the journey was originally published in 1602 under the title *Beschryvinge ende historische verhael vant Gout Konickrijck van Guinea* [Description and Historical Account of the Gold Kingdom of Guinea], and soon translated into several other languages. Modern-day scholars have classified his account as 'unrivalled' as a source for the early history of West Africa, providing much information on the 'character' of the people he encountered, as well as about the material culture in the region.[19] It is unfortunately quite unclear exactly what sources the author used when writing his account. Scholars generally assume that much of the information is based on personal observations. His personal experience of the Gold Coast was, however, possibly quite limited – he states himself that he visited the West African coast several times, but not exactly when or for how long.[20] De Marees did also make some use of other sources, even if this might primarily be concerning the natural history of the region.[21] One particular value of de Marees' publication is the number of illustrations included in it. It has been argued that they ought to be attributed at least the same value as a source material as the text in de Marees' book: even though the engraver of the copperplates most probably never had met Africans personally, the engravings were probably done after explicit descriptions by the author himself.[22] While many scholars argue that de Marees' account is highly valuable, and that the author was comparatively unprejudiced compared to many other Europeans at the time, it is also important to keep in mind that he was hardly completely free from the stereotypes about Africans that were prevalent in Europe at the time, moralizing not least about African women.[23]

*Nicolas Villault de Bellefond*

Nicolas Villault de Bellefond was a French merchant who participated on a Dutch voyage to West Africa in 1666–67. Once back in Europe, he wrote an account of the journey and his stay on the African coast, originally published in French in 1669 under the title *Relation des Costes d'Afrique appelées Guinée* [A Relation of the Coasts of Africa called Guinea], and translated into English in 1670.[24] Villault's account was according to his own description informed by his own observations and by information gathered from some of the Europeans stationed at Fort Fredericksburg on the Gold Coast, where the ship he travelled on lay anchored for a while. Some of the chapters were however, according to some previous scholars, clearly inspired by previous authors, such as Pieter de Marees.[25] As for its advantages, on the other hand, Jeffer Daykin has described the account as 'balanced', with comparatively few racial prejudices against Africans.[26]

*Olfert Dapper*

Though Olfert Dapper's *Naukeurige Beschrijvinge van Afrikaensche Gewesten* [An Accurate Description of African Places] (originally published in 1668) is not very intensively used in this study, it is worth a brief discussion not least because of the influence it had on later authors.[27] Dapper was a Dutch geographer, who compiled his account of Africa from what had been written previously on the topic. In contrast to many other authors on the topic, he is quite open with the fact that his work is a compilation, and that he explicitly referred to the previously discussed work of Pieter de Marees, as well as to the by then unpublished writings of a Samuel Blomert as important sources for the parts of his study concerned with West Africa.[28] Adam Jones has however shown that Dapper used more than a hundred different sources when compiling his account. Since many of these sources have since been lost, as far as is known today, Dapper occasionally contributes with the most primary source available for some aspects of African history, for example, when describing Benin.[29] Dapper's account came to be very influential for, and often plagiarized by, later writers on West Africa. One of the more blatant examples of the latter include John Ogilby's description of Africa which, it has been argued, was mainly a translation of Dapper into English, though without complimenting Dapper as the author.[30]

### *Wilhelm Johann Müller*

Wilhelm Müller was a German priest who worked on the Gold Coast for the Danish slave-trading company, from 1662 to 1669, and later wrote an account of this period in Africa. Müller provided many details of life and material culture on the Gold Coast at the time of his writing – in Adam Jones' mind 'a classic piece of systematic, almost pedantic, Teutonic scholarship'.[31] At the same time, he had most certainly read Pieter de Marees' work on the Gold Coast, and sometimes borrowed parts of what he wrote from him. Adam Jones has nonetheless argued that he was a rather critical reader who consciously chose what parts to borrow in order to produce an 'improved version' of the account, as Adam Jones has put it, at the same time contributing with many observations of his own.[32]

### *Willem Bosman*

Willem Bosman was a merchant working for the Dutch West India Company, stationed fourteen years on the Gold Coast, arriving there in 1698. His book *Nauwkeurige beschryving van de Guinese Goud-, Tand- en Slave-Kust* [English title: A New and Accurate Description of the Coast of Guinea, divided into the Gold, the Slave, and the Ivory Coasts] was published originally in 1704.[33] It is one of the first publications on West Africa by a writer who had spent a prolonged time in the region, and includes much information on the everyday workings of local society. J.D. Fage has argued that Bosman's book 'essentially [was] the fruit of his own fourteen years' residence on the Gold and Slave Coasts'.[34] Ivor Wilks has however belittled Bosman's work, arguing that Bosman hardly was a man of 'exceptional intellectual powers', and that he showed little interest in getting involved in local affairs, in contrast to some of the later writers of travel accounts.[35] Albert van Dantzig, who has studied the value of Bosman's accounts as a source for African history has, furthermore, argued that the book was written at least 'partly as a justification of his own actions', but added that it in general appears to be very accurate when it is possible to check factual statements against other records.[36]

### *Jean Barbot*

Jean Barbot was a French slave trader who undertook two voyages to West Africa, in 1678–79 and 1681–82, each time only staying a limited amount of time. His account of the voyages and his impressions of Africa, *A Description of the Coasts of North and South Guinea*, was not to be published until many years later, in 1732, which has created some confusion when Barbot's account has been used uncritically as a source for African history.[37] Further, the account is, to quite some extent, a compilation of information gathered from previous authors, primarily from the account of Olfert Dapper discussed above, and also from the accounts of Pieter de Marees, Nicholas Villault, Willem Bosman and some others.[38] Previous scholars have at the same time argued that Barbot nonetheless provided many unique observations in his publication, at least when he is describing some parts of the West African coast, including much information on daily life and material culture in the region. An edited volume of Barbot's account was published in 1992. The editors of the volume had then gone to great lengths to decompile Barbot, separating out what unique contributions he made himself from what he had borrowed from previous authors.[39] The edited volume has also been hailed by an expert, namely J.D. Fage, as having decompiled Barbot's account quite successfully.[40]

### *Ludewig Ferdinand Rømer*

Ludewig Ferdinand Rømer worked for the Danish slave-trading company, and was stationed on the Gold Coast from 1739–44 and 1745–49. His book *Tilforladelig efterretning om Kysten Guinea* [A Reliable Account of the Coast of Guinea] was first published in 1760, following a smaller pamphlet four years earlier.[41] Adam Jones has considered it the 'most important European source for the Gulf of Guinea composed between the works of Bosman (1704) and Isert (1788)'.[42] It is however known that Rømer to some extent borrowed some of his material from previous authors, most importantly Willem Bosman.[43]

### *Paul Erdmann Isert*

Paul Erdmann Isert was a German botanist and surgeon working for the Danish slave-trading company on the Gold Coast. He arrived on the coast in 1783, and stayed there for three years. His account, *Reise nach Guinea und den Caribäischen Inseln* [Voyage to Guinea and the Caribbean Islands], was first published in 1788.[44] It is to a large extent the fruit of his own experiences, but on some occasions he borrowed information from other authors, such as Ludewig Ferdinand Rømer, Chevalier de Desmarchais or William Snelgrave.[45] In his ethnographic observations, he tried to move away from many of the stereotypical descriptions of Africans, and according to Selena Axelrod Winsnes, 'Isert's book is notable for its attempt at objectivity and a scientific approach'.[46]

### *Henry Meredith*

Henry Meredith worked for the English company on the Gold Coast for a number of years in the early nineteenth century, and became the governor of the English fort of Winneba for a couple of years at the end of his life. His *Account of the Gold Coast of Africa* was first published in 1812, the same year that Meredith died, and was written based primarily on personal observations. The publisher wrote in the introduction to the book that a 'few observations' had been added to the manuscript by an unnamed gentleman to whom Meredith had entrusted the manuscript – but these additions were supposedly only done in notes to the manuscript 'not in any way to alter the original work'.[47] The book contains comparatively much information on local conditions and material culture.

### *William Hutton*

William Hutton accompanied the more often-cited author Joseph Dupuis on his mission to Asante in 1820.[48] Hutton did however stay somewhat longer in Asante than Dupuis did. Based on his own observations and enquiries during his stay on the African coast, he wrote his book *A Voyage to Africa*, first published in 1821, purportedly after being 'flattered by some respected friends into a belief that they were of sufficient importance to deserve publicity'.[49] The book contains many more observations on local conditions and material culture than Joseph Dupuis's rather more famous book does.

## ***Other travel accounts from the Gold Coast***

Occasionally, this book will make use of other primary sources describing living standards or material culture on the Gold Coast. These sources are generally far from as detailed on this topic as the sources discussed above are, and are therefore not used to the same extent as sources in this book. For whatever evidence these sources provide, however, some of them seem to be quite reliable per se. One example is the account of John Atkins, published in 1735. Atkins was a surgeon on a British slave-trading ship, visiting the Gold Coast in 1721. Most of his account has been considered to have been based on original, personal observations.[50] Another example is the account written by Sarah Bowdich, later remarried as Sarah Lee, who lived on the Gold Coast for a number of years in the early nineteenth century. Lee was a naturalist who made many important contributions to the development of natural sciences by her explorations of tropical botany in West Africa. She also published a book of 'stories', including a number of stories from her stay on the Gold Coast. It is unclear if the 'stories' are to be interpreted as supposedly true accounts throughout, or whether some degree of poetic licence was included in them. The stories are however written as if self-experienced, or – in some cases – as told to the author by an informant. The stories clearly shed some light on the life and customs among the local population on the Gold Coast, not least due to the lengthy notes where the author commented upon various details in the stories.[51] Sarah Lee's contribution in the field of African anthropology has rarely been recognized, perhaps since she has been overshadowed by her much more well-known husband Thomas Edward Bowdich (author of the often-cited book *Mission from Cape Coast Castle to Ashantee*, in 1819).[52]

Other sources describing the Gold Coast have been considered more controversial by modern scholars, most importantly because of extensive plagiarism. One example is the account of William Smith, published in 1744. While Smith certainly did visit West Africa himself, much of what he included in his publication – particularly the sections on the Gold Coast – was borrowed from Willem Bosman.[53] The Norwegian author Johannes Rask, whose account was published in 1754, on the other hand borrowed much of his material from Dapper. In the early nineteenth century, the Danish author H.C. Monrad, in turn, borrowed much material from Johannes Rask, but also from Ludewig Ferdinand Rømer and Paul Erdmann Isert.[54] An attempt has therefore been made to only cite such authors, if and when they contribute seemingly unique observations.

### *Travel account from other places along the West African coast*

Occasionally, some people describing other parts of the West African coast will be referred to in this study, in the belief that their observations can help to put the evidence from the Gold Coast into perspective and to determine whether the case of the Gold Coast was common or unusual compared to other coastal societies in West Africa. One example is the account of Anna Maria Falconbridge, the author of *Narrative of Two Voyages to the River Sierra Leone*.[55] The material for her book had been gathered when accompanying her husband Alexander Falconbridge – a surgeon on slave ships during the late eighteenth century, later turned abolitionist – when he came to be employed by the Anti-Slavery Society and the Sierra Leone Company to travel to the company's recently established colony in Sierra Leone. In 1802, Anna Maria Falconbridge published an account of her experiences from her stay in Sierra Leone. The book was based on her own, often very detailed, personal observations of the African coast, focused on the area of Sierra Leone in particular. Through this book, Falconbridge became the first English woman to publish a travel account of her experiences in West Africa, which is why it might provide important insights not least into the gender relations in Sierra Leone. Deirdre Coleman has, furthermore, argued that Anna Maria Falconbridge probably was comparatively free from much of the racism that permeated many other travel accounts from the region.[56]

Another example of this is the account of Francis Moore, published in 1738. Francis Moore spent four years in Senegambia, from 1730 to 1735, and also based much of his writings on personal observations noted in a journal at the time. A problem when using it as a source for African history is that when publishing his account of his stay in West Africa, Moore did introduce some anachronistic information in it, about events that took place after when the journal was supposed to have been written, confusing chronological dating of events.[57]

The account of Joseph Hawkins, published in 1797, has on the other hand been considered problematic for the simple reason that it is uncertain exactly what part of West Africa he is writing about: J.D. Fage has argued that the geographical information he provides does not fit with the exact area that he claims to be describing, and therefore suggests that Hawkins might have been mistaken as to which part of West Africa he actually had visited.[58]

As for a number of other travel accounts used briefly as a source for the research in this book, some of them have been frequently used in previous scholarship on other topics, and have then been considered quite valuable and reliable as sources. They are all included in the guides to African primary sources produced by leading experts in the field, without any indication that they would be unreliable for one or another reason discussed above. Because of the very limited role they play in the analysis in this book, a more in-depth attempt to find whether anything of what they had written might have been borrowed from some earlier author has not been undertaken for each and every one of them, but it seems reasonable to assume that this might have occurred at least to some extent.

### *Local correspondence*

The evidence from the travel accounts will be complemented by the use of sources that were unpublished at the time, in the form of the correspondence of the agents of the English Royal African Company as well as the Danish Vestindisk-Guinesisk Kompagni [West Indian-Guinean Company]. As for the English company, a large number of volumes in the British National Archives hold correspondence from the agents in West Africa, to the board of the Company in England. This correspondence has, to a very large extent, already been researched by previous scholars in the field. Robin Law has however made an enormous contribution by compiling and publishing the local correspondence between the various agents of the Royal African Company present on the coast.[59] A vast selection of documents from the correspondence of the Danish slave-trading company on the Gold Coast has, furthermore, been edited and published by Ole Justesen.[60]

This correspondence has been searched for any statements that provide evidence either of the operations of local markets, of conditions for the working classes of the local population, or of material living standards in general. The correspondence, it turns out, contains some amounts of information on how the local markets operated, as well as some information about the conditions for the working classes (in particular people working for the companies, both free and slave labourers). Hardly any statements in the correspondence relate to the material living standards of the population more generally.

The type of statements to be found in these sources occasionally provides considerably more down-to-earth and precise evidence of African societies than what can be found in the published travel accounts. In the travel accounts, the authors were generally attempting to explain the condition of African societies and peoples on a general level for a presumably quite ignorant audience of readers in Europe. In order to provide a complete and intelligible picture of the topic dealt with in the account, many of the authors also resorted to borrowing and plagiarizing from previous authors, as was noted above, to fill in the gaps between their own personal observations. The letters between the agents of the African company on the African coast are on the other hand sent between agents who (presumably) were all quite familiar with local conditions, since they were all living there. There was thus no need for the same type of general explanations or overviews about African societies. The correspondence can therefore be both much more detailed and more nuanced in its descriptions of particular issues or events, wherever such descriptions can be found between all correspondence dealing just with internal matters of the companies.

## Quantitative analysis

To accompany the qualitative analysis, the book will also use some quantitative analysis of data from primary sources. This will draw heavily on data assembled from the economic accounts produced by the English Royal African Company (RAC), and its successors, a source material that is called the T70 series in the British National Archives.[61] The Royal African Company was established as a slave-trading company in the seventeenth century. For a couple of decades, the company had a monopoly on all English slave trading. This was followed by a period where the monopoly was gradually dismantled, and the company was put in charge of maintaining the English forts and castles along the African coast. From the economic accounts of the RAC, it is possible to gather much important information which can be used for a study of the work and living conditions of the common population on the Gold Coast.

The accounts are kept in the British National Archives, dating from the establishment of the Company in the 1680s until a successor company was disbanded in 1821 and the Gold Coast was taken over as a formal colony by the British Crown. The accounts are not always useful for the purposes of this book. In practice, the quantitative analysis of the book will focus upon the period of 1699 to 1760, because of data availability in the source. There are also many gaps in the accounts, so it is not possible to construct a complete series of quantitative data even for all these years using this source. There are primarily two sorts of information that will be used from the accounts: information on the goods traded on the local markets (most importantly basic foodstuffs), and information on employments of and wage payments to various labourers working for the European company. This information has been assembled into two different databases, which henceforth will be referred to as the Gold Coast Pre-Colonial Price Database (GCPPD) and the Gold Coast Pre-Colonial Labour Database (GCPLD).

### *The Gold Coast Pre-Colonial Price Database (GCPPD)*

The RAC purchased a lot of different foodstuffs on the African markets, in order to provision not just the staff employed at the forts and castles but also – and perhaps primarily – the slave-trading ships visiting the forts and castles. The accounts also keep track of the European goods sold on the coast. From the accounts of these transactions, we can gather information about what goods were purchased, and the price they were purchased at, and similarly about European goods sold on the coast. The prices are all accounted for in gold dust and/or pound sterling (normally with an exchange rate between the two also reported). The source enables the construction of a price series for several different basic, local foodcrops, as well as for the European goods sold on the African markets.

Information on prices for specific crops can be found in this source for the period 1699–1760. Prior to 1699, the source did not record the prices of individual goods bartered for. After around 1760, the Company did not barter for most of the basic foodstuffs more than very rarely, making it impossible to construct any meaningful price series after this year. Furthermore, the Company then seems to be purchasing what little foodstuffs it needed from a middleman, thereby being considerably more insulated from price-movements in the local markets.

All transactions from this period, where the Company is purchasing foodstuffs (either in gold currency, or bartering in exchange for European goods) or selling a set of core European goods have been assembled by the author of this book in a database to be used for quantitative analyses. The database will henceforth be referred to as the Gold Coast Pre-Colonial Price Database (GCPPD). At the time of writing, the database in total contains 14,321 individual price observations.

### *The Gold Coast Pre-Colonial Labour Database (GCPLD)*

The RAC also employed a lot of labourers at the forts and castles. It is possible to divide these into three broad groups: European staff, free African labourers and African castle slaves. The staff of European descent was the largest group of free employees working at the forts and castles of the RAC. In this book, however, only the two latter groups – free or enslaved African labourers – are of interest.

All wage payments to all staff have been included in a second database constructed by the author of this book for this research project. This second database will henceforth be called the Gold Coast Pre-Colonial Labour Database (GCPLD). At the time of writing this, the database in total contains 36,687 observations, out of which 16,448 refer to African labourers (free and enslaved). A further 2,151 refer to 'mulatto' labourers, or labourers of mixed European/African descent (while the rest are wage payments to staff of European descent).

Both the African free labourers and the slaves could hold a number of different occupations (which are all recorded in the accounts). The number of individuals holding a special occupation varied enormously: for some occupations, there are many dozens of simultaneous observations. The Company did, for example, at times engage more than fifty free canoemen at the same time. For other occupations, there might only be one single or a handful of individuals occupied at the same time. This is often the case with interpreters or more skilled, free craftsmen employed by the Company. That the sample sizes vary depending on what occupations are analysed must therefore be kept in mind during the analyses.

The company kept account of all payments to people working for the Company, including both free and enslaved labour, on very detailed lists of the labourers for each month (or, in some cases, for two or three months at a time) of each year. Many of these lists have been preserved, and from these lists, one can gather information about virtually every individual labourer at the fort: their name, occupation, place of work, ethnicity/nationality (if not English), any disabilities, and the wages paid to them.

The Company generally separated the account books between two categories of workers: on the one hand, were all those included on so-called 'Pay Bills' and on the other hand, those included on so-called 'Slave Lists'. The division into these two different lists in itself suggests that the people included on the Pay Bill were not enslaved, but free labourers. All the employed Africans on these Pay Bills were, however, not necessarily free: there is at least one example where labourers that the English thought were free when they employed them, later turned out to be the slaves of a local African *caboceer*.[62] Even if not owned by the Company itself, Africans on the Company's Pay Bill might thus have been the slaves of other slaveholders. The fact that the Company actually took care to record this particular incident, when it was found that they had employed people who turned out to be slaves, does suggest, on the other hand, that it might have been an exception to the rule. It therefore seems quite reasonable to assume that the people on the Pay Bill in general were not enslaved, neither as castle slaves owned by the Company, nor by any other slaveholder.

The labourers – both free Africans and slaves – were all paid wages by the Company. These wages can be used for an analysis of wage differences and material living standards of the population. Wage payments can be found for some groups of employees throughout the same period as for price observations, that is. 1699–1760. Individual African employees are only recorded starting in 1707. Wage payments to individual slaves are only recorded starting in the 1750s – prior to this time the wage payments to the castle slaves are only reported as a lump sum to the whole collective of slaves.

The Pay Bills were in turn normally divided into two parts, along status or class lines: in the first part are people holding high-pay and high-status occupations such as the governors, factors, merchants, surgeons, writers and high-ranked militaries; in the second part are people holding lower-status occupations, including all the craftsmen, soldiers and more unskilled assistants and labourers. The only general difference, seemingly, between the two parts of the bills is that the high-status people received an extra bonus payment for the 'diet', separate from the wages they were paid. No such extra bonus for food was reported for the common employees.

The ethnicity of the individual labourers is to a large extent revealed in the accounts. In some cases, the name alone might suggest that the person was of African descent. In a number of cases, people with European-sounding names were, furthermore, explicitly reported as being 'negro', 'black', or 'native'. It is unclear if the specific wording was intentional to signify ethnic differences between these labourers, or whether the terms were considered as synonymous. In some cases, some staff was also described as 'mulatto' (either consistently, or interchangeably with the descriptions 'black' or 'negro'). Nationality was also noted if the labourer was of non-English, but European, origin – for example, some Dutch or Portuguese labourers employed by the Company. It is possible that the accounts might have under-reported the non-English labourers: on some Pay Bills, some specific individual might be reported as 'black', whereas the same information might be left out on some other Pay Bills. It is thus not possible to tell for certain exactly how many people of African descent were employed by the Company. It does seem, on the other hand, safe to assume that the number of African labourers is not over-reported, at least.

Full names were given for all staff of European descent. The fate of individual Europeans can therefore be followed in the accounts, and those who survived all the endemic diseases on the coast can be followed over many years. Many Africans are on the other hand not always identified individually by name, and even when they are, they might only be accounted for by a first name. This makes it almost impossible to link many of the records of the African employees with each other, not least since some names were quite popular (e.g. Coffee or Cudjoe, two of the Akan names given to men based on the weekday of their birth).

### *Welfare ratios*

One core contribution of this book is to estimate quantitatively the living standards of the population – for different social groups, and how it changed over time. To the knowledge of this author, this is the first book that attempts to do this in a systematic manner, for any African population during the pre-colonial period. To do this, a method called *welfare ratios* (or more specifically subsistence ratios) will be employed. The method has been pioneered by Robert Allen in a number of studies, in order to be able to compare historical material living standards between countries around the world.[63]

The method entails estimating the real wage of a population, by dividing the nominal wage a labourer could earn from working (assuming an average of 250 days worked per year) by the annual cost of subsistence. The annual cost of subsistence is constructed by calculating the price of a hypothetical basket of consumer goods. It is possible to think of many ways of constructing such a basket. The method that will be used here, of calculating 'subsistence ratios', entails calculating the price of a barebones basket of absolutely necessary goods. The basket contains only the most inexpensive staple foods available locally, in an amount that could provide the calories and proteins, respectively, that a human absolutely needs as a minimum to stave off starvation, as well as some other basic non-food necessities such as fuelwood and housing. The subsistence basket then provides us with a form of absolute benchmark against the cost of which one can compare the income of the household. The subsistence ratio could thus be estimated for any category of people for which there is information on local wages and prices. In practice, the method has so far primarily been used in studies comparing the subsistence ratios of unskilled wage workers, in order to enable a comparison of living standards between countries (see Chapter 1).

The method makes a number of assumptions in order to enable a comparison between countries. First, it is assumed that the caloric requirements are roughly equal for all adult human beings around the world, a simplification assumed in order to avoid the endogeneity in human stature (people who consume enough food during their youth might grow taller, but taller persons might then require more calories for their sustenance). The exact contents of the consumer basket are on the other hand allowed to differ between countries, to reflect that different countries' diets are based on different staple crops. The exact basket of goods used in this particular study is reported in Table 3.1. A person consuming these goods would certainly be very close to minimum needs for a working person, but would at least not starve.

Second, it is assumed that the wage-earner has to support a whole family on the wage earned. Further, since the previous studies so far have been based on the wages paid to male workers, the assumption is of a single male breadwinner family. Historically, this was hardly ever the case, as Jane Humphries has argued.[64] In most, if not all, historical societies women made crucial contributions to household income. These contributions are unfortunately all too often invisible in the historic source materials – women were often not employed as wage labourers to the same extent as men were, but were instead relegated to undertaking reproductive or household work, which do not figure in many of the source materials that have been kept. Estimating the 'subsistence ratio' of a household including only the male income, therefore, without a doubt underestimates the *absolute* subsistence ratio of the household. This absolute underestimate of the living standards must be kept in mind when interpreting any results. Since the method primarily was developed for *comparative* purposes, however, this is not necessarily a major problem, if women in the countries compared made similar

*Table 3.1* Gold Coast subsistence basket of goods

| | *Quantity (annual consumption)* | *Calories (kcal, daily intake)* | *Protein (grams, daily intake)* |
|---|---|---|---|
| 'Corn' | 200 kg | 2,000 | 52 |
| Yams | 50 kg | 162 | 2 |
| Meat/fish | 3 kg | 10 | 2 |
| Oil | 3.25 litres | 79 | 0 |
| Soap | 1.3 kg | | |
| Cotton | ⅓ 'piece' | | |
| Tallow | 2.6 kg | | |
| Fuel | 14 billets | | |

Note: In the accounts of the RAC, prices are reported for 'corn'. It is unclear if this refers to 'Indian corn' (i.e. maize) or 'Guinea corn' (i.e. sorghum), or both, see Chapter 2. It is here assumed that it primarily refers to maize. For a more detailed discussion of some of the challenges of conversion of the weights and measures used in the accounts, and making them comparable to the subsistence baskets used in other studies, see Rönnbäck, K., 'Living Standards on the Pre-Colonial Gold Coast: A Quantitative Estimate of African Laborers' Welfare Ratios', *European Review of Economic History*, 18 (2014), pp. 185–202.

relative contributions to household income (since the method presumably then would be underestimating the welfare ratios in *all* countries to a rather similar extent). It would, however, be problematic if the relative female contribution to family income differed drastically between societies, something that will be discussed in the book.

Third, the family is assumed to be of a specific size: two adults and four children. The assumption is based on estimates of normal household sizes in pre-modern Europe. If household sizes in practice differed drastically in other cultures, this might be problematic for the comparison. This is primarily an issue of how to interpret the welfare ratios estimated, since a high subsistence ratio means that the family could have had a real choice to have more children – an option that would have been impossible to a model family earning only a very low subsistence ratio.

The point of calculating subsistence ratios is to put household incomes relative to a universal baseline, common to all humans. A subsistence ratio of exactly one means that the (single male) breadwinner could just barely support a family on his wage, but had no surplus for any savings or luxuries whatsoever. If the subsistence ratio fell below one, this would mean that the male breadwinner was unable to support a whole family on his wage alone. In such a case, either contributions from the woman and/or from the children in the household would have been necessary to stave off starvation, or the adults would not have been able to provide for such a large family. If, on the other hand, a household had a subsistence ratio above one, they would not only have been able to purchase what was necessary for their basic survival, but would also have had some economic surplus that could be used for various purposes. What any such surplus was used for would naturally have been a reflection of the individual preferences of the members of the household (depending, of course, also on the power of the members of the household to have a say in how family incomes were spent), as well as on the social and cultural context influencing these preferences. In some cases, an economic surplus could be saved, perhaps in order to be used as investments in future economic activity, contributing to an accumulation of capital, or perhaps to be saved for if the family fell on bad luck, for example from sickness, accidents or sudden deaths in the family. In other cases, a subsistence ratio above one might imply that the members of the household would indulge themselves by purchasing not only the bare necessities, but also some luxuries. These might be of the everyday kind – a little bit of extra meat per person, some spices for the everyday food – or they might be of a more rare kind, like saving up to finance extravagant feasts on special occasions such as at a marriage of a family member. In yet other cases, being able to provide for a large family might have influenced a breadwinner's social status. In such a situation, a household with the possibility to do so (i.e. with a subsistence ratio above one if the family size is assumed to be six people in total, as noted above) would perhaps have chosen to use any economic surplus to increase the family size, rather than to indulge in any consumption of luxury goods, and to thus provide for a larger family than what in the model calculations were assumed to be a 'standard' family size.

What the subsistence ratio shows, then, is the household's *possibility for consumption or saving*, after the absolute necessities of life have been consumed. It does not reveal (let alone, for that matter, assume *ex ante*) anything about what this possibility actually was used for in any particular household.

One key point of estimating subsistence ratios is thus to be able to compare living standards in various societies across the world historically. The aim is to be able to say something not just about the living standards of the particular individuals or households studied but about broader groups in these societies. Lacking modern-day data on wages paid to large groups of people, some bold assumptions then have to be made about the representativity of the individuals in the samples studied. The assumption is, thus, that the wages paid to certain individuals are representative of the wages paid to the class or social stratum that they belong to. Many studies have been based on studying unskilled, urban day labourers on the one hand, and skilled, urban craftsmen on the other hand. The individuals for whom evidence on their wages can be found in the primary sources are assumed to be representative of these categories of workers, and then compared to similar groups in other societies around the world. Lacking reliable data or estimates of income for most of the rural population, most previous studies in the field have resorted to using wage data from (urban) day labourers as a proxy for living standards. The early modern economies were in general agricultural economies. A large share of the population produced goods for their own subsistence rather than for a market economy. Further, the urban population was in general quite small, and the share of wage-earners even in urban economies might have been limited. From that perspective, urban day labourers cannot automatically be considered as representative of the population at large in the country in which they live. It is instead often assumed that these ratios can be taken as reasonable proxies of living standards of more or less the whole society (e.g. a country or at least a region of a country), since social mobility (urban–rural mobility and other geographical mobility, as well as social mobility between occupations of similar social status and skill level) is assumed to even out wage differences between groups within this society on an aggregate level. Such comparisons are certainly not unproblematic. Kenneth Pomeranz has for example argued that the subsistence ratios of the urban unskilled labourers in China reveal little about the living standards of the vast mass of the Chinese population, because of institutions that guaranteed the rural population quite secure tenure to land, and thus a comparatively higher living standard relative to the urban population, than what might have been the case for the rural population in many other parts of the world.[65]

On a side note, the exact method for calculating welfare ratios has been revised slightly over time, in response to criticism against the method. The two main revisions to the method have been to revise upwards the amount of calories needed per person per year in order to avoid starvation, and the size of a 'standard' family. The caloric intake has been revised upwards from 1,900 calories per adult person and day in the earliest published studies of subsistence ratios, to 2,100 calories per person and day. As for family size, in some of the earliest published studies, it was often assumed that a wage-earner only had to support a family of four (two adults and two children). This has later been revised, so that more recent estimates instead assume that a wage-earner had to support a family of six (two adults and four children). Both these revisions lead to a lowering of the estimated subsistence ratios. These revisions must be kept in mind when comparing any estimates of subsistence ratios with each other. In the main, the *revised* assumptions about caloric requirements and family size will be used in this study. To enable comparisons with some previous research in the field, the unrevised assumptions will be resorted to in some of the graphs in Chapter 8. This will be noted explicitly in connection with the estimate, whenever it happens.

## Statistical analysis

The book will generally not employ any advanced statistical methods. Most of the empirical evidence of the study will instead be presented and analysed in the form of descriptive statistics in quite a straightforward manner, as tables or graphs. On two of the issues explored in the book, however, the data assembled will be employed for statistical analysis, using cross-sectional statistical regressions (ordinary least squares, OLS) for analysing the data.

In a first instance, in Chapter 5, the wages paid to the castle slaves will be analysed statistically in order to see what factors influenced the wages that the Company paid to the slaves. A cross section of 2,369 slave wage payments were used as the dependent variable in the OLS regression. The independent variables included the skill level (inferred from the stated occupation) of the slave, a dummy variable for slaves holding occupations requiring particular levels of loyalty, and separate dummy variables for the gender of the slave as well as for a slave who was a child or disabled, and finally a variable measuring the number of dependent children that adult (female) slaves were recorded to have in their care. A number of robustness tests were also carried out, for example excluding potential outliers, testing for occupational or time fixed effects, or changing the specification of the model tested. Overall, the results were highly robust to all of these changes.[66]

In a second instance, in Chapter 6, the data on prices will be analysed statistically in order to see what factors might have influenced the local prices of corn, yams and palm oil, respectively. Three separate cross-sectional OLS regressions were therefore run, one for each separate crop, using the price of the crop at each individual barter transaction as the dependent variable. The sample in each regression was comparatively small, ranging from 211 observations (yams) through 302 (corn) to 443 (palm oil), in all cases covering a period of thirty years. Independent variables included in the regression were the average temperature deviation from the norm in the year in which the transaction took place, the occurrence of war during the year in question, slaves exported in the year in question, the volume of the individual transaction, the season in which the transaction took place (in the form of a dummy variable) and a time-trend (see Table 6.1). A detailed description of how these independent variables were constructed can be found in a previous publication.[67] A number of robustness tests were also undertaken, for example, excluding outliers, including alternatives to the independent variables included in the baseline model, or including the possibility of non-linear effects or lagged variables.[68] In general, the results were highly robust to all of these changes in the model. Because some of the independent variables are only available on a yearly basis, this might create a problem for the statistical analysis, which unfortunately was impossible to avoid given what data there is available.

## A note on currencies

On the pre-colonial Gold Coast, the standard currency in use during the period of this study was gold, in the form of dust or nuggets. In the eastern part (from Accra and eastwards), cowries were also used as currency. For the geographical regions studied in the quantitative analysis in this book, gold was the only currency. Gold currency was divided in the following manner:[69]

1 mark = 8 ounces
1 ounce = 16 ackeys
1 ackey = 12 taku
1 taku = 2 dambas

Gold was also the unit of account in the primary source until 1730, when the Royal African Company started to keep all of their accounts in pounds sterling. Using pound sterling as unit of account seems to have been a mere translation of the gold prices, perhaps in order to make it easier for the managers of the Company in London to understand the figures – in the accounts, the exchange rate between pound sterling and gold is also reported (normally at £4 per oz of gold, or five shillings per ackey). Using this exchange rate, it becomes possible to convert the sterling prices into gold prices, or vice versa, in order to arrive at a price series denominated in the same currency throughout the period covered by this book. In this book, all prices and wages will be reported in the local currency, gold dust. Any prices after 1730 are thus a translation of the pound sterling prices reported in the primary source, using the exchange rates between the two also reported in the same source.

## A note on spelling

There is no consistent spelling of names in the primary sources used. This is most particularly the case regarding the names of individuals. Further, the spelling often differs from how the same name is spelled in modern times. In the accounts, it is for example possible to find a number of people named ‘Coffee’ (with a couple of variations to the exact spelling). The same name is still common in modern-day Ghana, being a traditional day name for men born on a Friday, but is normally spelt ‘Kofi’ or ‘Koffi’. In this book, I will not try to adapt the spelling of any names of individuals to modern standards, since it is impossible to tell whether the spelling was of their own choice (which might be the case for some of the free labourers, perhaps those who were able to read and write themselves, in particular) or not.

I have, on the other hand, attempted to systematically use modern-day spelling of geographical names. The accounts do, for example, then mention Succondee, which with modern-day spelling is called Sekondi, or Quittah (modern-day spelling: Keta).

## Notes

1 Ki-Zerbo, J. (ed.), *General History of Africa, vol. I. Methodology and African Prehistory* (Paris: UNESCO, 1989).
2 Vansina, J., *Oral Tradition as History* (Madison: University of Wisconsin Press, 1985), pp. 186–201.
3 Vansina, *Oral Tradition*, p. 190.
4 Yin, *Case Study Research*, pp. 118–23.
5 Jones, A., 'Drink Deep, or Taste Not: Thoughts on the Use of Early European Records in the Study of African Material Culture', *History in Africa*, 21 (1994), pp. 349–70.
6 Jones, A., *Raw, Medium, Well Done: A Critical Review of Editorial and Quasi-Editorial Work on Pre-1885 European Sources for Sub-Saharan Africa, 1960–1986* (Madison: University of Wisconsin, African Studies Program, 1987); Fage, J.D., *A Guide to Original Sources for Precolonial Western Africa Published in European Languages* (Madison: University of Wisconsin, African Studies Program, 1994); Alpern, S., *Original Sources for Precolonial Western Africa. An Updated and Expanded Supplement to Fage (1994)* (Madison: University of Wisconsin-Madison, African Studies Program, 2006).
7 The databases can be found at the following websites:

- The Making of the Modern World, Part I (MOMW): http://gdc.gale.com/products/the-making-of-the-modern-world-the-goldsmiths-kress-library-of-economic-literature-1450–1850/
- Early English Books Online (EEBO): http://eebo.chadwyck.com/home
- Eighteenth Century Collections Online (ECCO): http://gdc.gale.com/products/eighteenth-century-collections-online/
- Gallica: http://gallica.bnf.fr

8 See for example van Dantzig, A., 'English Bosman and Dutch Bosman: A Comparison of Texts', *History in Africa*, 2 (1975), pp. 185–216, being the first in a series of eight articles under this title in the same journal; Heintze, B., 'Translations as Sources for African History', *History in Africa*, 11 (1984), pp. 131–61; Hair, P.E.H., 'Portuguese Documents on Africa and Some Problems of Translation', *History in Africa*, 27 (2000), pp. 91–7; Jones, 'Drink Deep', pp. 355–7.
9 See for example Pratt, M.L., *Imperial Eyes: Travel Writing and Transculturation* (London: Routledge, 1992); Rubiés, J.-P., *Travellers and Cosmographers: Studies in the History of Early Modern Travel and Ethnology* (Aldershot: Ashgate, 2007).
10 Van der Linden, M., 'Studying Attitudes to Work Worldwide, 1500–1650: Concepts, Sources, and Problems of Interpretation', *International Review of Social History*, 56, Special Issue (2011), pp. 25–43.
11 Loomba, *Colonialism/Postcolonialism*, p. 104.
12 Applebaum, H., *The Concept of Work: Ancient, Medieval, and Modern* (Albany: State University of New York Press, 1992), pp. xii–xiii.

13 Waldman, L., 'An Unnoticed Aspect of Archibald Dalzel's the History of Dahomey', *Journal of African History*, 6(2) (1965), pp. 185–92; Akinjogbin, I.A., 'Archibald Dalzel: Slave Trader and Historian of Dahomey', *Journal of African History*, 7(1) (1966), pp. 67–78; Law, R., 'The Slave-Trader as Historian: Robert Norris and the History of Dahomey', *History in Africa*, 16 (1989), pp. 219–35.

14 See for example Rönnbäck, K., 'Enlightenment, Scientific Exploration and Abolitionism: Anders Sparrman's and Carl Bernhard Wadström's Colonial Encounters in Senegal, 1787–1788 and the British Abolitionist Movement', *Slavery & Abolition*, 34(3) (2013), pp. 425–45.

15 McCaskie, T.C., 'Drake's Fake: A Curiosity concerning a Spurious Visit to Asante in 1839', *History in Africa*, 11 (1984), pp. 223–36.

16 See for example Jones, A., *German Sources for West African History 1599–1669* (Wiesbaden: Franz Steiner Verlag, 1983); Jones, A., *Brandenburg Sources for West African History* (Stuttgart: Franz Steiner Verlag, 1985); Dapper, O., *Olfert Dapper's Description of Benin*, ed. A. Jones (Madison: University of Wisconsin-Madison, 1998); Barbot, J., *Barbot on Guinea*, ed. P.E.H. Hair, A. Jones and R. Law (London: Hakluyt Society, 1992 [1678–1712]), pp. xix–lxii; De Marees, P., *Description and Historical Account of the Gold Kingdom of Guinea (1602)*, ed. A. van Dantzig and A. Jones (Oxford: Oxford University Press 1987 [1602]), pp. xiii–xix; Jobson, R., *The Discovery of River Gambra*, ed. R. Gamble and P.E.H. Hair (London: Hakluyt Society, 1999 [1623]); Chouin, G., 'Seen, Said, or Deduced? Travel Accounts, Historical Criticism, and Discourse Theory: Towards an "Archaeology" of Dialogue in Seventeenth-Century Guinea', *History in Africa*, 28 (2001), pp. 53–70.

17 Hair, P.E.H., 'The Early Sources on Guinea', *History in Africa*, 21 (1994), pp. 87–126.

18 Fage, J.D., 'A Commentary on Duarte Pacheco Pereira's Account of the Lower Guinea Coastlands in his "Esmeraldo de Situ Orbis", and on Some Other Early Accounts', *History in Africa*, 7 (1980), pp. 47–80; Hair, 'The Early Sources', pp. 92–9.

19 De Marees, *Description and Historical Account*, p. xvi.

20 De Marees, *Description and Historical Account*, p. xv; Fage, J.D., 'Seventeenth Century Gold Coast', *Journal of African History*, 29(2) (1988), pp. 326–28; Iselin, R., 'Reading Pictures: On the Value of the Copperplates in the "Beschryvinghe" of Pieter de Marees (1602) as Source Material for Ethnohistorical Research', *History in Africa*, 21 (1994), pp. 147–70.

21 De Marees, *Description and Historical Account*, p. xv–xvi.

22 Iselin, 'Reading Pictures', p. 152; Sutton, E., *Early Modern Dutch Prints of Africa* (Farnham: Ashgate, 2012), p. 88.

23 De Marees, *Description and Historical Account*, p. xv; Morgan, J., ' "Some Could Suckle over their Shoulder": Male Travelers, Female Bodies, and the Gendering of Racial Ideology, 1500–1770', *William and Mary Quarterly*, 54(1) (1997), pp. 167–92; Sutton, *Early Modern Dutch Prints*, pp. 128–47.

24 Villault, N., *A Relation of the Coasts of Africk Called Guinee* (London, 1670) at MOMW [accessed 13 February 2012].

25 Thilmas, G. and de Moraes, N.I., 'Villault de Bellefond sur la Côte Occidentale d'Afrique: Les deux premières campagnes de l'*Europe* (1666–1671)', *Bulletin de l'I.F.A.N.*, 38 (1976), pp. 257–99.

26 Daykin, 'They Themselves Contribute', p. 628.

27 Dapper, *Olfert Dapper's Description*.

28 Hair, P.E.H., 'Barbot, Dapper, Davity: A Critique of Sources on Sierra Leone and Cape Mount', *History in Africa*, 1 (1974), pp. 25–54; Fage, J.D., ' "Good Red Herring": The Definitive Barbot', *Journal of African History*, 34(2) (1993), pp. 315–20.

29 Jones, A., 'Decompiling Dapper: A Preliminary Search for Evidence', *History in Africa*, 17 (1990), pp. 171–209.

30 Hair, 'Barbot, Dapper, Davity', p. 26.

31 Jones, A., 'Double Dutch? A Survey of Seventeenth-Century German Sources for West African History', *History in Africa*, 9 (1982), pp. 141–53, quote on p. 147.
32 Jones, 'Double Dutch', pp. 143–5.
33 Bosman, W., *A New and Accurate Description of the Coast of Guinea*, 2nd edn (London, 1721), at MOMW [accessed 13 February 2012].
34 Fage, 'Good Red Herring', p. 316.
35 Wilks, I., 'Bosman New and Costly', *Journal of African History*, 9(1) (1968), pp. 164–6.
36 Van Dantzig, A., 'Willem Bosman's "New and Accurate Description of the Coast of Guinea": How Accurate is it?', *History in Africa*, 1 (1974), pp. 101–8, quote on p. 105.
37 Barbot, J., *Barbot on Guinea*, ed. P.E.H. Hair, A. Jones and R. Law (London: Hakluyt Society, 1992 [1678–1712]).
38 Hair, 'Barbot, Dapper, Davity', pp. 29–32; Law, R., 'Jean Barbot as a Source for the Slave Coast of West Africa', *History in Africa*, 9 (1982), pp. 155–73; Barbot, *Barbot on Guinea*, p. cviii; Fage, 'Good Red Herring', pp. 316–18.
39 Barbot, *Barbot on Guinea*, pp. xix–lxii; Hair, P.E.H., 'On Editing Barbot', *History in Africa*, 20 (1993), pp. 53–9.
40 Fage, 'Good Red Herring', p. 319.
41 Rømer, L.F., *A Reliable Account of the Coast of Guinea*, ed. S.A. Winsnes (Oxford: Oxford University Press, 2000 [1760]).
42 Jones, A., 'A Danish Record of the Coast', *Journal of African History*, 31(1) (1990), pp. 143–4.
43 Winsnes, S.A., 'Voices from the Past: Remarks on the Translation and Editing of Published Danish Sources for West African History During the Eighteenth and Nineteenth Centuries', *History in Africa*, 14 (1987), pp. 275–85.
44 Isert, P.E., *Letters on West Africa and the Slave Trade*, translated and edited by S.A. Winsnes (Oxford: Oxford University Press, 1992 [1788]).
45 Winsnes, 'Voices from the Past', p. 279; Fage, J.D., 'Isert in English', *Journal of African History*, 33(3) (1992), pp. 489–91.
46 Isert, *Letters on West Africa*, p. 9.
47 Meredith, H., *An Account of the Gold Coast of Africa* (London, 1812) at MOMW [accessed 13 February 2012], p. viii.
48 Irwin, G., 'Precolonial African Diplomacy: The Example of Asante', *International Journal of African Historical Studies*, 8(1) (1975), pp. 81–96.
49 Hutton, W., *A Voyage to Africa: Including a Narrative of an Embassy to One of the Interior Kingdoms in the Year 1820* (London, 1821), p. vii.
50 Jones, A., 'Semper Aliquid Veteris: Printed Sources for the History of the Ivory and Gold Coasts, 1500–1750', *Journal of African History*, 27(2) (1986), pp. 215–35.
51 Lee, S., *Stories of Strange Lands; and Fragments from the Notes of a Traveller* (London, 1835) at Google Books [accessed 18 August 2014]; Beaver, D., 'Writing Natural History for Survival – 1820–1856: The Case of Sarah Bowdich, Later Sarah Lee', *Archives of Natural History* 26 (1999), pp. 19–31.
52 Bowdich, T.E., *Mission from Cape Coast Castle to Ashantee* (London, Frank Cass, 1966 [1819]).
53 Feinberg, H., 'An Eighteenth-Century Case of Plagiarism: William Smith's "A New Voyage to Guinea"', *History in Africa*, 6 (1979), pp. 45–50; Jones, A., 'William Smith the Plagiarist: A Rejoinder', *History in Africa*, 7 (1980), pp. 327–8.
54 Winsnes, 'Voices from the Past', p. 279.
55 Falconbridge, A., *An Account of the Slave Trade on the Coast of Africa* (London, 1788) MOMW [accessed 13 February 2012].
56 Coleman, D., 'Sierra Leone, Slavery, and Sexual Politics: Anna Maria Falconbridge and the "Swarthy Daughter" of Late Eighteenth Century Abolitionism', *Women's Writing*, 2(1) (1995), pp. 3–23.

57 Hill, M., 'Towards a Chronology of the Publications of Francis Moore's "Travels into the Inland Parts of Africa" ', *History in Africa*, 19 (1992), pp. 353–68.
58 Fage, J.D., 'Hawkins' Hoax? A Sequel to "Drake's Fake" ', *History in Africa*, 18 (1991), pp. 83–91.
59 Law, R. (ed.), *Correspondence of the Royal African Company's Chief Merchants at Cabo Corso Castle with William's Fort, Whydah, and the Little Popo Factory, 1727–1728* (Madison: University of Wisconsin-Madison, African Studies Program, 1991); Law, R. (ed.), *The English in West Africa 1681–1683. The Local Correspondence of the Royal African Company of England 1681–1699. Part 1* (Oxford: Oxford University Press, 1997); Law, R. (ed.), *The English in West Africa 1685–1688. The Local Correspondence of the Royal African Company of England 1681–1699. Part 2* (Oxford: Oxford University Press, 2001); Law, R. (ed.), *The English in West Africa 1691–1699. The Local Correspondence of the Royal African Company of England 1681–1699. Part 3* (Oxford: Oxford University Press, 2006).
60 Justesen, O. (ed.), *Danish Sources for the History of Ghana 1657–1754* (Copenhagen: Royal Danish Academy of Sciences and Letters, 2005).
61 National Archives, Kew, Surrey, Royal African Company, T70 (NA T70), volumes 376–486, 1007–15 and 1450–3.
62 Reese, 'The Drudgery'; Reese, 'Facilitating the Slave Trade'.
63 See Allen, 'The Great Divergence'; Allen, R. *The British Industrial Revolution in Global Perspective* (Cambridge: Cambridge University Press, 2009).
64 Humphries, J., 'The Lure of Aggregates and the Pitfalls of the Patriarchal Perspective: A Critique of the High Wage Economy Interpretation of the British Industrial Revolution', *Economic History Review*, 66 (2013), pp. 693–714; see also Allen, R., 'The High Wage Economy and the Industrial Revolution: A Restatement', *Economic History Review Early View Online* (2014).
65 Pomeranz, K., 'Ten Years After: Responses and Reconsiderations', *Historically Speaking*, 12 (2011), pp. 20–5.
66 Rönnbäck, K., 'Waged Slavery: Incentivizing Unfree Labour at the Cape Coast Castle in the Eighteenth Century', forthcoming in *Slavery & Abolition.*
67 Rönnbäck, K., 'Climate, Conflicts, and Variations in Prices on Pre-Colonial West African Markets for Staple Crops', *Economic History Review*, 67(4) (2014), pp. 1065–88
68 Rönnbäck, 'Climate, Conflicts', appendix I.
69 Daaku, *Trade and Politics*, p. 36; Kea, *Settlements, Trade, and Polities*, p. 191.

# 4 Work ethic and the division of labour

## Introduction

This chapter will study how European observers perceived the work ethic and the division of labour on the Gold Coast, in particular, and also put the evidence from the Gold Coast into a regional perspective. As was noted in Chapter 2, one of the features found in much of the early modern European literature on Africa is that Africans were described as 'lazy' or 'idle'. This stereotype would for a long time be a key explanation as to why Africans supposedly were so poor. Previous research has shown that the stereotype was part of a broader, racist European discourse on Africa. In this chapter, it is argued that an intersectional analysis – incorporating not only the issue of race/ethnicity and racism, but also gender and class aspects to the stereotype – is necessary in order to understand this particular stereotype in full. These three factors all intersected in the development of the stereotype, and how it was used as a justification for coercion of labour in the form of slavery. Most importantly, the gendered division of labour in the region was crucial for the development of this stereotype.

## Tropical exuberance and the need to work

It is easy to find European writers from the early modern period complaining over the African work ethic: a common European stereotype simply held that Africans were lazy. As many previous scholars have argued, this was often part and parcel of a broader, highly racist discourse about Africans. To take just one example, we can look at how the German explorer Johann Peter Oettinger generalized about Africans by the late seventeenth century: 'The character of the natives is thoroughly timorous, mistrustful, avaricious, cruel, thievish, vain and indolent'.[1] The stereotype of idleness was thus often, but not always, connected to a number of other racist stereotypes. The people living on the Gold Coast certainly fell victim to this stereotypical portrayal. Willem Bosman for example wrote about the work ethic of the local population on the Gold Coast by the early eighteenth century: vices such as craftiness and villainy, he then believed, 'are accompanied with their Sisters, Sloth and Idleness; to which they are so prone that nothing but the utmost Necessity can force them to Labour'.[2] Many other European authors writing about the Gold Coast also believed that the stereotype was very fitting.[3]

No matter who the observers were – as to occupation, nationality, or relation to the slave trade – a number of European writers who adhered to the stereotype can be found. It was thus not simply a self-serving justification used by people personally involved in the slave trade. Certainly, many people who were directly involved in this trade no doubt believed (or found it convenient to believe) in the stereotype. There were on the other hand also a number of other people, who were not necessarily involved in the slave trade themselves, but who anyway believed in the stereotype. Even some people who by the late eighteenth and early nineteenth century were sympathetic to the abolitionist cause believed in the stereotype. Further, the stereotype was not limited to, or seemingly more prominent among, people of any particular European nationality. Rather, the stereotype seems to have become pan-European very soon, and figured already in the earliest European accounts available from the fifteenth century. This is most certainly a reflection of how early accounts of West Africa were translated into various languages, and how some particularly influential works were read widely within interested elites across the continent. With the spread of the written accounts across national borders in Europe, the stereotypical portrayal of Africans also spread.[4]

In modern-day literature, work is often defined as the opposite of leisure: work is an activity (primarily) undertaken in order to earn a livelihood (for example by subsistence production or by waged work), whereas leisure is defined as an activity (primarily) undertaken for the sheer pleasure of doing the activity per se.[5] The distinction between work and leisure is crucial in order to understand the European discourse on 'laziness' among Africans. Many Europeans at the time believed, at least officially, in the Christian doctrine that work was virtuous per se. For people who did not adhere to this faith (or to some other faith propagating a similar work ethic), on the other hand, there was nothing inherently virtuous or positive in working. The point of work was then just a means to another end: to enable the person working to earn a livelihood, by subsistence production, wage-work or some other economic activity that might serve that purpose. The point of this, in turn, was to enable the person to consume goods and services of various kinds. These included, in the first place, various basic goods necessary for survival. What the existence of the stereotype of 'laziness' then perhaps suggests is that many people in the African societies that the European observers encountered *might not have needed to work* in order to meet their basic subsistence needs. This was indeed a very common explanation to the stereotype, suggested by many of the European authors at the time: people in Africa did not have to work very hard, since the land was very rich and bountiful, and everything one needed could easily be had without much work. This explanation is, as was mentioned above (see Chapter 2), also the one emphasized by most previous modern-day scholars of African history. This was indeed a common idea among many of the European observers writing travel accounts about the Gold Coast. Jean Barbot for example argued that the Africans 'are lazy, the result of the bounty and fertility of the land they occupy, which furnishes them with all that is necessary for life, in abundance and almost by nature alone'.[6] Paul Erdmann Isert produced one of the more positively formulated explanations on this theme when writing about people on the Gold Coast:

> Since the Blacks live in such an enchantingly delightful climate, it is no wonder that they have a taste for amusement. Their games are as numerous as they are inventive, and they spend most of their time in such enjoyment, the work necessary to support their existence requiring so little time.[7]

Similar arguments were repeated by other authors writing about the Gold Coast, including William Smith or the English governor John Hope Smith.[8] Many of the sources then seem to describe a Garden of Eden, where people can just pick the fruits from the trees without having to worry much about how they are to support themselves in the future. Work is just not necessary, and therefore not undertaken voluntarily. Indeed, 'abundance' and 'fertile' are words very frequently used in many of the primary sources, when describing the land and the natural resources available in the region. This supposed abundance had a very direct impact upon the perceived living standards in the region. Paul Erdmann Isert for example argued that: 'Poverty cannot easily occur here, for instance, but for a long-lasting drought. On the contrary, there are always fish in the sea and an abundance of game in the forest'.[9]

Related to the idea of tropical exuberance was also the idea that Africans exhibited few 'artificial wants'. Once one's basic needs were met, any economic surplus one has made from working can be used for the consumption of non-necessities, ranging from material luxuries to leisure time. How much work one is then willing to do, above what is necessary for sheer survival, depends on the individual's valuation of such material goods, versus his or her valuation of other social values (not the least leisure per se). Individual preferences of the good life are not exogenous, but the perceptions of this are to a very large extent determined by cultural factors, and can take on many different forms in different societies. The stereotype of 'lazy Africans' could thus also imply that people in Africa generally put other social values before material consumption (and thus work to finance the latter), and simply did not value material possessions in general as highly as many of the European observers did. Indeed, some of the European observers explicitly elaborated on the idea that people from many African societies had little demand for material wealth. Two of the English governors on the Gold Coast, Hope Smith and Winniett, for example, clearly believed that this was the case.[10] Other authors emphasized that the local population exhibited a whole host of social leisure activities, instead of valuing material wealth. While Paul Erdmann Isert, as was cited above, thought that Africans were brilliant at inventing new games, Pieter de Marees devoted a chapter in his book to the dancing of the people on the Gold Coast.[11] The supposed idleness was thus easily explained in the minds of many of the European authors: people were content with little material wealth. As we will see in Chapter 7, this was an issue some of the nineteenth-century authors argued changed over time, with the creation of increasingly 'artificial wants'.

Some authors did however caution against the belief in this natural abundance. As we saw above, Jean Barbot thought that Africans were lazy precisely because of the natural abundance of their lands. Elsewhere in the same book, however, he wrote:

> those authors deceive themselves who locate the Elysian Fields here, for apart from the fact that winter and its intemperate weather make this country a place of horror and unease during several months of the year, it is subject to great famines in the spring.[12]

The natural environment was, according to Barbot, thus simply not as abundant as some of his contemporary authors would like to imagine. Later in his book, he elaborated even further on the same topic, arguing that people rarely sowed more than they thought was necessary for their own consumption the coming year. Any crop failure, for example due to drought, war or locusts, could therefore have devastating effects, he argued: 'Their explanation is that they prefer to work little and eat less'.[13] Barbot's opinion was thus rather contradictory: on the one hand, he argued that there was a great abundance, and that people therefore did not have to work very much; on the other hand, he argued that this was not at all the case, and that people therefore regularly starved . . . Barbot's objections notwithstanding, the idea of 'tropical exuberance' was clearly very common among the European observers.

## The gendered division of labour – female occupations

The stereotype was at the same time clearly gendered: many of the European observers describing the African work ethic seem to believe that the supposed laziness was a *male* character trait, rather than a trait applying to men and women alike. William Smith for example claimed that the men on the Gold Coast 'being naturally of a lazy idle Disposition, insomuch that they seldom care to put their Hands to any Thing, but make their Wives do all Manner of Work for them, not only within Doors, but also in the Field'.[14] By the early nineteenth century, John Adams adhered to the same interpretation of the stereotype:

> The women here [on the Gold Coast], however, as well as in most other parts of Africa, sow and reap, grind corn, carry wood and water, and perform all the drudgery attendant on housekeeping; while their husbands are perhaps gossiping, drinking, or sleeping, except during the herring or fishing season, when the villages along the sea-coast present a scene of bustle and activity much beyond what they do in ordinary times.[15]

What many of these writers were used to from back home in Europe was that women were responsible for reproductive and household work. The women were, as many European men saw it, according to Olwen Hufton, 'providers of vital support services'.[16] In contrast, men generally thought of themselves as the main or even sole breadwinners, responsible for everything from farm-work to trade and craftsmanship, as well as military service. Obviously, this was not how the gendered division of labour always turned out in reality in Europe all the time. Many women did much work that in the hegemonic discourse was considered to be in the male domain, but this work was often made invisible and can sometimes be very hard to find in historical sources. Household and reproductive work was, furthermore, certainly not just a support service for male-coded types of work, but of crucial necessity to society. Nonetheless, the idea that this was a more or less natural or God-given way of dividing up the socially necessary labour no doubt permeated much European thinking.

On the Gold Coast, on the other hand, the European observers writing travel accounts came across a slightly different gendered division of labour. Just as in Europe, women were generally responsible for domestic and reproductive work. In one of her stories, Sarah Lee described how a girl on the Gold Coast was raised, so as to be able to fulfil a whole number of tasks:

> To attend on her kind hostess, to watch over the sick, to support the aged, to amuse the infant of a wearied mother, to protect the ill-treated slave, to prepare food in the most exquisite manner, to embroider cloths, to weave, to make mats and baskets, to carve calabashes, to string beads in beautiful patterns, and to net, were her chief occupations.[17]

Most male observers in contrast rarely took notice of who was responsible for the reproductive work in Africa. Furthermore, only in some cases would some of them note the undertaking of domestic work, such as that housekeeping in general was a female task. Cooking and preparing food were in particular described as female tasks in many areas along the West African coast, including the Gold Coast. Other household tasks explicitly described as female work, at least in some societies along the coast, included carrying wood and water, brewing beer and making palm oil.[18] These aspects of the gendered division of labour in West Africa were hardly very surprising to a European observer.

What was surprising, and seemingly also quite controversial, to the European observers was instead the amount of agricultural work that the women were responsible for on the Gold Coast. According to the European writers, women were responsible for virtually all agricultural work, including sowing and reaping the harvest. This was for example how John Beecham described the division of labour in both Asante and on the Gold Coast by the early nineteenth century:

> With regard to the employment of the female sex, it may be remarked, that the weightiest duties generally devolve upon the wife, who is to be found 'grinding at the mill', transacting business in the market, or cultivating the plantation.[19]

Some authors were also more detailed about some specific agricultural tasks. The grinding of corn and pounding of millet were then, for example, described as specific female tasks on the Gold Coast. Women could also be responsible for many other tasks aside from subsistence agriculture, including the production of handicraft (particularly spinning and weaving), or market trading.[20] Nicolas Villault for example argued that women on the Gold Coast were in charge of 'keeping their Markets' (just as John Beecham would argue much later as we saw in the quote above), whereas the men went fishing or built canoes.[21]

This description of the gendered division of labour was not without its sceptics at the time. The Danish physician Paul Erdmann Isert was one such sceptic, reacting to the otherwise common description of the gendered division of labour on the Gold Coast:

> Household work is the responsibility of the women alone. Sometimes they take part in the tasks of the men, such as cultivation or planting, but this is not common, and it is a fabrication to say that the Black women support the men completely.[22]

Regardless of whether Isert was right or not in this remark, the gendered division of labour that a clear majority of the Europeans perceived seems to have had a decisive impact upon what most Europeans thought of African men: just because the men did not do all the work that they 'ought to', according to the Europeans' way of thinking about the gendered division of labour (most importantly, then, much of the work in agriculture), the African men must be lazy, idle and slothful.

## The gendered division of labour – male occupations

Whereas women seem to have been in charge of reproductive and domestic work, as well as much subsistence agricultural work, the African men were responsible for a whole host of other economic activities, such as trading, hunting and fishing. By the late seventeenth century, Nicolas Villault wrote that the men on the Gold Coast: 'employ themselves abroad, either in matters of Trade, or in making of Palm-wine, or fishing, as every man's genius inclines him'.[23] Other male-coded economic activities included much craftsmanship, such as the work of carpenters or blacksmiths. In the 1660s, Wilhelm Johann Müller would list a few of them: 'The best known craftsmen are goldsmiths and blacksmiths, carpenters, potters, hatters and mat-makers, and people who make ivory trumpets, bracelets and combs'.[24] These occupations seem to have been gender-coded almost exclusively as male occupations. Other authors, such as Jean Barbot, added a number of titles to the list of male occupations: fishermen, canoe-makers and canoemen, merchants, woodcutters, house-builders, masons, thatchers, potters, porters/hammock-men and messengers.[25] The number of clearly distinct male occupations was thus quite limited, if the European sources are to be trusted.

Some European observers complained in particular about the skill level of the craftsmen. Müller for example complained about the lack of skilled carpenters on the Gold Coast:

> The whole country is full of carpenters; for each native understands how to build his own house and does not need to call on specialist carpenters. Yet not all of them know how to make a canoe in which to go out to sea.[26]

However, not all African labourers and craftsmen were belittled as unskilled. In general, the European observers seem to be pretty impressed, or at the very least content, with people of some occupations. Jean Barbot argued that the fishermen at Elmina on the Gold Coast were 'strong men and good fishermen', and the canoemen were 'the fittest and most experienc'd men to manage and paddle the canoes over the bars and breakings'.[27] The canoemen were thus not blamed for just trudging slowly over wet sand in search of an easy income, but were often hailed as hard-working professionals skilled at their work. These occupations might on the one hand arguably be considered to require lower skills than many of the particular crafts would. In a patriarchal tone, John Atkins on the other hand claimed that the craftsmen easily could be taught to become 'good Workmen', and that 'with very little Instruction'.[28]

One male occupation of key interest to the Europeans was certainly that of the canoeman, depicted in Figure 4.1. Their work was crucial in order to operate the trade along the coast. Since the Gold Coast had virtually no natural harbours, ships had to anchor off the coast in order to conduct trade. The canoemen – for it was undoubtedly a male task – were therefore necessary for carrying the European goods from these arriving ships to the shore, and to carry slaves and other African goods to the ships waiting off the coast. The canoes could be small – being handled by a single or a few men only – to very large vessels being paddled by several scores of canoemen. The main skill necessary for manoeuvring a canoe was the knowledge of how to cross the bar and the surf along the African coast.[29] In large canoes, all canoemen would presumably not have had to possess such skills, but could be included primarily in order to paddle rather than manoeuvre the vessel. Many of the people employed as canoemen on the Gold Coast were still, or had previously been, fishermen according to Henry Meredith.[30] This is also what is illustrated in Figure 4.1.

*Figure 4.1* Fishing from canoes on the Gold Coast.

Source: Illustration from the manuscripts of Jean Barbot, British National Archives ADM 7/830B. Reproduction by the author.

The timing of some of the work undertaken by the men might have influenced the stereotype about the 'lazy African man', simply because the men might have worked other hours than when the Europeans were observing them. Godefroy Loyer for example claimed that, on the Gold Coast, many of the male fishermen embarked in the evening, and stayed out fishing throughout the night, only to return in the morning: 'Ils envoyent le jour leurs femmes au marché pour y vendre leur pêche, tandis qu'ils se reposent [in the day they send their wives to the market to sell their catch there, while they themselves rest]'.[31] It is not impossible that many of the European observers might have interpreted these men as just lazing around throughout the day, without understanding or recognizing the work they did at night.

## 'Othering' as justification of coercion

Aside from race/ethnicity and gender, a third factor – class – is also necessary in order to understand the stereotypical description of the African work ethic. 'Lazy' and 'idle' were after all labels that Europeans attached not only to some exotic 'Other', but often also to the domestic working classes in Europe. The stereotype therefore seems to be a reflection of contradictory class interests: the upper classes' interests in expropriating surplus value from the working classes (and thus get the workers to work as long hours as possible), and the working classes' interests in not working more than was absolutely necessary. That the stereotype of the 'lazy African' partly is a reflection of class relations, is suggested by some scattered evidence from some of the accounts from the region. One of the first accounts of this can be found already in one of the very earliest accounts attributing idleness to the African population, an anonymous Portuguese report from Elmina on the Gold Coast, dated to 1572. In the report, the author believed in the idea that the Africans were lazy:

> In the same way as is done in Spain to vagabonds who seek out masters and travel about for work, it will be necessary to force all these blacks to work, punishing them, in pecuniary and even corporal terms, when they fail to work, for they are the most idle, do-nothing people in the world.[32]

What is striking here is that the author does not describe this supposed laziness as a character trait specific for or unique to the Africans on the Gold Coast, but on the contrary very similar to what the author believed was the case among segments of the population ('vagabonds') living back home on the Iberian Peninsula.

A completely different class aspect of the stereotype was on the other hand suggested by the Englishman William Hutton, writing about people on the Gold Coast in the early nineteenth century. In contrast to how the stereotype could be used within a European context, Hutton turned the issue around, arguing that idleness 'appl[ies] chiefly to those natives of the higher orders, who have little or nothing to do; but those who are poor, and are slaves, are constantly kept at work'.[33]

According to Hutton's observation, laziness was thus not really an African character trait at all, since the 'poor' all had to work hard for their livelihood. It was, furthermore, not a character trait of the lower classes, as so many other authors argued both regarding the working classes in Europe and in Africa. Hutton's very radical argument was instead that laziness was a trait of the upper classes in African society – exactly those who could exploit the work of others, and thus were not compelled to work. Hutton's claim does however seem quite apart from what most other European observers at the time thought.

The really exoticizing and racist aspect of the stereotype of the 'lazy African' was perhaps not in the claim that some segments of society or other (e.g. men or the working class) were supposedly lazy. The racist aspect of the issue was perhaps rather in what conclusions were drawn from this stereotype. The supposed idleness among the European working class, and how to deal with it, was to some extent debated among upper-class intellectuals: could the working classes be encouraged to work harder somehow, for example, if they were allowed to 'taste the fruits of their industry', as the Irish bishop Berkeley put it, or would they have to be coerced to work?[34] At least some people seem to have believed that the former option posed a real alternative to various forms of coercion, even if poor or vagrancy laws often contained highly coercive elements. For that purpose, class interests joined forces with religious doctrine: Christian doctrine often attempted to internalize a work ethic in the congregation, labelling work as virtuous and idleness as sinful, most famously known from Weber's claim about a special Protestant work ethic.[35]

In the West African context, however, hardly any such dissenting voices are to be found in the sources for a very long period of time. Many of the European observers wrote about the supposed idleness in highly moralizing and pejorative terms, often with explicit references to Christian doctrine, reminiscent of how religious doctrine in Europe attempted to instil a work ethic in the believers. Ludewig Ferdinand Rømer, working as a merchant for the Danish slave-trading company, for example morally condemned what he thought were the lazy people of the Gold Coast:

> How the Almighty has blessed this land which these lazy natives do not know how to utilize! God has undoubtedly left them to their evil nature, and they consider good to be evil and evil good, since they consider all work too demeaning, and beneath them.[36]

It does not seem unreasonable to assume that the work ethic was an issue raised in missionary activities in Africa. Missionary activity did however virtually cease in pre-colonial West Africa from the second half of the sixteenth century.[37] Christian doctrines could therefore hardly contribute to fostering a work ethic that satisfied the European observers' demands. On the contrary, already from the very earliest accounts on the topic, the European observers seem to have been determined that simple propagation of a Christian work ethic would not suffice. Herein lies perhaps the greatest difference between the discourses about the work ethic of the European and the African working classes, respectively. The primary conclusion that the early modern European observers seem to have drawn from their belief in African laziness, for a very long period of time, was simply that Africans *had to be coerced* in order to work. The coercion would, further, need to be not just vagrancy or poor laws, which served to discipline much of the working class in Europe, but of the most severe kind – slavery. The stereotype thus already from the very early years of direct contact between Europe and West Africa came to be used as a justification for enslavement.

## The idle and the industrious

Even though the stereotype of the 'lazy African (male)' soon became hegemonic in European thinking about Africans and their work ethic, it did not pass by completely unquestioned. Many Europeans clearly realized that many Africans – both male and female – often were very industrious at their respective occupations. A most explicit account suggesting this can be found in the travel account published by Nicolas Villault: 'So great an aversion have these people against idleness, that among them the aged men and women are not allow'd it, but are constrained to get their livelihood by such employments as their age and infirmities will bear'.[38] Jean Barbot, for his part, made a geographical distinction between people on the Gold Coast, when he wrote that people in the inland 'prefer to work little and eat less. It is true that, as I have said, the peoples beside the sea are more hard-working, especially those at Axim, Anta, Abroby, Mouree, Anamabou, and Cormentin'.[39] Paul Erdmann Isert similarly described the Fante living on the Gold Coast as 'industrious'.[40] What is striking in many of these accounts is that they all seem to operate with the stereotype of the 'lazy African' as the default assumption, but find exceptions to this rule in some particular case or cases. They also seem to find that these supposedly industrious peoples are worthy to mention just for the particular reason that they are thought to be exceptions to a rule. For a long period of time, no one really seems to have questioned the stereotype as such.

## The Gold Coast in regional perspective

How the Europeans described and explained the work ethic of people on the Gold Coast was in no way unique to how they described people in West Africa in general. On the contrary, the claim of African laziness was repeated over and over again in European travel accounts, reports and correspondence from all over West Africa throughout the period studied in this book. The stereotype of laziness can be found already in some of the first European accounts from the continent. In 1453, Gomes Eanes de Zurara (chronicler of the Portuguese explorations of the African coast) argued that the Africans lived like beasts, 'and worse than all, through the great ignorance that was in them, in that they had no understanding of good, but only knew how to live in a bestial sloth'. The argument was used as a direct excuse for slavery, since 'their lot was now quite the contrary of what it had been', once they had been enslaved by the Portuguese.[41] Cadamosto, writing about people in Senegal by the late fifteenth century, similarly believed that the people there were 'very bad labourers – unwilling to exert themselves to sow more than will barely support them throughout the year'.[42] One can then find the stereotype frequently applied to virtually any people that the Europeans wrote about, all along the West African coast – from the Cape Verde and Senegal, through Sierra Leone, the Gold Coast all the way to the societies on the Slave Coast – and beyond.[43]

The idea of the 'lazy African' soon became quite ubiquitous among Europeans who travelled in and reported from pre-colonial West Africa. No wonder, then, that the idea found its way into both literature and secondary scholarly accounts dealing with West Africa, and soon seems to have become a hegemonic idea in the European discourse on Africa. One example was the French *Encyclopédie*, published in 1780, wherein it was argued that Africans 'are blamed for ferociousness, cruelty, perfidy, cowardice, laziness. This accusation is but too true'.[44] Another example comes from the Swedish natural scientist Carl Linnaeus who, in the twelfth edition of his famous *Systema Naturae*, classified Africans as 'niger, phlegmaticus, laxus' [black, phlegmatic, lax], and later in the same entry adds that they are 'vafer, segnis, negligens' [cunning, lazy, negligent].[45]

On the other hand, just as some people on the Gold Coast were described as being 'industrious', a number of descriptions of a similar industriousness can be found in accounts of societies and peoples from all over coastal West Africa, ranging from Senegambia in the west all the way to Ouidah and Dahomey in the east. Even if descriptions of industrious Africans are not as frequent as those of idle Africans, the number of authors describing some society or other as industrious is quite surprising. The patterns are in no way systematic, so a group or society described by one author as being made up of idle people, could very well be hailed as industrious by another author. Just as in the case of the Gold Coast, this stereotype of 'industriousness' was then often discussed, explicitly or implicitly, as an exception to the more general stereotype of 'idleness'.[46]

The idea that tropical exuberance can explain the phenomenon of 'idleness' can be found in European accounts concerned with virtually any part of the West African coast. One of the earliest accounts that seem to believe that this exuberance explained the phenomenon of the 'lazy African' was published in the year 1600, by the German explorer Johann von Lübelfing. In his account, he argued that people on the Guinean coast 'do not take the trouble to work, either: they live on the fruits of the country and on their livestock'.[47] This idea was in turn intimately connected with an idea that much of West Africa was a very fertile region. One of the first to describe West Africa (more specifically Senegambia) in such terms was Cadamosto, who thought that the African lands south of the river Senegal were very fertile, in contrast to the 'dry and arid land' north of the river.[48] The argument was later repeated by a large number of observers, of a range of different European nationalities.[49]

The gendered nature of the stereotype was likewise not an idea unique to the accounts dealing with the Gold Coast. It was on the contrary first described much earlier, from the Upper Guinea coast. What might be the first description of this relationship comes from Pieter van de Broecke, in his journal of a journey to Cape Verde from 1605–6. The men at Cape Verde, van den Broecke wrote, 'keep wives as their slaves. They must plough the land with hoes, which is heavy labour, and then seed and weed'.[50] The claim was later repeated by a whole number of European authors, writing about various parts of the West African coast.[51] Anna Maria Falconbridge was the first European woman to write about pre-colonial West Africa, based on her travels in Sierra Leone. In her book, she too described a highly patriarchal labour regime: 'They [the women] are not only obliged to till the ground, and do all laborious work, but are kept at a great distance by the men, who seldom suffer a woman to sit down or eat with them'.[52]

The gendered division of labour naturally differed somewhat between West African societies. Agricultural work in particular was however described as female work by a whole number of authors describing societies from Senegambia in the west to Benin and Ouidah in the east. Even the task of preparing the fields, using slash-and-burn techniques, was sometimes described as a female task in some areas along the West African coast. In some parts of coastal West Africa, women were also described as responsible for fishing and the building of huts and houses, but these latter examples might be exceptions to a more common pattern of the gendered division of labour.[53] Male occupations, when described, were on the other hand seemingly quite similar throughout much of the region relative to how they were described on the Gold Coast.[54] The illustration in Phérotée de Lacroix's book on West Africa (see Figure 4.2) might however seem to depict the grinding of corn as a male task. This could on the other hand be a reflection of the gender-bias not only of the author but also of the engraver.

The class aspect of the stereotype can also be found in the account of Anna Maria Falconbridge. In her journal, Falconbridge claimed that the British colony in Sierra Leone had problems employing local labourers since 'when they get their wages, like our English tars, they quit work while they have money'.[55] Again, the description of the behaviour Falconbridge thought was common among the African labourers was not exoticized, but rather considered to be quite similar to how English labourers also supposedly behaved.

Some of the evidence from the region would however suggest one further aspect to the stereotype of 'idleness', which is not to be found in the evidence from the Gold Coast in particular: that the stereotype was related to a market failure. If people were unable to sell surplus goods that they were able to produce, or were unable to purchase goods that they wanted on the markets, they would most certainly have found little reason to work much more than was necessary for their own subsistence. The issue would then not be a high valuation of leisure (or a culture without 'artificial wants') per se, as so many authors argued at the time. This is seemingly just what the English explorer Mungo Park was arguing, when he objected to characterizations of Africans as being lazy: they were not lazy 'when occasion requires', he argued, and continued: 'but not having many opportunities of turning to advantage, the superfluous produce of their labour, they are content with cultivating as much ground only as is necessary for their own support'.[56] Exactly why the Mandingos, which Park was exemplifying with, did not have

*Figure 4.2* Inhabitants on the Gold Coast grinding millet. The picture also illustrates parts of the interior of a house, with some household possessions.

Source: Illustration from Phérotée de Lacroix's *Relation universelle de l'Afrique* (1688). Reproduction: Jörgen Dahlberg, Norrköpings Stadsbibliotek, Sweden.

'many opportunities' in this case – if this was a problem of finding a buyer for their produce, or of finding goods that they were willing to buy in return – is unfortunately not elaborated upon by Park, but it might seem as if he suggests that their opportunities to sell produce were limited. Some writers, such as Brodie Cruickshank, attributed this market failure to the idea that people in many African societies were unaccustomed to monetary transactions.[57] Cruickshank's claim seems ignorant of the fact that many pre-colonial African societies actually did have some form of money (see Chapter 6), even if this money was not always in the form of coins as in Europe at the time. That this particular argument had any bearing had also been refuted by other authors already before Cruickshank published his book. So, for example, argued the American merchant Samuel Swan (*c.* 1815), that the Kru 'had never seen coin till they received it from the [Sierra Leone] company', but that that 'experience' soon taught them the value of money.[58]

Experience indeed seems to have taught many people – not just the Kru from Sierra Leone, but also many other people – not only the value of money, where it was used, but also how to bargain for the most favourable terms of employment. As will be shown in a later chapter (see Chapter 5), the European companies operating on the Gold Coast seem to have had no problem employing people on a monthly wage, paying them either in gold or in kind, and often had to negotiate the terms under which people were employed.

Perhaps it was not the (supposed lack of) means of monetary payments that constituted a hurdle, but rather what the money could purchase. In practice, if all one can exchange one's goods or labour for on a market are other very similar goods, there is little point in working very hard beyond subsistence needs, since the marginal utility of basic subsistence goods rapidly decreases. The so-called consumer revolution in early modern Europe, it has been argued, essentially created a culture of 'industriousness' among the working population in many European countries just for this specific reason – when a growing number of various luxury goods became available to a wider audience, it gradually became more interesting to work and people correspondingly increased the hours they worked, that is, increased the labour supply on the labour market.[59] That the European presence, and the goods that they brought with them for trade with the Africans, could induce a more industrious behaviour among African workers was also the conviction of some European observers. One example was the Englishman Philip Beaver, in charge of an attempt to establish a colony on the island of Bulama, one of the Bijagos Islands (off current-day Guinea-Bissau), by the late eighteenth century:

> I never saw men work harder, more willingly, or regularly, generally speaking, than those free natives whom I employed upon the island of Bulama. What induced them to do so? Their desire of European commodities in my possession, of which they knew that they would have the value of one bar at the end of a week, or four at the end of a month.[60]

To Beaver's mind, it was precisely the preference to consume (European) goods that enticed people to work voluntarily for his company. Key to Beaver's argument was also that the people working for him did so because they, in his opinion, could not get hold of the coveted European goods in any other way than accepting an employment position. We will return to this issue in Chapter 6, studying the development of markets in pre-colonial West Africa.

In conclusion, the descriptions that Europeans gave of people on the Gold Coast are often very similar to those that are given of people elsewhere along the West African coast. This is partly no doubt a reflection of the fact that many Europeans generalized wildly about Africans, but partly might also be a reflection of quite similar socio-economic contexts. One example is the gendered division of labour, where many European observers seem to describe a similar gender-coding of much of the agricultural work. This was also one of the key aspects of the stereotypes the Europeans adhered to concerning the West African work ethic throughout the region, including the Gold Coast. The Gold Coast did however seemingly differ in one aspect: whereas people in some other parts along the coast were described as not wanting to work for a wage simply because the factor or commodity markets were functioning badly, the sources describing the Gold Coast do generally not seem to have resorted to any such explanation.

## Questioning the stereotype

There was a great continuity in the European ideas about the West African work ethic, for a long period of time. By the late eighteenth century, however, some people's perceptions on the topic started to change, and they started to question the stereotype of the 'lazy African' completely. This questioning of the hegemonic discourse was clearly related to the emergence of an anti-slavery ideology, and the abolitionist movement, in the Atlantic region – most importantly in Britain and the British colonies in America. The first author to attempt such a questioning was perhaps the American abolitionist Anthony Benezet. Benezet had never visited Africa himself but undertook an alternative reading of some of the key publications on West Africa available at the time, including Willem Bosman's *A New and Accurate Description of the Coast of Guinea*, Jean Barbot's *A Description of the Coasts of North and South Guinea*, and Francis Moore's *Travels into the Inland Parts of Africa*. His conclusion from these readings was one quite contrary to what these authors themselves deduced from their observations, since Benezet, after quoting from the previous authors at length, argued that:

> the Foregoing are sufficient to shew them to be entirely different from the stupified and malicious People some would have them thought to be. They have the Judgement and Industry sufficient to cultivate their Country, which in most Parts abounds in the Necessaries of Life.[61]

Other abolitionists came to concur with Benezet. The French *philosophe* and abolitionist Condorcet in 1781 published a pamphlet entitled *Réflexions sur l'esclavage des Nègres*, under the pseudonym Mr Schwartz. In the pamphlet, he put forth an argument very similar to Benezet's, but also added that laziness was a 'fate of slaves' rather than any 'natural' trait of Africans.[62] For Condorcet, then, idleness was induced by the state of slavery, rather than the opposite causal relationship that many previous authors had argued in favour of (a sort of 'natural' idleness among Africans, necessitating coercion). Olaudah Equiano, an abolitionist of African origin himself, published his memoirs in 1789. In an early chapter, devoted to his memories of life in Africa, Equiano would argue that 'we are all habituated to labour from our earliest years. Every one contributes something to the common stock; and, as we are unacquainted with idleness, we have no beggars'.[63] The list could be made longer, including for example the Swedish scholar-turned-abolitionist Charles Bernhard Wadström, or the English naturalist Henry Smeathman.[64] By the early nineteenth century, the stereotype was almost turned on its head by some authors, arguing that idleness was a trait that Africans had learnt from the Europeans, and that the institution of slavery in the Americas by itself proved that it was the Europeans (and their American descendants) that were the really lazy ones, and for that particular reason found it necessary to try to coerce others to work for them.[65]

## Conclusion

This chapter has studied the development of a long-lasting stereotypical description of Africans' work ethic: the supposed 'lazy African'. This chapter has shown how this racist stereotype can be found already in some of the very first European accounts of contact with Africans. The stereotype soon came to be frequently used by a great number of European writers in describing the Gold Coast as well as many other parts of the West African coast. The stereotype of the 'lazy African' is thus a prime example of the European 'othering' of Africans.

In his classic study of West African economic history, Anthony Hopkins argued that the stereotypical picture of the African work ethic might have been the result of a market failure, where factor markets either failed to employ people who actually were willing to work, or commodity markets failed to provide the types of goods that people might have been interested in purchasing (which in turn would have induced them to earn an income to be able to buy the coveted goods). Once these failures were addressed, for example, by the growing imports of consumer goods addressing the latter failure, some European observers experienced little problem in finding locals, in various places along the coast, who would work both willingly and hard for them. Interestingly, however, this explanation for the stereotype was not to be found in the travel accounts dealing with the Gold Coast in particular. This might, on the one hand, be due to the descriptions on this topic found in the sources simply being too short and too poor to include all aspects of the phenomenon. It does on the other hand not seem unreasonable to also interpret it, at least partly, as a consequence of the comparatively high degree of market orientation of Gold Coast society, with comparatively well-functioning markets (an issue that will be dealt with in depth in Chapter 6). It would in any way seem unsatisfactory to explain the stereotypical portrayal of the African work ethic solely by this factor, since – as has been shown in this chapter – the work ethic of the people on the Gold Coast was portrayed in the same stereotypical way as that of most people along the West African coast.

One of the key explanations to the stereotypes about the African work ethic given by many contemporary authors themselves was the idea of a tropical exuberance. This has also been emphasized in much modern-day scholarly research into the history of the stereotype. It is therefore possible that the stereotype might reflect a rather high reservation wage among the local population. In particular, the Europeans were perhaps not always able to find a large number of people willing to work for whatever wages that the Europeans might have been willing to offer, if alternative economic activities offered better opportunities. This unwillingness to accept waged employment for the European companies, in particular, might have been wrongly interpreted as evidence of an innate idleness among the population.

Further, as has been shown in this chapter, the gendering of the division of labour is also of the utmost importance to understand the European ideas of stereotypes about the West African work ethic. West African societies – including the Gold Coast in particular, and many other coastal societies – had a clear division of labour along a couple of different dimensions. One was occupational specialization, based on certain skills, as we have seen many examples of in this chapter. Another was a gendered division of labour. What many Europeans encountered, and wrote about, was a gendered division of labour that was quite unlike what they were used to in Europe. The evidence from the sources is pretty scattered, and we cannot get a systematic picture of the gendered division of labour throughout the region. The silences in many of the accounts also give rise to many uncertainties about how to interpret the available evidence. There can however be no doubt that the women of the Gold Coast, in particular, and in West Africa, in general, certainly were not just providers of 'support services'. They were undoubtedly doing much of the core work necessary in West African societies. Most importantly, women seem to have played a key role in subsistence agricultural production throughout West Africa, and played a much more important role in this sector than how the European observers imagined it was like back home. The majority of the evidence from the Gold Coast, in particular, and most other parts of the West African coast, in general, thus indicates that this was generally coded as female work. Ester Boserup once suggested that the stereotype of laziness only applied to African men. Her suggestion was largely based on a reading of twentieth-century anthropological studies of more modern African societies, and has unfortunately received quite little attention among African historians. In this chapter, it has been shown that Boserup's hypothesis certainly has much explanatory value for the long historical development of the stereotype as well. Women were commonly described as being expected or forced to do much of the drudgery and hard work in West African economies. As a consequence, the men – who the Europeans thought avoided doing this work – easily came to be seen as lazy.

Alberto Memmi once argued that racist stereotypes, such as the accusation of laziness, served the purpose of justifying economic exploitation of colonized peoples. Other scholars have since argued that such stereotypes also came to be used as a justification for coercion of labour, in the form of slavery. Some scholars have even argued that the stereotype was developed more or less consciously for that specific purpose. This aspect certainly seems to have played a part from the start in the European 'othering' of West Africans, including the people living on the Gold Coast.

## Notes

1 Jones, *Brandenburg Sources*, p. 193.
2 Bosman, *A New and Accurate Description*, p. 101.
3 See for example Barbot, *Barbot on Guinea*, pp. 527–8; Rask, J., *A Brief and Truthful Description of a Journey to and from Guinea. Two Views from Christiansborg Castle, vol. I*, translated by S.A. Winsnes (Accra: Sub-Saharan, 2008 [1754]), p. 111; Uring, N., *A History of the Voyages and Travels of Capt. Nathaniel Uring* (London, 1726) at

ECCO [accessed 1 February 2013], p. 156; Smith, W. *A New Voyage to Guinea* (London, 1744), at ECCO [accessed 1 February 2013], p. 143; Rømer, *A Reliable Account*, pp. 217–18; Oldendorp, C., *Tillförlåtlig underrättelse om negrerne på Guineakusten* (Uppsala, 1784), p. 138; Meredith, *An Account of the Gold Coast*, p. 96; Adams, J., *Remarks on the Country Extending from Cape Palmas to the River Congo* (London, 1823), pp. 96 and 130; Cruickshank, B., *Eighteen Years on the Gold Coast of Africa* (London: Frank Cass, 1966 [1853]), pp. 284–5.

4 Rönnbäck, K., 'The Idle and the Industrious: European Ideas about the African Work Ethic in Precolonial West Africa', *History in Africa*, 41 (2014), pp. 117–45.

5 See for example Osberg, L., 'Leisure', in S. Durlauf and L. Blume (eds), *The New Palgrave Dictionary of Economics*, 2nd edn (Palgrave Macmillan, 2008), at www.dictionaryofeconomics.com [accessed 30 July 2014].

6 Barbot, *Barbot on Guinea*, p. 84.

7 Isert, *Letters on West Africa*, p. 136.

8 Smith, *A New Voyage*, pp. 28–9; John Hope Smith in Metcalfe, G.E., *Great Britain and Ghana. Documents of Ghana History 1807–1957* (Accra: University of Ghana, 1964), p. 2.

9 Isert, *Letters on West Africa*, p. 142.

10 Metcalfe, *Great Britain and Ghana*, p. 2; Curtin, *The Image of Africa*, p. 454.

11 De Marees, *Description and Historical Account*, pp. 171–2.

12 Barbot, *Barbot on Guinea*, p. 76.

13 Barbot, *Barbot on Guinea*, pp. 527–8.

14 Smith, *A New Voyage*, p. 145.

15 Adams, *Remarks on the Country*, p. 40.

16 Hufton, O., *The Prospect Before Her: A History of Women in Western Europe, 1500–1800* (London: Fontana Press, 1995), p. 153.

17 Lee, *Stories of Strange Lands*, pp. 39–40.

18 See Rönnbäck, 'The Men Seldom Suffer'.

19 Beecham, J., *Ashantee and the Gold Coast* (London: John Mason, 1970 [1841]), p. 129.

20 See Rönnbäck, 'The Men Seldom Suffer'.

21 Villault, *A Relation of the Coasts*, p. 216.

22 Isert, *Letters on West Africa*, p. 136.

23 Villault, *A Relation of the Coasts*, p. 158.

24 Jones, *German Sources*, p. 253.

25 Villault, *A Relation of the Coasts*, p. 214; Barbot, *Barbot on Guinea*, pp. 516–33; see also Isert, *Letters on West Africa*, pp. 135–6; Hutton, *A Voyage to Africa*, p. 91; Bowdich, *Mission from Cape Coast*, pp. 309–13.

26 Jones, *German Sources*, p. 254. See also Bosman, *A New and Accurate Description*, pp. 408–9.

27 Barbot, *Barbot on Guinea*, pp. 381–2.

28 Atkins, J., *A Voyage to Guinea, Brazil and the West Indies* (London: Frank Cass, 1970 [1735]), p. 100.

29 Barbot, *Barbot on Guinea*, p. 382; Lee, *Stories of Strange Lands*, p. 125.

30 Meredith, *An Account of*, p. 22.

31 Loyer, G., *Relation du voyage du royaume d'Issyny* (Paris: Seneuze & Morel, 1714), p. 162. See also Villault, *A Relation of the Coasts*, p. 220.

32 Da Mota, A.T. and Hair, P.E.H. (eds), *East of Mina: Afro-European Relations on the Gold Coast in the 1550s and 1560s. An Essay with Supporting Documents* (Madison: WISC, 1988), p. 84.

33 Hutton, *A Voyage to Africa*, pp. 157–8.

34 Hatcher, J., 'Labour, Leisure and Economic Thought before the Nineteenth Century', *Past & Present*, 160 (1998), pp. 64–115

35 Applebaum, *The Concept of Work*, chapter 14.
36 Rømer, *A Reliable Account*, pp. 217–18.
37 Curtin, P., 'The West African Coast in the Era of the Slave Trade', in P. Curtin, S. Feierman, L. Thompson and J. Vansin (eds), *African History from Earliest Times to Independence*, 2nd edn (London: Longman, 1995), p. 191.
38 Villault, *A Relation of the Coasts*, pp. 195–6.
39 Barbot, *Barbot on Guinea*, pp. 527–8.
40 Isert, *Letters on West Africa*, p. 173.
41 De Zurara, G.E., *The Chronicle of the Discovery and Conquest of Guinea*, vol. I (Cambridge: Cambridge University Press, 2010 [1453]), pp. 84–5.
42 Cadamosto, *The Voyages of Cadamosto* (London: Hakluyt Society, 1937), p. 42.
43 For a detailed analysis of descriptions adhering to this stereotype from all along the West African coast, see Rönnbäck, 'The Idle and the Industrious'.
44 Cohen, *The French Encounter*, p. 68.
45 Linnaeus, C., *Systema Naturae per Regna Tria Naturae* (Vindobonae, 1767) at Biodiversity Heritage Library Online [accessed 19 June 2013]), p. 29.
46 Rönnbäck, 'The Idle'.
47 Jones, *German Sources*, p. 11.
48 Cadamosto, *The Voyages of*, p. 27.
49 See for example Jobson, *The Discovery*, p. 275; Jones, *German Sources*, p. 150; Struys, J.J., *The Voiages and Travels of Jan Janszoon Struys* (London, 1684) at EEBO [accessed 27 April 2012], p. 11; Bosman, *A New and Accurate*, pp. 14–15; Moore, F., *Travels into the Inland Parts of Africa* (London, 1738) at MOMW [accessed 13 February 2012], p. xi; Smith, *A New Voyage*, p. 33; Watt, J., *Journal of James Watt: Expedition to Timbo Capital of the Fula Empire in 1794*, ed. B. Mouser (Madison: University of Wisconsin-Madison, African Studies Program, 1994 [1794]), p. 27; Winterbottom, T., *An Account of the Native Africans of Sierra Leone*, vol. 1 (London, 1803) at MOMW [accessed 13 February 2012], p. 11; Froger, F., *A Relation of a Voyage* (London, 1698) at EEBO [accessed 27 April 2012], p. 31; Durand, J.P.L., *A Voyage to Senegal* (London, 1806) at MOMW [accessed 13 February 2012], pp. 38, 61, 163.
50 Van den Broecke, P., *Pieter van den Broecke's Journal of Voyages to Cape Verde, Guinea and Angola (1605–1612)*, translated and edited by J.D. La Fleur (London: Hakluyt Society, 2000), p. 38.
51 For a detailed analysis of this topic, see Rönnbäck, 'The Men Seldom Suffer', pp. 211–27.
52 Falconbridge, A.M., *Narrative of Two Voyages to the River Sierra Leone* (London, 1802), at MOMW [accessed 13 February 2012], p. 77.
53 See Rönnbäck, 'The Men Seldom Suffer'.
54 See for example Ritchie, C.I.A., 'Impressions of Senegal in the Seventeenth Century', *African Studies* 26(2) (1967), pp. 85–6; Matthews, J., *A Voyage to the River Sierra Leone* (1788) at ECCO [accessed 23 May 2012], p. 107; Winterbottom, *An Account of*, p. 89; Stanfield, J.F., *Observations on Guinea Voyage* (London, 1788) at ECCO (accessed 25 April 2012), pp. 21–2.
55 Falconbridge, *Narrative of Two Voyages*, p. 204.
56 Park, M., *Travels in the Interior Districts of Africa* (New York, 1800) at MOMW [accessed 6 June 2013], pp. 277–8.
57 Cruickshank, *Eighteen Years*, p. 43.
58 Brooks, G., 'A View of Sierra Leone ca. 1815', *Sierra Leone Studies* 13 (1960), pp. 24–31, quote on pp. 30–1.
59 De Vries, *The Industrious Revolution*.
60 Beaver, P., *African Memoranda: Relative to an Attempt to Establish a British Settlement on the Island of Bulama* (1805, London) at MOMW [accessed 6 June 2013], pp. 385–6.

61 Benezet, A., *A Short Account of the Part of Africa, Inhabited by the Negroes* (Philadelphia, 1762) at MOMW [accessed 28 January 2013], pp. 18–19.
62 Condorcet, *Réflexions sur l'esclavage des Nègres* (Neufchatel, 1781) at Classiques des Sciences Sociales, http://classiques.uqac.ca [accessed 30 January 2014], p. 21.
63 Curtin, P. (ed.), *Africa Remembered. Narratives by West Africans from the Era of the Slave Trade* (Madison: University of Wisconsin Press, 1967), p. 76.
64 Rönnbäck, 'The Idle'.
65 Rönnbäck, 'The Idle'.

# 5 Work and wages at the Cape Coast Castle

## Introduction

This chapter will attempt to study the issue of work and working conditions on the Gold Coast utilizing data from a different primary source: the accounts of the English Royal African Company, operating the Cape Coast Castle and a number of outposts on the Gold Coast. In these accounts, it is possible to find evidence of many African labourers either owned or employed by the Company. The chapter will attempt to study who these labourers were and what they did. It will also attempt to study what material remuneration these labourers received for their labour and the conditions they worked under.

## Working at the Cape Coast Castle

When Europeans started to establish forts and castles along the African coast, they soon found that the climate on the West African coast created an environment that came to be called 'the white man's grave': endemic tropical diseases, such as malaria and yellow fever, increased mortality levels among the settler population to record-high levels.[1] It was for that reason not easy to sustain a European labour force at the forts big enough to undertake all the necessary work. In that respect, the European castles and forts on the African coast faced a situation similar to that of the plantations in the Americas, where it also was hard to keep any European population alive because of the endemic diseases.[2]

The European companies therefore began to acquire local African labour in order to do all the daily chores at the forts and castles. There were two ways the European companies could acquire such labour. On the one hand, they could do it by purchasing slaves who could be used for a variety of tasks. We will return to these so-called 'castle slaves' below. On the other hand, the companies soon also started to employ some labour that was not enslaved, from the nearby towns and villages. In the case of the Royal African Company, they employed many labourers from the town of Amanforo (later renamed Cape Coast), which was situated very close to the fort, as Figure 5.1 illustrates.

Evidence of employed labourers can be found in the accounts of the European companies operating on the Gold Coast. The qualitative sources indicate that it posed little problem to the European companies to employ free labourers on the

*Figure 5.1* Cabo Corso castle and town.

Source: Illustration from the manuscripts of Jean Barbot, British National Archives ADM 7/830B. Reproduction by the author.

Gold Coast. In the journal of the Danish slave-trading company one can, for example, find evidence that people from nearby towns on many occasions were hired to help with construction work, such as quarrying and carrying stones, already in the early eighteenth century.[3]

That free labour could be hired along the coast is also supported by evidence from the correspondence of the English Royal African Company. In one letter, John Roberts, president of the Cape Coast council, argued that a British captain by the name of Bignal ought to be reprimanded for his mistreatment of local canoemen at the Cape Coast, after he had refused to pay the canoemen their wages and wounded one of them in the shoulder with his sword. Roberts explicitly argued:

> They are free people and work only for their hire and not to be abused, beaten or starved by those who have no right to exercise such cruelty upon them especially as they are very willing and desirous to do any work . . . for pay and good wages.[4]

This was not unique to the Gold Coast in particular. In another letter, Abraham Duport wrote from Ouidah, further east along the coast, to the factors at the Cape Coast Castle, to ask whether he could be allowed to employ a particularly useful freeman, skilled as a blacksmith, in the Company's service.[5]

As was discussed in Chapter 3, a number of employed labourers – people of African, European and mixed descent – can be found on the Royal African

Company's 'Pay Bill', ranging from the top officials such as the governor, factors and merchants of the Company, to the lowest soldiers and assistants. Virtually all of these were men: only rarely do women figure in these lists during the period studied in this book. The women who do figure in these accounts all seem to be of European descent, judging from the fact that they arrive on the coast at the same time (and, when this is specified in the accounts, on the same boat) as their husbands.[6] There is thus virtually no information on free, African women being employed by the Company until the late eighteenth century, when Ty Reese has found some occasions when women were employed for various construction projects.[7]

With a few rare exceptions, all the high-status occupations were reserved for people of European descent. The career opportunities for the European staff were nonetheless quite limited: most of the staff never advanced at all, or advanced only to some limited extent – some soldiers being promoted into sergeants or gunners, an apprentice being advanced to writer, and so on. There were however rare examples of individuals who switched class completely. One such example can be found in the case of Andrew Lewis Dettmere, who arrived from England on 17 October 1720. He started out his career as a cooper, a position he held for a little over four years. After this time, his career started to take off: in January of 1725, he was advanced to steward, and then a few years later to surveyor. By 1733, he had achieved the position as chief (of one of the outforts), and by 1734 factor. By 1739, he was called inspector general, and from then onward he shifted between the last three positions. Another example is James Craik, who managed to advance all the way from starting out as a soldier in 1724, to being a highly paid accountant for the company by the late 1740s.[8]

As for free African labourers, quite a few of them were employed on a temporary basis, and paid piecework wages – as messengers, taking a letter from one fort to another; as canoemen employed to carry goods from ship to shore, and paid for the loads they carried; or as craftsmen employed to do a specific job, such as constructing a building or building a canoe. The European companies also found it necessary to employ some free African labourers on a steadier, long-term basis. These people could occasionally be quite highly paid. One example was Thomas Awishee, 'a black' according to a note on one of the Pay Bills, who was employed as a 'linguist' on the first of April 1707. Whether Thomas Awishee (or, for that matter, any of the other interpreters employed by the English Company) ever had any role as interpreter or linguist for the chief in an African community, or just was an ordinary (multilingual) interpreter, interpreting between the different languages spoken on the coast, is not evident from the source. Awishee doubled as a soldier during the first month of his employment for the Company, indicating that he might have been of quite humble origins. At this time, he was to be paid an annual wage of 6.75 oz of gold, similar to what the soldiers in general were paid. Soon, he specialized in being employed just as a 'linguist'. He then started to experience a quite important rise in the wage he received from his European employer. Awishee stayed with the Company, and became one of the most long-lasting employees. He was still on the Pay Bill of May/June 1744 – thirty-seven years after he was first employed. By this time, he had advanced to being paid a wage of 18 oz of gold per year. Given that the cost of subsistence around this time cost less than 1 ounce of gold per year (see Chapter 8), Thomas Awishee must have been able to afford a quite respectable life. Then, he suddenly disappeared from the Pay Bills, without any note of his fate.[9]

Other staff of African descent included everything from craftsmen to manual labourers. On the Pay Bill, one can therefore find people such as the carpenters Bass John and John Coffee; the cooper Black Tom; the caulker Richard Perry; the canoemen Coffee Quashoe and Quacoe Saffoe; the sailor Thomas Cecil; the linguist Quaw Butty; the messenger George Banishee; the writer Frederick Adoy; the overseers Peter Penin and Peter Comma; the trumpeter Isaac Moore; the soldiers John Quamino, Peter Powell and William Ugly; the gunsmith John White; and the brickmaker Quashee Ansah. All of these individuals were explicitly described in the accounts as being of African descent, just as in the case of Thomas Awishee above. Bass John was on some of the Pay Bills for example described as 'a Black Portuguese', John White was described as a 'negro', and many others were simply just called 'black', or in some rare cases 'native'.

The information about the African labourers is often far from as detailed as it is for the staff of European descent. In a vast amount of cases, as was noted in Chapter 3, the accounts only report a first name of the Africans being paid wages, such as the sailors Boneta or Chassy, the linguist Cudjoe, or the canoemen, Daddie and Mumfoy.[10] Further, some entries do not report any name at all, but only that wages were paid to a certain number of workers of a specific occupation. In the 1730s, many of the Pay Bills noted that around fifty (the exact figure varied between the Pay Bills) canoemen, with only a few of them named, were paid a wage every second month, specifying the wage paid to each individual canoeman (equal for all able-bodied canoemen) and the total sum for the whole group.[11]

The list of occupations showed a great variety, as the examples above give ample proof of, ranging from some of the most unskilled tasks (such as the plain labourer) to some occupations requiring quite advanced skills, such as the writers or the gunsmith.[12] One important task for the carpenters in particular was, most certainly, that of building canoes for the Company – a work that can be seen depicted in Figure 5.2. The company also purchased a number of canoes of its own annually, and employed an even greater number of canoes owned by local Africans, in order to transport goods between ships and the European forts along the coast.[13]

Unfortunately, the accounts do not reveal much information about more complex issues regarding the social aspects of the work process. Some observations are, however, possible to make regarding the ethnic aspects of the social relations at the Cape Coast Castle. For starters, the Africans were generally denied any of the more high-ranking positions in the Company. The only exceptions found were a couple of writers of African or mixed descent, employed by the end of the period under study in this book.[14] Further, the Africans were often paid much lower wages than Europeans holding the same type of occupation, and were also often cheated when their wages were paid (two issues we will return to below). Most certainly, then, the free African labourers were thus discriminated against in a number of different ways.

*Figure 5.2* Carpenters on the Gold Coast building a canoe.

Source: Illustration from Phérotée de Lacroix's *Relation universelle de l'Afrique* (1688). Reproduction: Jörgen Dahlberg, Norrköpings Stadsbibliotek, Sweden.

## Payments to the free African staff

The European companies had to offer competitive wages to attract the free workers. This could be the cause of tension between the European companies, as is evident in a letter by the Danish governor Andreas Wærøe who, in 1734, complained to the directors of the Danish slave-trading company: 'As for the Mulattoes, they have almost all gone, for when they become old enough to carry a flintlock, they immediately run off to the English, who pay them 10 rdl. in monthly subsistence'.[15]

The regular employees at the forts and castles of the English Royal African Company were paid wages every month, or every second month. The wages paid to the African staff employed by the Company varied considerably between the individuals, and was determined primarily by the occupation that the individual employee held. Some of the most highly skilled labourers could earn very high wages indeed: by the 1760s, the Company employed a couple of 'black' writers, including Frederick Adoy and William Ansah, paying them each the equivalent of a wage of 25 to 30 oz of gold per year. This enabled them to live a life of quite some material luxury (see more on this in Chapter 8). An experienced 'linguist' (i.e. interpreter), such as Thomas Awishee, mentioned above, could normally earn some 12 to 18 oz of gold per year. The African craftsmen, such as the carpenters, caulkers or coopers, employed by the Company were paid a wage of around 4 to 6 oz of gold per year.[16]

For some occupations, the wages paid to the workers were quite standardized: the canoemen were almost universally paid 2 ackeys of gold per month, that is, 1.5 oz per year. The only exceptions were disabled canoemen (some were described as blind), or young boys (called 'canoeboys'), who both received half pay of what the able-bodied adults received. For most of the employed labourers, however, wages were not standardized in this way.[17] The rather large variance in wages between individuals holding the same occupation, instead suggests that the wages normally were the result of a process of bargaining between the Company and the individual labourers.

The inference that wages generally were the outcome of a bargaining process is also supported by qualitative evidence. In 1693, Nicholas Buckeridge – factor at Winneba fort on the Gold Coast – wrote to the factors at Cape Coast Castle about his attempts to hire bricklayers to help out with the construction of the fort:

> The two black bricklayers which formerly advised of will not worke unless you will allow them 3½ an per month each, I mean the 4 weeks, wherefore pray let me have your advise. I am forced to make use of them at present by reason 2 of the whites have every other day a feavour & ague.[18]

Clearly, Buckeridge had attempted to hire the bricklayers at a lower wage, but they – knowing their worth, and possibly also in the know about the situation that the Company was in – simply would not accept such a low wage. Another example comes from Henry Meredith, who was an English governor on the Gold Coast by the early nineteenth century. Meredith argued that the porters and canoemen employed by the Europeans often were paid an all too high wage:

> These men are paid in goods or gold, to about the value of five shillings each man for their trip; beside which, they have subsistence and liquor. This appears but moderate pay for such laborious employment: but when it is considered, that a Black can be victualled sumptuously, agreeably to the custom of the country, for ten shillings per month, it is too much: and it is very probable, if Europeans, at a future time, should have occasion to hire free labourers for purposes of cultivation, they will regret that such high pay has been given to hammock-men and canoe-men; as it may be urged against them as a precedent for giving high wages.[19]

The wage payments were clearly discriminatory: Europeans holding the same type of occupation were often paid considerably higher wages than the African

*Table 5.1* Wage discrimination of free African labourers at the Cape Coast Castle, 1730s

| | *African mean wage (oz)* | *European mean wage (oz)* | *Wage ratio (African/ European wages)* |
|---|---|---|---|
| Carpenter | 4.2 | 9.0 | 0.47 |
| Cooper | 4.8 | 11.1 | 0.43 |
| Gunner | 3.8 | 9.4 | 0.40 |
| Soldier | 4.4 | 6.7 | 0.66 |

Source: GCPLD.

labourers were. This is evident from the 1730s, when the accounts report quite a large number of different African free labourers on the Pay Bills. It then becomes possible to compare the wages paid to the labourers of African and European descent, respectively. This is reported in Table 5.1 for the four occupations where people of both backgrounds were employed.

While a carpenter of African descent, for example, Bass John mentioned earlier, was paid a wage of around 4 oz of gold per year in the 1730s, a carpenter of European descent, such as James MacDowall working at the Castle around the same time, was paid an annual wage of around 9 oz. Least discriminated against were perhaps the soldiers, at least in nominal terms: quite a few of the African soldiers employed at the forts were even recorded as being paid the same nominal amount (6.75 oz of gold per year) as all the European soldiers received, which is why the wage ratio between the groups is considerably higher for this category of employees than for all the others.[20]

During the first half of the eighteenth century, the Company employed no free female labourers. As was noted above, Ty Reese has found two occasions by the late eighteenth century (in 1769 and 1775, respectively) when the Company did do this, participating in construction work. The women were then on both these occasions paid lower nominal wages than the male workers employed for the same project: on both occasions, the women earned three-quarters of what the male workers earned when working on the same construction project.[21]

While the wages reported on the Pay Bills are reported in monetary terms (in amounts of gold dust or pounds sterling), this is not how most of the workers actually were paid. In reality, most of the African staff working for the Company were paid in kind. They could then be paid either with provisions (including local provisions such as corn or palm oil, or European provisions such as beef, bread or cheese) or with European trade goods, such as alcohol, textiles, tobacco or any other goods the Europeans sold. The labourers were then given an amount of these goods that was considered equivalent to the wage they were supposed to have received.[22] It is evident from the accounts that the Company often tried to cheat the African staff out of part of their wages, when estimating the value of the goods paid to them in kind: the price that the Company used for this accounting was often inflated relative to the price at which they could sell their goods on the local markets, or compared to the price they could purchase local provisions for.

*Table 5.2* Royal African Company's mark-up of price of goods when paid as wages in kind to African employees, relative to the price when purchasing/selling goods on the local markets, 1740 and 1752

| | *1740* | *1752* |
|---|---|---|
| *Local provisions (mark-up vs purchase price)* | | |
| Corn | 8% | 60% |
| Palm oil | 0% | . |
| *European trade goods (mark-up vs sale price)* | | |
| Guinea stuffs | 0% | 41% |
| Meat | 50% | 50% |
| Tallow | 15% | 4% |

Source: GCPPD.

Table 5.2 shows the mark-up that the Company added to the price when paying wages to the Africans in kind, for two years where there is overlapping data, so that prices charged can be compared.

As can be seen in the table, the mark-up differed greatly between the goods: in some cases, such as palm oil or tallow there was no or only a comparatively small mark-up on the price charged to the African labourers, relative to the going market prices. In other cases, such as with the meat paid to the labourers, or both corn and guinea stuffs in one of the two years compared, the prices were substantially higher than the local market prices, when the Company tried to buy or sell similar goods on the markets. The practice of cheating was, furthermore, clearly discriminatory against the Africans: the Company did not try to cheat the European staff in the same way. On the contrary, the European staff, when paid in kind, are many times charged a price for the goods that is *lower* than what the Company would have received if it had sold the goods on the local market. Consistently, for all years and all commodities where it is possible to compare the data, the prices charged to the Africans for goods paid in kind are 50 per cent higher than the prices charged to the European staff, when they were paid in kind. Even if some African and European employees were paid a similar nominal wage, the real purchasing power for the Africans was therefore considerably lower because of how they were cheated when paid in kind.

The wages paid to these labourers were regular, monthly wages. In some cases, it is possible that the labourers might have supplemented these incomes through *dashes* (gifts and gratuities) or through business on the side of their employment. It is not difficult to imagine that some of the canoemen employed by the company might have earned extra money from dashes, from participating in some trade themselves, or from fishing during slow periods of work. Further, in early modern Europe, many employees who had a monthly wage were also provided with food, in addition to the monthly wages they were paid.[23] It is possible that this practice was the case also at the Cape Coast Castle. The sources are not clear on this issue, but it is how K.G. Davies interpreted the evidence, simply assuming that the staff also was provided with food.[24] The monthly wages that an employee earned would thereby not have to be used to pay for food (not at all, or only to some extent), but could be used for other purposes. Ty Reese has however argued that, at least in the case of the slaves, they were expected to pay for their own subsistence using the wages they were paid.[25] It is, however, unclear what evidence there is supporting this interpretation. As was mentioned previously, there are in general figures on the Pay Bills for extra payments for the 'diet' for the (European) staff of higher social status, such as the factors and governors. The accounts do not make any such distinction between wage payments and payments for the 'diet' for staff of lower social status, including the African labourers.

## The castle slaves

The free labourers only constituted a minority of the labour force at the Cape Coast Castle and the other European forts. Most of the manual labour was instead undertaken by a large number of slaves owned by the European companies. In the primary sources, they are called 'castle slaves', and were clearly separated from the 'trade slaves' – the slaves that the Company were selling for transport to the Americas.[26]

The castle slaves were the slaves retained at the forts on the African coast, in order to do all the chores that needed doing. The Company's choice to exploit some slaves for daily chores at the forts and castles on the African coast must have been an easy one, once the transatlantic slave trade had started to take off in the region (see Chapter 2). The Company then could tap into the same supply in order to acquire castle slaves as they did when purchasing slaves for the transatlantic trade. A drawback of purchasing castle slaves was, however, that it possibly could compete with the Company's own business – that of selling slaves overseas. Rebecca Shumway has, therefore, argued that many of the castle slaves in practice came to be the 'refuse' slaves, that is, the slaves that the Company for some reason was unable to sell to any buyer.[27]

The castle slavery regime could undoubtedly be a highly brutal one. Ray Kea has found the testimonies from a trial held in 1736 of the Danish governor Andreas Wærøe, charged with mismanagement. One question and the response by Wærøe during the trial shed some brief light on a brutal practice that otherwise often went by without much notice in accounts or day books:

> And isn't it well known that most of the Company's slaves who died, died of hunger and brutal treatment?
>
> Response. Yes! In God's truth this is known, that they were brutalized because of onerous work.[28]

While Wærøe's statement referred in particular to the Danish castle slaves, there is no reason to assume that other European companies treated their castle slaves very differently. Unsurprisingly, many of the slaves attempted to run away or rebel against the European companies. This is one of the recurring events reported in the journals and correspondence of the companies on the Gold Coast. In August of 1699, the journal from the Danish slave-trading company reported that three company slaves had run away after having been sent to the forest to gather firewood.[29] On another occasion, in 1730, two canoemen assigned to assist a sloop, attempted to run away after having set the sails of the sloop on fire.[30] In 1752, a company slave by the name of Mamma assigned to guard duty one night was blamed for helping two female slaves escape during the night.[31] Even more serious, in the eyes of the Company, was the fact that company slaves sometimes tried to rebel, for various reasons.[32] In at least one of these attempts, the rebellion was thwarted since some other company slaves reported the plans to the managers of the Company in time for the latter to counteract.[33] These examples certainly show how valuable it was for the company to gain the loyalty of the company slaves.

The work that these slaves did is to some extent revealed from the very detailed 'Slave Lists' that the English Company kept. These lists report a name of all the slaves owned by the Company, as well as the gender, occupation and if they have any disabilities. The lists also reported wages paid to the slaves. Each Slave List can contain up to a couple of hundred slaves of various occupations. On the Slave List, one can, for example, find the sailor Boneta (who also was recorded as being 'Master of Ye C Boat'), being paid a wage equivalent of 2.25 oz of gold per year; the gunner Cudjoe being paid the equivalent of 3.75 oz of gold per year; or the labouress Abbah (recorded to also have had two children to care for), being paid 2.25 oz of gold per year for herself and her children. One can also find disabled slaves on the list, such as the blind carpenter Cudjoe Dragon or the 'mad' labouress Ambah. Presumably only disabilities that might impact their work performance were reported on the lists. From the occupation, it is to some extent also possible to tell whether the person was an adult or a child (children all have the title of 'boy' or 'girl', but in the case of the boys usually also associated with some specific occupation, such as the 'carpenter's boy' Arrotee, or the 'canoeboy' Appah).[34]

The male slaves were designated to do a whole range of different tasks, ranging from unskilled manual labour to presumably quite highly skilled tasks as craftsmen or foremen. The list of specific male occupations – aside from those who simply were categorized as labourers – is quite long, including armourer, blacksmith, bomboy (i.e. assistant or foreman), bricklayer, brickmaker, canoeman, captain of the canoemen, carpenter, cook, cooper, doctor, drummer, gardener, goldsmith, goldtaker, gunner, labourer, linguist (i.e. interpreter), sailor, sawyer, soldier and stockkeeper. The list of specific female occupations is significantly shorter: cook, doctress (possibly a midwife?), hospital tender, and washerwoman. Another difference between the genders is that while the unspecified labourers were a minority among the men (only 24 per cent of the male slaves were categorized as labourers only), virtually all (97 per cent) of the female slaves were categorized as such. Whereas quite a large share of the male slaves thus had been allowed to learn – either as slaves, or prior to being enslaved – at least some particular skill, most female slaves were not recorded as having any particular occupation or skills.[35]

This might, of course, to some extent be a reflection of how many men belittled female activities, not necessarily recognizing the skills necessary for, for example, reproductive or domestic work – or, as was described in Chapter 4, the agricultural work that many women were expected to do.

Clearly, the slaves often held the same type of occupation as some of the free African labourers employed at the forts. The Company did also see the free and enslaved workers as interchangeable to some extent. It, therefore, became a practical issue of profit maximization to decide whether to employ free labourers, or to exploit castle slaves, for a specific task. This is evident from a letter written by Abraham Duport, factor at Ouidah, to the factors at Cape Coast Castle, in 1727. In the letter, Duport argued that the fort at Ouidah needed regular repairs, but that he would

> leave you to judge whether it's the Company's Interest to hire free People to do it (for it must be done) or keep their own Slaves, which are not too many to keep it in repaire. As for my part it's equal to me to hire free People as to compell [sic!] the Slaves to do it.[36]

Unfortunately, the records of the Royal African Company only report a first name of each slave for almost all of the slaves. Further, the number of different names is quite limited – there are for example quite a few of the male slaves named Coffee or Cudjoe, and a large number of the female slaves names Abbah, Effebah or Aggubah. On some of the lists, there is also a 'tally number' that generally seems to be associated with a particular slave, but these are not kept consistently and there are a number of cases where several different slaves have the same 'tally number'. It therefore becomes hard to link the individuals in different records with any certainty, and follow their fate over time.[37]

The accounts also take explicit note of a couple of human pawns. One example is the 'Company pawn Ampha', reported to be a canoeman on some of the lists in the 1740s. The number of pawns is however very small compared to the number of people included on the Pay Bills and Slave Lists in total. Most of these pawns were nonetheless stationed at Accra in particular, and were then reported to work as canoemen there.[38]

## Wage payments to the slaves

It is clear from the 'Slave Lists' that the castle slaves were paid regular wages. The wages paid to the castle slave labourers were, furthermore, comparatively high – substantially higher than what would be expected if the purpose of the wage only was to make sure that the slaves could acquire basic subsistence necessities for themselves. Detailed data on an individual level on the wages that the slaves were paid are available from the 1750s. By this time, the cost of subsistence – including basic foodstuffs of a quantity large enough to provide the calories and proteins necessary to avoid starvation, some cheap textiles for clothes, and some housing and energy costs – was around 0.3 oz of gold dust per single adult per year (see Chapter 8). An unskilled male slave – the lowest paid among the male adults – was at this time paid a nominal wage of around 1.5 oz of gold per year – five times the cost of subsistence of a single individual (see Chapter 8 for an in-depth discussion on this topic). Many of the more skilled craftsmen among the slaves, such as the carpenter Akassie or the blacksmith Coffee Bob could earn up to 3 to 4 oz of gold per year. A few individual craftsmen, such as the gardener Limas or the cooper Quobino Dick were occasionally paid upwards of 6 oz of gold per year. Slaves who also were foremen, such as the head cooper Qui or the bomboys, Quamino and Coffee, were paid even more than that.[39] It is clearly not the case that the wages paid to the slaves were only supposed to pay for their own basic subsistence. The question of what motivated these comparatively high wages then becomes of interest.

Some payments to the slaves were in the form of bonuses for 'overwork', that is, for working beyond the set hours.[40] What is further obvious from the accounts is that the regular, bi-monthly wages paid to the slaves differed significantly between individuals – the wages paid ranged from the equivalent of 0.75 oz of gold per year for some of the lowest paid female or child slaves, to more than 6 oz of gold per year for the single best paid slave labourer, the head cooper. One of the key factors behind the wage differences was gender. Table 5.3 shows the mean and median wages of male and female slaves in the sample studied. The data shows that the female slaves were paid almost exactly half of what the male slaves were paid, regardless of whether we study the mean or median wage.

This lower wage to the female slaves is not just an effect of the fact that male slaves were designated more specific (and higher paid) occupations than the female slaves were. The female slaves were also paid less than the male slaves even when they had exactly the same occupational title: a male cook could for example be paid a nominal wage of 3.4 oz of gold per year, while a female cook only was paid 2.3 oz of gold per year.

There were also large differences in pay depending on the occupation of the slave. This is shown in Graphs 5.1a and 5.1b, separated by gender. The graphs show the wage premium for the various specific occupations the slaves were assigned to, relative to the wage paid to an unskilled slave labourer of the same sex.

As can be seen in Graphs 5.1a and 5.1b, there are some quite systematic patterns to the wage differentials among the slaves. It is unknown if there is a selection

*Table 5.3* The annual wage paid to all adult slaves at the Cape Coast Castle (oz gold/year), 1728–60

| | *Mean* | *Median* | *n* |
|---|---|---|---|
| Female | 1.0 | 0.75 | 4,032 |
| Male | 1.8 | 1.5 | 3,828 |
| All | 1.4 | 1.5 | 7,860 |

Source: GCPLD.

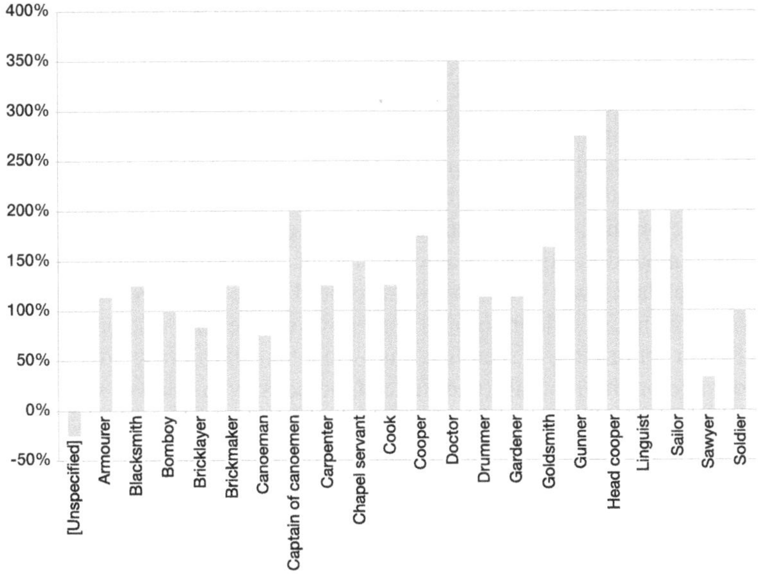


*Graph 5.1a* Wage premium for male slave occupations, relative to wage paid to unskilled male slave labourer, 1728–60

Note: calculated as the premium on median wage.

Source: GCPLD.

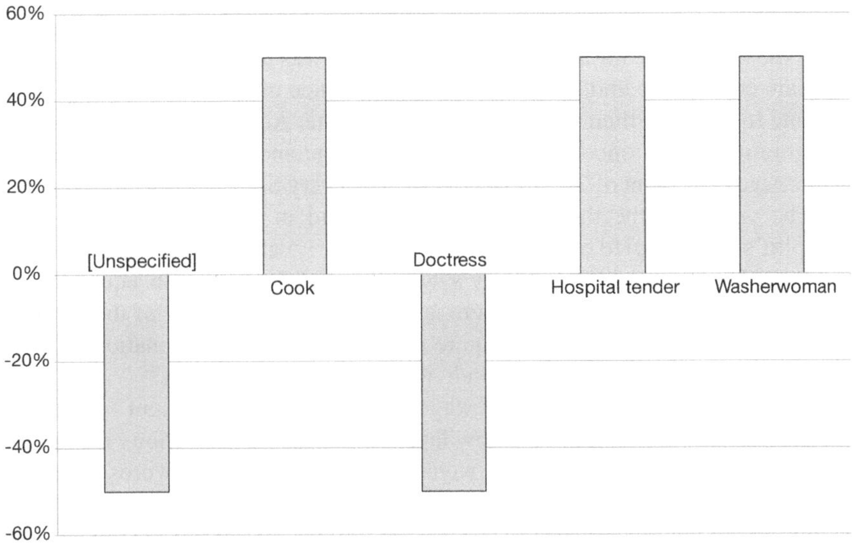


*Graph 5.1b* Wage premium for female occupations, relative to wage paid to unskilled female slave labourer, 1728–60

Note: calculated as the premium on median wage.

Source: GCPLD.

bias in who were appointed to a specific position: it is possible that more productive or loyal slaves were rewarded by being taught a particular craft. The wage structure does however show a very distinct skill premium. Craftsmen were on average paid around double the wages of the unskilled manual labourers. Canoemen were paid more than 50 per cent higher wages than the unskilled labourers. A doctor, if skilled at his work, could possibly save many lives among both the castle and trade slaves, and could then also save the Company a lot of money. It is therefore not very surprising that the doctors were paid a substantial wage premium – around five times the amount of what an unskilled manual labourer received. Female slaves who were recorded to hold some specified occupation, such as a washerwoman, cook or hospital tender, were in general also paid a wage premium. Rather surprising is therefore the result that the female 'doctresses' received no wage premium at all (and, indeed, perhaps even a lower wage than the 'labouresses'). Why that is so is unfortunately not revealed from the accounts.

There are also a number of other factors influencing the wage differences between the individual slaves. Disabled slaves were paid a lower wage than the able-bodied ones, and children were paid a lower wage than the adults. Some of the women also had to care for small children, who were unable to take care of themselves. These women generally received some extra payments for the dependent children.

Furthermore, while the wages paid to the slaves often were set at a specific rate over time for most individuals, some experienced more flexible wages. Take for example the slave cooks, in the accounts named Porridge, Dumplin, Dunsee, Quow, Doc, Akenequo, Yan Terry and Eukebah, respectively. The only female cook among them, Eukebah, was paid a wage of 1.5 oz except for one single month when she had to care for a couple of children, and was paid extra for that. Among the male cooks, Doc and Akenequo only figure once in the accounts, so it is not possible to compare their wage payments over time. Among the slave cooks that do figure more than once in the accounts, Porridge and Quow were both paid a stable wage equivalent of 2.25 oz of gold each on every Slave List that they featured on. The wages of the three remaining cooks did in contrast vary over time. Dumplin's wages varied between the equivalent of 1.5 and 2.8 oz of gold per year, and both Dunsee's and Yan Terry's wages varied between the equivalent of 1.9 and 3.4 oz of gold per year. There is no progression in either of these cooks' wages, but they go up and down quite randomly, with no explanation given in the accounts as to the level of the individual's wage each month.[41]

Given the quite large number of wage observations, almost eight thousand in total, it becomes possible to test how large an impact all the various factors had upon the individual slave's wage payments. This is done in a cross-sectional multivariate regression analysis. The occupational title is used to determine a skill level of the individual, assuming not only that all the slaves were skilled enough for the tasks they were performing but also that the Company was exploiting all the skills that the castle slaves possessed to the full. The coding of this skill level follows the Historical International Standard Classifications of Occupations (HISCO) and the Historical International Social Class Scheme (HISCLASS).[42]

A special 'loyalty'-dummy variable is also created, given the value of one for all occupations where the individual slave either had access to arms (i.e. soldiers or gunners), or had an occupation where they generally worked outside the forts (and then plausibly could escape from slavery more easily, i.e. sailors or canoemen). The results of the cross-sectional analysis are reported in Table 5.4.

The Company thus developed a rather intricately differentiated wage system to the slaves. But why would the Company pay these high wages in the first place? Presumably, given that these people were enslaved, they were never given any choice as to work or not, and would not have been able to negotiate directly for their wages. Common practice under slavery was instead to try to compel the slaves to work, using violence and coercion if necessary. There were however reasons for the company to try to use positive incentives, as a complement to the negative incentive of coercion. Coercion of slaves could lead to drastically reduced productivity of the slaves, if they were beaten so much that they became disabled, temporarily or permanently, or large capital costs if the slaves were killed. From that perspective, it might be rational even for the most brutal and racist slaveholder to attempt to foster loyalty, obedience among the slaves, and inspire them to work hard through positive incentives. One way of doing this would be to use positive incentives such as economic rewards, possibly as a substitute for or more probably as a complement to coercion. Whether to use the carrot or the stick thus became an economic issue.

Instead of being considered as subsistence payments, it thus seems more plausible to interpret the wages paid to the slaves as a form of incentive system. By differentiating the occupational positions and the wages, it became possible for the Company to 'promote' particular slaves, and to let the slaves 'advance' *within* the system of the slavery. Slaves who misbehaved could consequently be punished not just by violence and coercion, but also by being reduced in rank and

*Table 5.4* Determinants of the wage differences among the castle slaves at the Cape Coast Castle, 1750s

| *Variable* | *Impact on wage* |
|---|---|
| Gender | –35% for women, compared to men |
| Skill premium | +23% per skill level, on a scale of 1–4 (where 1 is unskilled and 4 is highly skilled) |
| Loyalty premium | +23% for occupations where the slaves were armed, or had a better chance to escape |
| Child labour | –50% for child slaves, compared to adults |
| Disability | –41% for people with any recorded disability, compared to able-bodied people |
| Dependent children of adults | +12% to the woman for every dependent child in her care |

Note: n = 2,764. All results are statistically significant at the conventional level of confidence (5 per cent). The variables in the table explain 31 per cent of the variation in the sample.

Source: GCPLD.

pay. This interpretation is perhaps also supported by anecdotal evidence in the qualitative sources. In 1695, John Pinck, factor of the Dixcove fort, wrote to the factors at Cape Coast Castle: 'We have two slaves that work very well and are very servicable in the building, they therefore desire you would be pleased to advance them'.[43] It is not entirely clear how to interpret the specific meaning of the wording ('to advance them'), but it might perhaps indicate that advancement, as synonymous to promotion, could be a reward for good conduct. With promotion then also followed a higher wage. Such an interpretation of the wage payments to the slaves therefore also provide a rational explanation to many of the wage differences found among the slaves, from the point of view of the slaveholder. The variation in wages paid to some of the individual slaves, discussed above, could reflect a bonus paid for good behaviour or hard work during that particular month (or months, if paid for several months at a time).

From the slaveholder's point of view, it was also rational to try to foster loyalty among key segments of the slave population. One such group were the slaves with access to arms (such as gunners or soldiers) who might become a hazard for the Europeans, should they try to rebel against their fate as slaves. The loyalty bonus paid to slaves that carried arms was therefore not very surprising. Another group of slaves, particularly important to keep loyal, were those that regularly might have to work far away from the fort, such as the canoemen and sailors, since they otherwise might attempt (and also have a better chance at being successful in their attempts) to run away from the slaveholder. It also seems rational for the Company to pay a skill premium. Since skilled slaves sold at a premium, and it took time and capital to train an unskilled slave by oneself, the Company stood to lose more if a skilled slave either idled at work or tried to rebel or run away from the slaveholder, than they would if a presumably less costly and less productive unskilled labourer would do the same.

It might on the other hand make less sense to try to incentivize certain other groups to work very hard. This would include women, disabled or child slaves. For one thing, they might have been easier to coerce than the able-bodied/adults were, and there might have been less risk to coerce them since they might have had less chance to resist and rebel than the able-bodied, adult male slaves did. For another thing, the productivity (at least of the disabled slaves) might have been quite low, even if they were to work hard. The gender differences in wages, finally, might to some extent be explained by two further factors. On the one hand, there was an idea among the Europeans that African women in general were more industrious than the 'lazy' African men (see Chapter 4). Even though the stereotype was unfounded in actual fact, the idea could nonetheless have influenced how the Europeans acted in relation to African populations. On the other hand, many Europeans also saw African women as more docile, and less prone to resist, either by running away or by rebelling.[44] Given such ideas, it seems rational to pay higher wages to able-bodied, adult men in particular, in order to foster loyalty and reduce any incentive to resist the institution of slavery per se among them.

## The choice between slave and free labour

One of the key choices faced by the Company when attempting to acquire labour was whether to attempt to employ free labourers, or whether to purchase slaves to undertake the work. Opinions on the value of slaves and free labourers, respectively, differed between different observers. In a resolution from the Danish slave-trading company from the middle of the eighteenth century, it is, for example, stated that – since the Danish company at the time owned very few slave canoemen (*remidors*) – 'when something of urgency arises, the Noble Company incurs great expenses hiring free *remidors*'.[45] The slaves thus seem to have formed the core, permanent labour force for the company at the time, supplemented by more expensive free labourers only on a temporary basis. On the Gold Coast, many of the free, hired labourers seem to have received a nominal wage on a par with that paid to the slaves. This is evident in the wage data from the accounts of the company, but is also revealed in the correspondence of various English company agents. The English governor Mutter argued by the late seventeenth century that:

> As to company slaves, it would undoubtedly be necessary to have a supply of them, but till they could be procured, free labourers might be hired, and they would come full as cheap as company slaves, but then they must not be relied on entirely, for if they once saw you could not proceed without their assistance, extravagant wages and insolent behaviour, would in spite of the greatest indulgences, knock all our schemes in the head.[46]

Another governor, Charles Bell, agreed with Mutter that the free labourers often could be hired at a similar cost to the Company as it cost to purchase a slave, the only drawback being that 'I am obliged however to give them goods in advance'.[47]

At first, similar nominal wages to both free and slave labourers might seem counter-intuitive, given the fact that the slaveholder had to invest capital in order to purchase a slave. What was then the point of acquiring slaves at all; why not just employ only free labourers, in order to save the capital investment of purchasing a slave? One reason is suggested in the correspondence of the English Company: that a slave, since they could be coerced to work, was a more reliable labour force than the unpredictable freemen. This is what Thomas Bucknell, the governor of the English fort at Sekondi experienced, when asking the factors at the Cape Coast Castle for advice about how many slaves to keep 'for a constancy', since 'the towns people are of such a sordid nature that sometimes they will be hyrd to help us and sometimes they will not'.[48] Bucknell unfortunately never elaborated on why the townspeople only accepted to work for the Company on some occasions.

Akosua Perbi has suggested a complementary reason for purchasing slaves instead of employing free labour: that the owner could coerce the slaves to work longer hours per day than they could request of freely employed staff.[49] Using data on the wages paid to the workers (slaves and free), as well as the prices paid to purchase slaves, it becomes possible to calculate how much more time per day

*Table 5.5* The cost of slave versus free labour, 1730s

| | | |
|---|---|---|
| A | Purchase price of an adult, male slave | 1.40 oz |
| B | Purchase price of slave, including discounting of capital cost (10 %/year) | 2.23 oz |
| C | Annual median wage of slave labourer | 0.75 oz |
| D | Annual cost of slave labourer (= C + B/10) | 0.97 oz |
| E | Annual median wage of free labourer | 0.75 oz |
| F | Cost ratio (slave/free labourer = D/E) | 1.30 |

Note: a discount rate for capital of 10 per cent per year is assumed. It is, furthermore, assumed that a slave could be exploited for a period of ten years on average.

Sources: data for purchasing price of slaves (A) from Richardson, D., 'Prices of Slaves in West and West-Central Africa: Towards an Annual Series, 1698–1807', *Bulletin of Economic Research*, 43(1) (1991), pp. 21–56. Annual wages of slave and free canoemen from GCPLD.

the slaves must have worked in order to motivate the capital investment in purchasing a slave. This is shown in Table 5.5.

The wage and price data from the Gold Coast canoemen thus suggests that a slave labourer had to work around 30 per cent longer per day than was customary for free labourers to work, for it to be economically rational for the Company to purchase slaves to do the same work that they otherwise could employ a free labourer to do.

Anecdotal evidence suggests that the slaves indeed were forced to work longer hours. There is unfortunately no information in the accounts on how many hours per day the individual labourers employed by the RAC worked. One indication of how long a time this might have been can, however, be gathered from the correspondence of the English Company. In 1753, Mr Apperley, chief engineer at the English outfort Anomabo on the Gold Coast, wrote in a letter that 'The white bricklayers can work but five hours a day and the blacks seven hours in the day'.[50] A Danish source on the other hand suggests that the Danish slaves on the Gold Coast were expected to work 9 hours per day, in contrast to the free labourers who were expected to work 7 hours per day only. This source might be biased, attempting to portray the Danish company as more humane than it really was.[51] Nonetheless, the ratio between the hours expected from the slaves relative to the free labourers would, according to this source, amount to 1.29, thus very similar to the ratio estimated as necessary for it to be profitable to the Company to exploit slave labour, even if forced to pay a wage to them too.

## Reproduction and health among the staff and slaves

As was noted previously, the accounts do not record any free African women, and there is no information on the family structure of any of the free employees (except for a few European males who were accompanied by a wife and/or children). Little can, therefore, be known about the reproduction and reproductive work of the free labourers. A number of the female slaves were, as mentioned previously, recorded as having dependent children to care for. This is recorded in a column for 'Comments' on the Slave Lists. The labourer Aggubah ('tally number' 10, since there were quite a few female labourers by this name) was for example recorded as having two children. A single woman at most had five children in her care, as for example the labourer and washerwoman Abinnebah. The records do not state exactly who these children were, but presumably they were the offspring of the slaves. It is however uncertain whether these children necessarily were the offspring of the particular women in charge of caring for them.[52]

There are reasons to believe that the Company accountants might not have bothered to record the infants completely systematically or minutely, so that the real number of infants and children might be underreported in the source. There are two main reasons to believe that this might have been the case. First, the records otherwise hint at an implausibly large number of the women giving birth to three or more children at the same time, since many of them go from having none to having so many children to care for just between two consecutive lists of wage payments (i.e. from one month to the next). Second, some of the children seem to disappear from the accounts quite suddenly. In some cases, this might naturally reflect infant or child mortality. One example of this is the labouress Abbah ('tally number' 13), who on the list of July/September 1760 was recorded as having a child in her care. She is however not recorded as having any child to care for either prior to or after this particular record. Perhaps she gave birth to a child at this time, who did not survive until the next wage payments were due to the slaves. More complex is the case of Aggubah ('tally number' 23), who on one list was recorded as caring for three children. On the list for the following set of months, however, no children were recorded as being in her care, but this was followed by another list, where she yet again was recorded as being in charge of three children.[53]

One possible explanation for these anomalies is thus that the accountants were sloppy when recording the (slave) children, and that they simply missed or neglected to record all children all of the time. There is, however, another possible explanation that could fit with both types of anomalies in the records: that some of the female slaves were assigned as wet-nurses or caretakers of a group of infants and children, who might not always have been their own offspring. This could explain why some women all of a sudden have to care for a large number of – up to three or four – children at the same time. They might thus have been assigned to be the wet-nurses or caretakers not just of their own children, but also of other women's children at the same time, perhaps in order for the Company to maximize the exploitation of the female slave labour force. It could also explain why the number of children in a specific woman's care could change so drastically between the months – it is perhaps not only an issue of child or infant mortality, but also that there were shifts in which women were assigned as caretakers. The unsatisfactory conclusion is unfortunately because the records provide no more detailed information to settle this issue further.

Turning instead to the issue of the health and sickness of the population, both slaves and free employees, the accounts, unfortunately, do not record temporary sicknesses, but only permanent disabilities, among the staff. Assuming that all who were not explicitly recorded as having any particular disability were able-bodied, very few of the labourers were disabled in any way. As has been noted in passing previously, there were a certain number of the people on the Pay Bills and the Slave Lists of the Company that for one reason or another were disabled. The accounts record this factor, since the disabled Africans were paid a lower wage than the able-bodied ones. A blind man for example received only half the wage of what a man who could see received. This was the case for a couple of blind canoemen, for the soldier Frederick Stackmore or the carpenter Cudjoe Dragon. The slave Coffee, simply described as 'a Lunatick', received even lower payment. There are also those who simply are described as 'disabled', without any specification of the disability. One example was Quashee Ansah, described as a 'disabled freeman'. Ansah turns up on the Pay Bill for the first time in 1752. Prior to this time, the Slave Lists were not detailing the names of the slaves, so it is impossible to check if, and for how long, Ansah had been a castle slave of the Company. Neither is it possible to determine whether he became disabled while working for the Company, or was disabled even prior to that. It does not seem unreasonable to assume that Ansah was manumitted by the Company in order for them to reduce any costs of providing for a disabled slave.[54]

The Company could however keep disabled labourers on the payroll for many years. The disabled Quashee Ansah continued to work for the Company for many years – he can be found in the accounts for at least eight years after first being included on the Pay Bills, all the way to 1760, at least. Another example is the soldier Peter Cloice, who started working for the Company in 1727. In 1729, after less than two years of service, he had become blind. The accounts do not tell what happened – whether it was by an accident, an injury of war, or from some disease – but simply recorded the disability. His wages were also reduced by half as a consequence. Cloice continued to serve for the Company for more than thirty years after being disabled – throughout the period at a wage half of that of the able-bodied soldiers.[55]

The accounts do not reveal any information on why the Company chose to keep these people on the payroll, even though they were disabled. Given that the Company was involved in what might have been the most dehumanizing trade possible, it does not seem plausible that the governors of the Company allowed it as an act of charity or kindness. It seems more reasonable to assume that they simply could find some use even for these disabled slaves or free labourers, so that the Company could profit from employing them – at least at the reduced wage rate – just as they could from employing all the other staff and castle slaves.

## Conclusion

This chapter has shown how the English Royal African Company, and its successors, employed labourers on the Gold Coast. Much of the previous literature on pre-colonial Africa has emphasized the importance of domestic slavery, and other forms of unfree labour such as pawnship. Many scholars have questioned whether free labour existed at all in this part of the world prior to the slow death of slavery during the nineteenth and the twentieth centuries. This chapter has shown that there indeed was free labour on the Gold Coast already in the eighteenth century. From the sources available, it is unfortunately impossible to tell how common free labourers really were. There is at least no indication in the consulted primary sources that the Company had any major problems employing free labourers at virtually any time that they wanted to. On the contrary, what evidence there is, rather suggests that free labourers most often could be employed quite easily if or when the Company so desired, in virtually any part of the Gold Coast for which there is evidence in the primary sources. The question for the Company was instead whether it was economically profitable for them to hire labourers, or to purchase slaves instead.

The free African labourers held a number of different occupations, ranging from unskilled manual labour to potentially quite highly skilled positions as writers. The wages were for employees of many occupations (particularly occupations requiring some specific skills) the outcome of a bargaining process. Some of the labourers were then in a position to demand comparatively high wages relative to others. Given that the Royal African Company required labourers of many different skills, and that the mortality among the staff of European descent was very high, the Company might many times have been forced to accept what demands these labourers required. The wages were however clearly discriminatory: African labourers were consistently paid much lower wages than European ones holding the same type of occupation, and the Company often tried to cheat the African staff out of part of their wages. What purchasing power these wages entailed will be discussed further in Chapter 8.

One alternative to employing free African labourers was to utilize castle slaves to undertake what labour was necessary at the forts. Another alternative was to exploit the labour power of human pawns. While a couple of human pawns do occur in the accounts of the Royal African Company, castle slaves seem to have made up the core group of labourers at the forts in terms of numbers. In many respects, castle slavery on the Gold Coast is similar to slavery elsewhere in the world, including viewing the slaves as property, as well as the brutal exploitation of the slaves. Strikingly, however, the system of castle slaves was in one aspect quite unusual in a global comparison: the castle slaves were namely paid regular monthly wages. The wages were many times higher than the cost of subsistence of the individual slave, so it does not seem reasonable to argue that the wages were just subsistence payments, as some previous scholars have done. Instead, it was argued in this chapter that the wages were used as an incentive system. On the Cape Coast, the Company had developed a system of regular, generally quite high, but differentiated wages. The differentiation of the wages along a number of dimensions served as a means of introducing positive incentives in the form of the possibility of 'advancement' or 'promotion' for the slaves – but advancement *within* a system of slavery. This should in no way be interpreted as a claim that the slavery regime at the Cape Coast Castle was more humane or less exploitative than slavery elsewhere in the world. It merely shows the existence of an additional form of punishment, complementary to sheer coercion: to punish shirking or disobedient slaves by reducing them on the socio-economic ladder introduced through the differentiated wages.

## Notes

1 Curtin, P., *Disease and Empire: The Health of European Troops in the Conquest of Africa* (Cambridge: Cambridge University Press, 1998).
2 McNeill, J.R., *Mosquito Empires: Ecology and War in the Greater Caribbean, 1620–1914* (Cambridge: Cambridge University Press, 2010).
3 Justesen, *Danish Sources*, pp. 188, 734–5.
4 Quoted in Gutkind, 'Trade and Labor', p. 33.
5 Law, *Correspondence of the*, p. 18.
6 National Archives, Kew, Surrey, Royal African Company, T70 (NA T70).
7 Reese, 'Wives, Brokers, and Laborers', pp. 298–9.
8 Gold Coast Pre-Colonial Labour Database (henceforth GCPLD), based on NA T70.
9 GCPLD.
10 GCPLD.
11 GCPLD.
12 GCPLD.
13 Gold Coast Pre-Colonial Price Database (henceforth GCPPD), based on NA T70.
14 NA T70.
15 Justesen, *Danish Sources*, p. 496.
16 GCPLD.
17 GCPLD.
18 Law, *The English in West Africa 3*, Letter 1069.
19 Meredith, *An Account of*, p. 59.
20 GCPLD.
21 Reese, 'Wives, Brokers, and Laborers', pp. 298–9.
22 NA T70.
23 See for example Clark, G., 'Farm Wages and Living Standards in the Industrial Revolution: England, 1670–1869', *Economic History Review*, 54 (2001), pp. 477–505.
24 Davies, *The Royal African Company*, p. 252.
25 Reese, 'Facilitating the Slave Trade', p. 372.
26 NA T70.
27 Shumway, 'Castle Slaves'.
28 Quoted in Kea, *A Cultural and Social History*, p. 140.
29 Justesen, *Danish Sources*, p. 130.
30 Justesen, *Danish Sources*, pp. 436–7.
31 Justesen, *Danish Sources*, pp. 886–7.
32 Justesen, *Danish Sources*, pp. 545–8, 770–3.
33 Justesen, *Danish Sources*, pp. 770–3.
34 GCPLD.
35 GCPLD.
36 Law, *Correspondence of the*, p. 12.
37 NA T70.
38 GCPLD.
39 GCPLD.
40 Reese, 'Wives, Brokers, and Laborers', p. 309.
41 GCPLD.
42 Leeuwen, M., Maas, I. and Miles, A., *HISCO – Historical International Standard Classifications of Occupations* (Leuven: Leuven University Press, 2002); Leeuwen,

M. and Maas, I., *HISCLASS – A Historical International Social Class Scheme* (Leuven: Leuven University Press, 2011).
43 Law, *The English in West Africa 3*, Letter 89.
44 Meillassoux, C., 'Female Slavery' in C. Robertson and M. Klein (eds), *Women and Slavery in Africa* (Madison: University of Wisconsin Press, 1983), pp. 49–66.
45 Justesen, *Danish Sources*, pp. 935–6.
46 Quoted in Reese, 'The Drudgery', p. 283.
47 Quoted in Reese, 'Facilitating the Slave Trade', p. 368.
48 Law, *The English in West Africa 2*, Letter 50.
49 Perbi, *A History of Indigenous.*
50 Quoted in Reese, 'The Drudgery', p. 283.
51 Hernæs, 'Fort Slavery', p. 209.
52 GCPLD.
53 GCPLD.
54 GCPLD.
55 GCPLD.

# 6 Domestic markets for goods

## Introduction

As was noted in the chapter on previous research, very much attention has been given to the African export trade during the period studied. Considerably less attention has been given to the domestic trade and domestic markets. This chapter will discuss how the local markets for basic foodstuffs operated on the Gold Coast: What goods were bought and sold? How did the markets function? What factors influenced the pricing of goods on the local markets? The questions will be analysed both qualitatively and quantitatively. The chapter will also deal with the question of whether the demand for provisions to the slave ships played any role for the development of commercial agriculture in Western Africa. In this chapter, an attempt will therefore be made to analyse quantitatively the suggestion that the demand had a substantial impact upon this development.

## Local markets in European travel accounts

Many European observers writing about pre-colonial West Africa described the markets they encountered. One of the most detailed descriptions of these markets can be found in the accounts of Pieter de Marees. In this account, he provides a detailed description, along with an illustration (see Figure 6.1), of the market at Cabo Corso – 'just over a mile to the east of the Castle de Mina'. According to de Marees, this was 'a good trading-place, having the finest Market of all the Towns'.[1] The accounts of the Dutch merchant Pieter van den Broecke who visited the Gold Coast briefly just a few years later also reported that Cabo Corso 'is now one of the principal trading places on the entire coast'.[2]

According to de Marees, the markets in the towns on the Gold Coast provided all 'such necessaries as people in the Coastal towns need to buy'.[3] The markets were also frequented by the Dutch to provide for their castles and forts. De Marees was unclear as to how regular the markets were. He only stated that 'If one Town has its great Market-day on one day, another Town has its market on another day: thus they keep their Market-days on separate days'.[4] The demand for products sold on the markets would thus not seem to have been big enough at this time to support a daily market at any specific place.

The markets shifted character in the course of a market-day. In the early morning, de Marees described, peasants brought sugar-cane for sale. Given that sugar-cane deteriorates rapidly once harvested, it made sense to try to sell it early in the morning. This was followed by the peasant women bringing corn, fruits, chicken and other staple goods. During the midday, finally, peasants selling palm wine arrived.[5] The market was quite strictly organized geographically, according to de Marees' description:

> all these Market-vendors know their place where they must stand with their goods or Wares: those who come to Market with Fruits have their place on one side; others, who bring Sugar-cane, on another side; others, who come with wood, water and bread, have their place to sit or stand on another side; then those bringing Palm Wine from Inland have their Market on another side. Thus each has his own place and they do not stand higgledy-piggledy.[6]

The illustration in de Marees' book (see Figure 6.1), and the caption to it, also show how the market was organized geographically into different sections, each specializing in different goods – according to the illustration, the market was divided into ten different sections: corn and rice, fruits, meat, palm wine, chicken, fish, wood, fresh water, sugar-cane and European textiles, each had their own separate section.[7]

Nicolas Villault, Wilhelm Johann Müller and Jean Barbot all described the market at Cabo Corso, in their accounts of West Africa from the second half of the

*Figure 6.1* Markets on the Gold Coast.

Source: Illustration from Pieter de Marees's *Description and Historical Account of the Gold Kingdom of Guinea* (1602). Reproduction: Ann-Sofie Persson, Kungliga Biblioteket, Stockholm, Sweden.

seventeenth century. Barbot then noted that the Cape Coast market was not the only market on the Gold Coast by then. According to Barbot, 'each village has its own, but at these only the necessities of life and the products of the land are sold'.[8] Müller agreed, further explaining that there were what he called 'general markets' daily in Fetu, Cabo Corso and Friederichsburg.[9] The market at Cabo Corso was however the largest market on the whole of the Gold Coast and, according to Barbot, even in the whole of West Africa: 'It is held daily, in a large open space at the end of the town, where the traders of the place and the neighbourhood gather together from daybreak, with those goods produced locally and those obtained from the Europeans'.[10] Nicolas Villault agreed, and added that there also were yearly fairs held throughout the country.[11] The fact that a market might have been held daily at Cabo Corso by the end of the seventeenth century could then be an indication of a market growth, enabling vendors to find an outlet for their products every day of the week, compared to when Pieter de Marees wrote about the same market a century earlier. As Anthony Hopkins has argued, the periodicity of markets was primarily a function of the volume and spatial distribution of purchasing power.[12] A shift from a periodic to a continuous market might thus indicate a quite important improvement in the purchasing power in the region.

Barbot also noted that the market was highly organized geographically, just as de Marees had described it.[13] Market trading was, according to these authors, primarily done by women: 'Apart from the peasants who bring palm wine and sugar-cane to market every day, there are no men who stand in public markets to trade but only women'.[14] Barbot also described the rather great variety in goods sold on the market:

> The goods always sold there are the following: sugarcane, plantains (*bananes*), bananas (*baccovens*), [sweet] potatoes, yams, lemons, oranges, rice, millet, maize, maniguette [pepper], bread, cakes, fish (raw, boiled or fried), palm-oil, eggs, pumpkins, purslane, the beer called *pitou*, fire-wood, roofing material, and country tobacco in untreated leaves. The other traders of the coasts also bring there many kinds of European goods, which they buy from the whites. In the afternoon the peasants arrive with their palm wine and the fishermen with their fresh fish.[15]

The travel accounts thus shed light on many facets of the market economy on the Gold Coast. For one thing, markets were (or possibly became, in the course of the seventeenth century) ubiquitous throughout the Gold Coast. Certainly, markets in many of the small villages only traded in 'the necessities of life and the products of the land', as Barbot put it. This is, however, perhaps just what ought to be expected from a village market, and most certainly also the number of village markets in Europe at the same time that could have been described. If there was little else than the 'products of the land' to buy on these local markets, the producers might have been paid in the universal means of exchange on the coast, that is, in gold, which they later could use to purchase goods either from travelling merchants, or if visiting fairs or more specialized markets in larger towns or cities such as the Cape Coast. The market at Cape Coast, in contrast, was considerably more richly stocked than the village markets, just as would be expected from a larger market. In Barbot's description, everything from basic foodstuffs to European luxury goods could be bought here. There was also a great variety in the foodstuffs sold – including a number of different fruits, vegetables and staple crops. There thus existed a plethora of goods to buy for anyone with the purchasing power to enjoy them.

It is also interesting to note what none of these authors mentioned as being traded on the market: neither slaves nor locally produced luxury goods. First, neither of these two authors mentions anything at all about slaves being traded on the marketplace that they described. The transatlantic slave trade had certainly not begun from the Gold Coast when de Marees wrote his account, and had barely more than begun when Barbot's description was first written. Nonetheless, many modern scholars have noted that there was a domestic demand for slaves on the Gold Coast – for the gold mines, as domestic servants, or elsewhere.[16] What the accounts of de Marees and Barbot indicate, then, is that to the extent that these slaves were bought and sold locally, it seems to have been a business quite clearly separated geographically from the marketplace for goods described by the European observers. Second, neither of the authors describe that any locally produced luxury goods were sold on the markets. Much previous literature has noted that there did exist a local production of and trade in various goods that could be considered as luxuries in pre-colonial West Africa: locally produced textiles which in some cases could be quite luxurious, handicraft including jewellery of gold and other precious metals, and foodstuffs such as kola.[17] As was described in Chapter 4, many of the European authors of travel accounts described that there existed some special occupations, such as goldsmiths, devoted to producing such handicraft. It therefore remains curious why the Europeans described no such goods being traded on the Cape Coast market. One possibility is of course that there were no such goods for sale. A more plausible alternative is perhaps instead the possibility that the Europeans simply were quite uninterested in such goods, and that they primarily took note of the trade in goods that they found of interest – such as gold, European trade goods, or foodstuffs that could be bought for provisioning forts and ships.

## Patterns to the barter trade

The peasants and merchants trading on the Cabo Corso market did 'not use any money or coins to pay each other', according to de Marees. Traditionally, he argued, most trade was instead undertaken through barter, but people on the Gold Coast had come to use gold dust as a universal means of exchange, so 'when they buy anything they pay each other with Gold, using weights'. The only exception to using gold dust as a means for exchange were for very small transactions, where a more or less standardized 'small square piece of Gold' (known as *kakra*, 'little', gold), or 'little Pins, about the length of a finger' were used.[18]

In the eighteenth century still, a large share of exchange between the Europeans and local agents was through direct barter trade, where no currency – not even gold – was directly involved in the exchange. Slaves were therefore paid for, not necessarily in gold, but with a number of 'trade ounces' worth of commodities.[19] The 'trade ounce' was simply a combination of European goods presumably once worth the equivalent of 1 oz of gold. The (gold) ounce was therefore a means of accounting and negotiating, even if not always used in the actual exchanges. Exactly what combination of goods were included in this 'trade ounce' was however not predetermined. On the contrary, it differed over time, depending on the geographical location of the barter, and depending on the types of goods exchanged. Whereas European or Asian textiles for example could be very popular at certain times, or among some of the African agents that the Europeans traded with, alcohol or arms could be very popular at other times or among other customers.

There are some persistent aggregate patterns to the barter trade, something which becomes evident when the data for a large number of barters is aggregated. This is shown in Graph 6.1, showing what different types of goods were bartered for. The graph is based on a database of transactions, including all transactions undertaken by the English Royal African Company (RAC) every fifth year from 1725 to 1745. The graph is based on a total of 1,268 barter transactions, involving a total of 8,698 European commodities bartered.

The bar furthest to the right in the graph shows what the Europeans purchased for *all* the goods they sold on the coast during the years in the sample. In total,

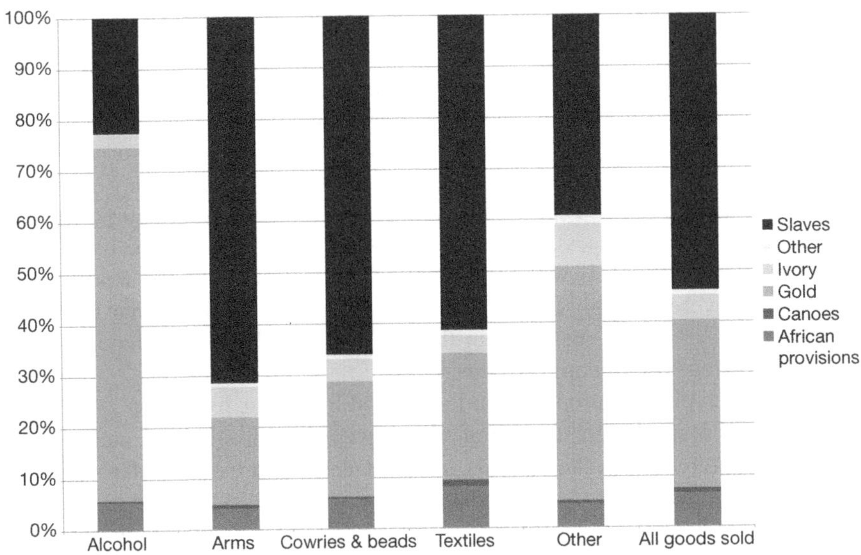


*Graph 6.1* The payment for African goods, by type of European commodity sold, 1725–45

*Source*: database assembled from BNA T/70/389–421.

some 55 per cent of what all of these goods were worth was used to purchase slaves, some 35 per cent was bartered for gold, and the rest was shared between a number of other goods bought from Africans including ivory, canoes and African provisions. If the trade is disaggregated by the type of European goods sold in the barter transactions, however, some interesting features emerge, where specific commodities sold by the Europeans were in particularly high demand among certain African buyers. In total, various sorts of textiles were without a doubt the most important commodity sold on the coast at this time. The patterns for the textile trade were for that reason very similar to the pattern for the overall sales, aggregating the data on all European goods sold on the coast. The patterns of what two other types of commodities – arms and alcohol – were bartered for do however differ quite substantially from the overall pattern.

Starting with the alcohol, many contemporary abolitionists could blame the slave trade on the sale of alcohol. Alcohol, it was argued, was consciously used by Europeans to make African agents (not the least kings and chiefs) dependent alcoholics, so that they easily could be manipulated into selling slaves to the Europeans. Even if this practice indeed was a conscious practice among Europeans, it was of rather limited importance at least on the Gold Coast. As can be seen in Graph 6.1, more than 70 per cent of all alcohol sold on the Gold Coast, even at this time when the slave trade had reached its first peak, was used to purchase gold – not slaves. Just one-fifth of the alcohol sold was exchanged for slaves. The share of alcohol bartered for gold is substantially higher than the aggregate gold purchases, which accounted for only some 35 per cent of all the RAC's purchases at this time. Apparently, alcohol was in particularly high demand among African agents controlling the gold production and/or trade (rather than among the slave traders). The close relationship between gold sales and alcohol purchases thus seems well in line with what previous research on local alcohol consumption has argued: that imported alcohol could be a means for transforming material wealth into social status.

In contrast, arms were clearly used in order to purchase slaves in particular: more than 70 per cent of the value of all arms sales were used to buy slaves (in contrast to aggregate purchases, where slaves only made up some 50 per cent of the value of the purchases). The demand for guns from agents selling slaves therefore seems to fit nicely with the hypothesis of a special 'guns-for-slaves' trade, where arms were in high demand specifically among those agents in Africa directly involved in the enslavement themselves, or at least were having direct business dealings with people who were.

One of the types of European goods included in the bar for 'other' goods was various forms of metalware, including everyday items such as knives, cutlery, pots and basins. Interestingly, these goods were to a very large extent bartered for one of the minor trade goods: ivory. Perhaps, this is a reflection of the demand from the hunters who gathered the ivory – and were not able to or interested in purchasing status items such as foreign alcohol to the same extent as the more wealthy local elite – and settled for purchasing these everyday respectability items.

What the data shows in aggregate, therefore, is that there existed what might be called different 'cycles' or 'spheres' of trade, as has been suggested in some previous research. The patterns reflect a functional aspect of the barter economy, where the non-monetized exchange was influenced by the use value of the products bartered, rather than just the exchange values of the commodities dominating the terms of exchange in a fully monetized economy. Arms were for example to a large extent bartered for slaves since the African agents selling slaves found a high use value in the arms, as a means for further enslavement.

## Prices for local goods

While much of the trade was barter trade, gold was indeed used as a currency throughout most of the Gold Coast. It is also in this currency that the Europeans keep account of their trade, for a very long time, even if no gold was directly involved in every single transaction. In the travel accounts from some European observers, one may occasionally find observations of market prices of local goods. This information is very scattered, and many observers noted the prices primarily or only when they for some reason deviate from what was perceived to be a normal price. By the late seventeenth century, Jean Barbot for example noted that 'The locusts have raised the price of Indian corn to ten pieces-of-eight for a bin of two bushels', without clarifying what the normal price would have been in years without locusts.[20] In the correspondence of the European companies, it is not rare to find examples where the governors complain of the high prices, for one reason or another.[21] Ludewig Ferdinand Rømer was slightly more informative when writing, in the late eighteenth century, that

> The price of *millie* [corn] can rise and fall swiftly, according to conditions inland. You may at one time be unable to finish eating bread purchased for 10 bos, and perhaps a month later a bread or *boller* [buns], costing 20 bos might be as small as a dove's egg, or even smaller.[22]

From such anecdotal information, dating from specific points in time, it is very hard to get a clear idea of what the price of various commodities really was in general, and – not the least important – how it might have changed over time.

The archives of the European companies trading in West Africa do, however, provide a rich source of information on the prices of various goods. These companies purchased considerable quantities of staple goods every year from local producers in Africa, in order to provision staff employed at the forts and castles, as well as to provision the slave ships leaving the coast. In October of 1699, the RAC for example bartered a number of European trade goods for African corn. The Company then purchased sixty-three chests of corn from local suppliers, paying them in kind with goods considered to be worth 5 oz, 14 ackeys and 6 tacus of gold – amounting to 1.5 ackeys per chest of corn. One month later, the Company made another barter involving corn, now purchasing twenty-four chests with goods worth 2 oz and 4 ackeys of gold (again 1.5 ackeys per chest of corn). From these accounts, it is thus possible to assemble prices for some of the most important basic foodstuffs on the coast. Some core foodstuffs – such as fish, plantain or rice

– can be found in the accounts, but only at irregular intervals. It was for example only possible to find purchases of fish ('framfrah fishees') at twelve occasions throughout the period 1699–1760. The prices fluctuated around 0.2–0.3 ackeys per 100 fishes. Plantains were purchased seven times only, at a price of 0.6 ackeys per 100 plantains. Rice was purchased thirteen times during the period, at a price around 2 to 4 ackeys per hundredweight. Salt was purchased more often, at a price of 1.5–2 ackeys per chest of salt. Because of the low number of observations for each of these basic commodities, however, it becomes impossible to try to construct any meaningful long-term price series for many of these locally produced goods.[23]

Three African foodstuffs – corn, palm oil and yams – were however very regularly purchased by the Company over a long period of time (all three can be found in the accounts virtually every year for which the account books have been preserved, and in most years they are purchased several times per year). The prices for these three goods are reported in Graphs 6.2a–c, showing the annual weighted average price of each respective commodity that the Company had to pay when purchasing these goods in the local markets (either through barter or using gold dust). The average price is weighted by the volume of each transaction, so that it is not unduly influenced by small but comparatively expensive or cheap transactions. The error bars in the graphs show the minimum and maximum price paid by the Company each single year for each respective foodstuff. Error bars are missing for some years of the period studied: in the early period, this is due to a small number of observations, so that either there is only one single observation per year, or the few observations that are there all report the same price. At the end of the period studied, however, there are, on the other hand, quite a large number of observations per year, but for some of the commodities they all reported the same price. The reason for this, it seems, is that the Company by then had started to purchase their provisions from one single supplier (possibly starting in different years for different foodstuffs: the source reports identical prices for all purchases throughout a year from 1752 for palm oil, 1758 for yams, and 1760 for corn) – and a supplier who, furthermore, seemingly was one of the employed factors of the Company – so the prices reported in the source probably reflected local market prices poorly, at best, from this period onwards.

As can be seen in the graphs, the prices for the three staple crops varied considerably over time – both within a single year, and over a number of years. Within a single year, the prices normally varied around ±15 per cent for yams, ±20–30 per cent for corn, and ±25–45 per cent for palm oil, relative to the annual weighted average price for that crop. In some rare instances, the Company was lucky to purchase these foodstuffs at much lower prices – in some transactions at less than a fifth of the annual weighted average price. The Company was also on some occasions prepared to pay considerably higher prices than the annual weighted average prices; in some transactions, the price that the Company paid for one of these foodstuffs was more than three times that of the annual weighted average price. To a large extent, the latter phenomenon might reflect that the Company experienced shortages shortly before the harvest season, indicating that they might have had problems planning for what large stores they needed until the

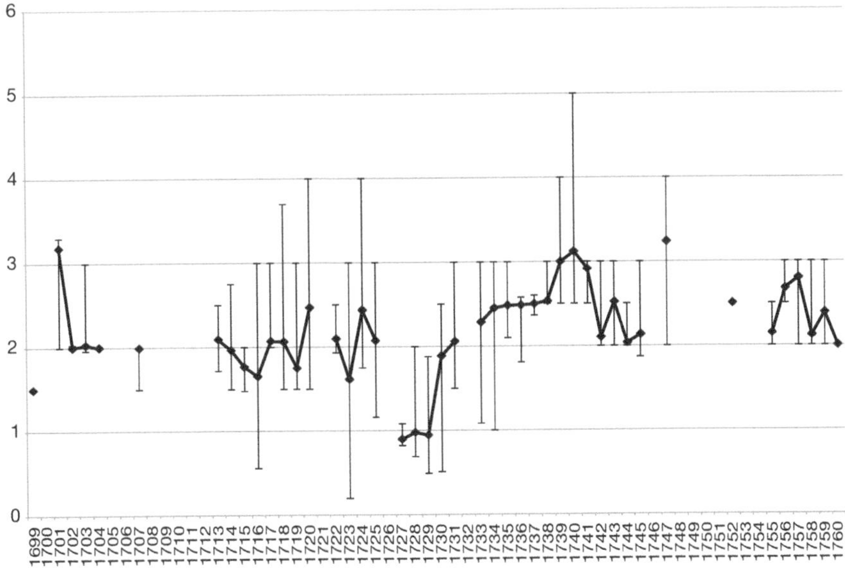


*Graph 6.2a* The price of corn on the Gold Coast, 1699–1760 (ackeys gold/chest, weighted average price with minimum and maximum prices)

Note: n = 302.

Source: GCPPD.

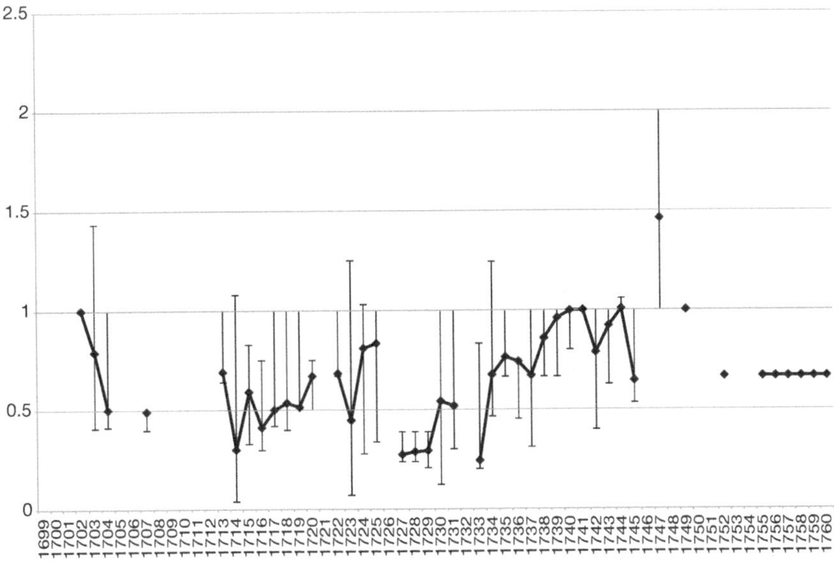


*Graph 6.2b* The price of palm oil on the Gold Coast, 1699–1760 (ackeys gold/gallon, weighted average price with minimum and maximum prices)

Note: n = 443.

Source: GCPPD.

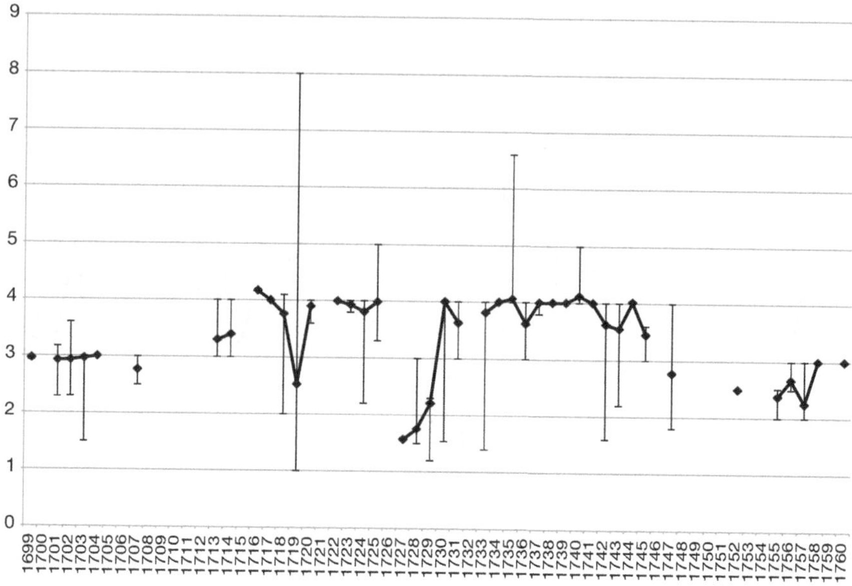


*Graph 6.2c* The price of yams on the Gold Coast, 1699–1760 (ackeys gold/100 yams, weighted average price with minimum and maximum prices)

Note: n = 211.

Source: GCPPD.

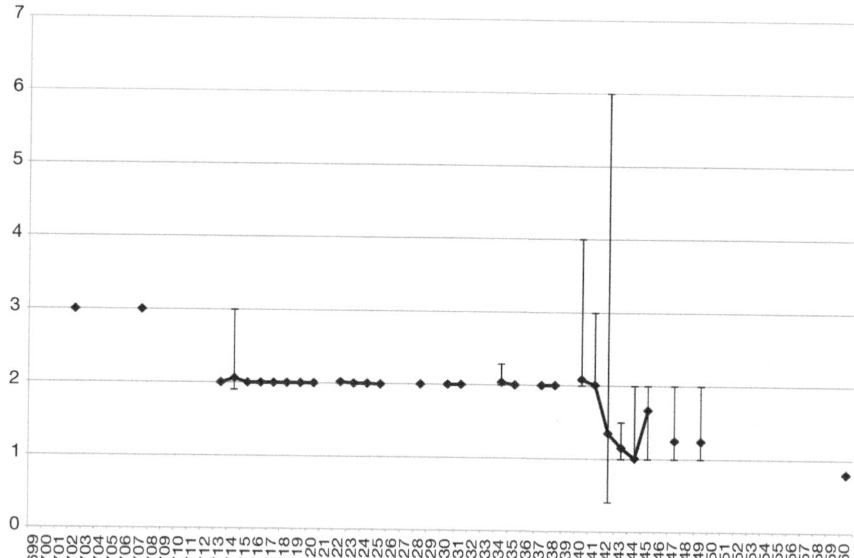


*Graph 6.2d* The price of firewood on the Gold Coast, 1699–1760 (ackeys gold/100 billets, weighted average price with minimum and maximum prices)

Note: n = 165.

Source: GCPPD.

next harvest. Between the years, the annual weighted average price also varied considerably, normally within the range of ±50–60 per cent of what the average price for the whole period amounts to, but on some rare occasions increasing more than 100 per cent relative to the average for the whole period. There is no obvious trend over time, so the prices fluctuated around quite a stationary mean price.

Ray Kea has reported some Gold Coast price data for various goods from the 1650s–70s, unfortunately not specifying either the year or the particular source for each specific price observation. The data he has assembled shows, however, that the price of palm oil (96 damba per anchor, which translates into 1 ackey per gallon) around this time seems to have been on a par with the prices reported in Graph 6.2b. The price he reported for yams, on the other hand (2 dambas each, i.e. 8.3 ackeys per 100 yams), was considerably higher than that reported in the accounts of the Royal African Company reported in Graph 6.2c. The price reported for *millie* is harder to compare with the prices from the Royal African Company's account, since Kea's *millie*-price is accounted for by the stalk (24 dambas per 1,000 stalks), while the Royal African Company accounted for the prices by the chest of corn. Assuming an average weight of 100 grams per stalk, as is suggested in the previous literature, the price would compute to around 2.15 ackeys per chest, that is very similar to the prices from the Royal African Company reported in Graph 6.2a.[24]

Apart from foodstuffs, another key provision both for the forts and castles, as well as for the slave ships, was firewood. Much of the firewood used or sold by the Company was acquired directly from nearby forests by the castle slaves – the accounts occasionally record such expeditions, and how the slaves then supplied large amounts of firewood to the castle. In such cases, the accounts do not record any price or value of the wood acquired. On other occasions, however, the Company purchased firewood from local suppliers, and the accounts do in these cases report the price of the firewood purchased in a similar manner as they did for all other goods purchased. The price is then reported per 100 'billets' of firewood, but how large such a billet was is not made clear in the accounts. This price is reported in Graph 6.2d.

In contrast to the prices of foodstuffs, the price of firewood might at first glance seem to be dropping during the period, from a high of around 3 ackeys per 100 billets of wood in the early years of the period, to a low of less than 1 ackey per 100 billets at the very end of the period. Most of the time, however, the price is quite stationary at 2 ackeys per 100 billets, with no, or extremely little, variation in the price within a single year. Since there are a lot of years of missing data, and the downward trend mainly depends on three specific datapoints, one should probably be cautious before drawing any conclusions about any long-term trends in this case.

## Negotiating the market prices

It is certainly no surprise that the prices that the English Royal African Company and its successors had to pay did fluctuate over time. Evidence from the qualitative sources confirm that the prices on the Gold Coast could be the object of negotiations between the sellers and the buyers, where both parties had to agree on a price. This is shown by the correspondence of the RAC. While much of this correspondence only survives in summary form, detailed correspondence between the company's agents along the Gold Coast on the everyday running of the company's affairs have been preserved from a number of years during the late seventeenth century. Here, the local factors of the minor English forts on the Gold Coast were writing to the chief merchants at the main castle, Cape Coast Castle, about events in the outforts. On a few occasions in this correspondence, the factors ask to get orders, permission or advice about what goods to buy and sell, and at what prices. In 1682, Richard Thelwall wrote from Anomabo, in response to a previous request from the chief merchants at Cape Coast Castle to buy corn to be shipped to the Cape Coast. The corn, Thelwall wrote,

> may be got in a shorte time, but the people here wont take under 1 angle and a halfe. I told them your honour paid but 1 angle, but they told mee that all Fetue had not corne enough for 2 shipps and then must be forced for to give a larger prices, these people are cunning rogues; soe if please to in order to gett itt at 1 angle and halfe itt may be done.[25]

It thus seems as if Thelwall had tried to follow orders to purchase corn for one angle per chest, but had failed at doing so since the current market price was considerably higher. The same complaint came from James Nightingale, who wrote from Komenda in the same year.[26]

It is also evident from the correspondence that the local African agents were well accustomed to exploit competition among buyers in order to make a profit. Important competition came not least from the local inhabitants living in the towns along the coast. This was exactly what John Rootsey experienced when trying to acquire provisions, as is evident in his letter from Anomabo, in April of 1695. The local traders, he argued, refused to sell any corn below 3 ackeys per chest, since they otherwise could sell it 'per the taccoe' (i.e. for small amounts, and thus in small volumes) to the local population in Cape Coast: 'I have had a long palaver with them about their asking so extravagant a rate but it signifies little, they knowing your necessity and they will have their own price and that goods they please'.[27] A few months later, Rootsey again wrote to the Cape Coast asking whether he should purchase corn since, by this time, the traders only demanded 1.5 ackeys per chest.[28]

The competition could also come from elsewhere, aside from the local townspeople. In February 1687, William Cross reported about a palaver at Komenda with the local *caboceers*, finding they would not accept a price for corn lower than 2 ackeys per chest, since 'hereing corn is scarce elcewhere'.[29] A few weeks later, Cross was apparently under pressure from his superiors at Cape Coast Castle to procure more corn, but replied 'I shall endeavor to purchase what I can and have hopes of a considerable quantity in a short time, but I partly find they keep up their corn in expectation of raising it, hearing it is very scarse to leward'.[30]

That many of the local producers attempted to profit from such scarcities was also the experience of Ralph Hassel, chief at the Anomabo fort. In a letter to the Cape Coast factors, he thus argued that the people of Annishan 'know when it is their harvest time to reap both the benefitt and gather the gleaning'.[31]

Another factor that influenced the supply to the local markets was the occurrence of wars. In the first half of 1687, several of the chiefs of the English outforts reported that local supply of corn at various places of the coast was low, simply because the local traders were refusing to sell anything in the run-up to an expected war, possibly expecting to profit more if they held on to what stocks they had. Ralph Hassel wrote from Anomabo: 'They ask very dear for corn, and say they will not take less than two angles per chest, and say it will grow dearer, they pretend a great scarcety by reason of the warr'.[32]

The prices that Europeans had to pay for goods they purchased thus depended on a complex interplay between supply and demand in each local market. Both sides to the trade certainly had to agree on a price in order for there to be any trade. From what scattered remarks there are in the correspondence, it seems as if the Royal African Company in general was a price-taker on the local markets, and often simply had to accept the prices that the African sellers requested for their goods. Further, what the sellers requested was to a large extent determined by the demand from local inhabitants in the towns and cities on the Gold Coast.

The European factors on the other hand had slightly more room to bargain for the price that they could demand when selling their own trade goods. Some correspondence contained complaints that no goods could be sold, since other European traders were selling their goods at a substantially lower price.[33] Other letters described a process of negotiations over the prices charged. In 1695, John Browne reported about negotiations over the price of bafts at Agga factory, which finally could come to a satisfactory conclusion.[34] In 1696, Thomas Buckeridge wrote from Dixcove to the factors at the Cape Coast that they must 'putt a small price upon the sayes, which otherwise, being no commodity in this country, will lie untill they are worth nothing'.[35] The price that the Company demanded for its own trade goods would seemingly impact, not least, how fast they could be sold. Given that some of the products were perishable in the tropical climate, making a profit could thus be a race against time.

That the pricing of goods was a matter of negotiation is also evident in the mark-up of the trade goods that the Europeans sold on the coast. In the accounts, the Company records the original price that they had to pay for the goods that were sent from England, as well as the 'coast price' of the commodities, that is, the price that they could charge when selling the goods in question. Previous scholars have argued that the Company in general used a rule-of-thumb to double the price of the goods when selling them on the African coast. While they might have attempted to apply such a rule-of-thumb in theory, the practice was more complex. In reality, the mark-up varied considerably between goods and over time. In the case of guinea stuffs, for example, the mark-up ratio varied between 1.1 and 6.6, but was mostly in the range of a mark-up ratio of 2 to 3. The mark-up ratio for tallow sold on the coast, on the other hand, varied between 1 and 3, and the mark-up ratio for meat varied between 1 and 2.5.[36] Contemporary estimations done by representatives of the Danish slave-trading company indicate mark-up ratios of the same order of magnitude.[37]

The complexity of the interplay between supply and demand is also reflected in the variation in prices that the Europeans had to pay for crops in every individual port. That people occasionally could travel long distances in order to purchase staple foodstuffs is shown in the correspondence of the Company. In 1687, Thomas Bucknell wrote from Sekondi that: 'canoes comes from all parts both windward and leeward, from Axim to Annamaboe, hither to buy corn and give any rate for't, here comes at least 20 canoes every day'.[38] The distance between Sekondi and Anomabo is approximately 70 km. Bucknell's letter thus suggests that some people could travel quite a substantial distance just to purchase basic foodstuff.

Would such long-distance trade have enabled an integration of the market prices for foodstuffs on the Gold Coast? The qualitative evidence in the correspondence that has survived is unfortunately too scattered in time to enable a comparison between different geographical locations. We can instead again turn to the economic accounts of the Royal African Company. In this source, it is possible to study prices at each individual port along the coast since they – at least for a part of the period under study in this book – take note of the port at which each individual purchase was done. For some ports, there are only a handful of observations, which makes it very hard to draw any conclusions (since the prices for those individual transactions might have been impacted by several confounding factors). From a couple of ports there are, however, enough observations to enable comparisons. More than half (55%) of all price observations come from the Cape Coast. Six other ports (Accra, Komenda, Dixcove, Sekondi, Tantumkweri and Winneba) each account for some 6 to 8 per cent of the number of observations. While prices to some extent fluctuated in parallel – increasing in certain years and decreasing in others – there are some important differences between the ports. Graph 6.3 therefore illustrates whether there is any relationship between the geographical distance between two ports, and the degree to which the prices between them were correlated over time.

As can be seen in Graph 6.3, there does not exist any clear relationship between distance and price correlation between two ports: the prices on markets very close to each other geographically could be as correlated with each other as ports that were several hundred kilometres apart. It instead seems reasonable to interpret this as showing that virtually all the ports along the coast were impacted by the same, or at least similar, exogenous factors determining the price level in general. We, therefore, need to turn to the question of what these exogenous factors might have been.

## Explaining the price variations

That prices could fluctuate is of course not surprising in itself. More important is instead the question of why prices fluctuated and what determined these

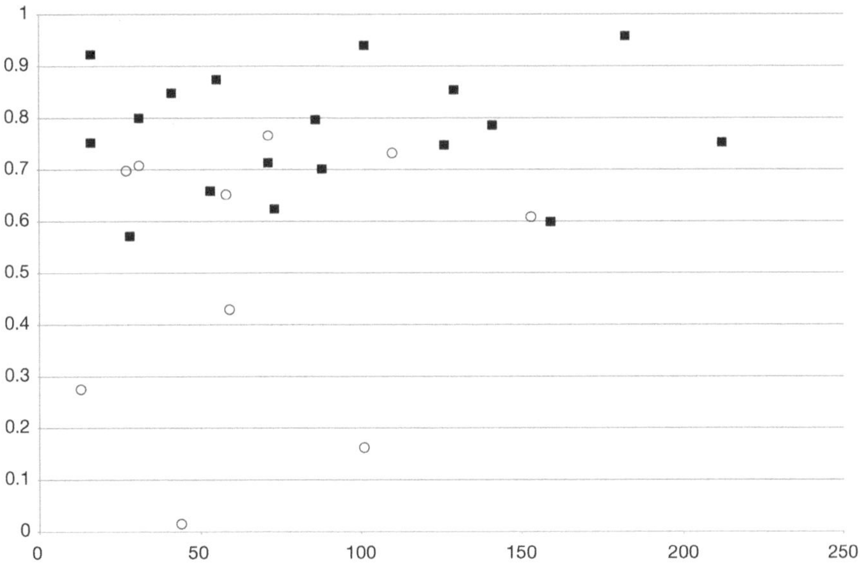


*Graph 6.3* Geographical distance (km) between ports and the correlation of prices of corn, 1713–47

Note: black squares show statistically significant results, circles show statistically non-significant results.

Source: GCPPD. Geographical distance (x-axis) estimated as a straight line between two locations.

fluctuations. Is it possible to make any sense of how the prices for these goods varied over time? An attempt to do so is presented below, based on an econometric OLS regression to determine the impact that several different factors had upon the market prices for the three core foodstuffs. The model estimated included a set of explanatory variables: the impact of climate (temperature) deviations, wars and the volume of the external slave trade in the year that the transaction took place (previous year for climate deviations); seasonal fluctuations; volumes purchased in each specific transaction; and long-term time trends to the price. The results from this exercise are reported in Table 6.1.

The regression equations use information from the 956 transactions where Europeans purchased any of the three goods from African sellers during the period in question, in order to determine each variable's specific impact upon the prices of the staple crops. There were two variables that had a quite consistent impact on all the three crops studied: the climate and the occurrence of war.

One of the most important factors for determining the price on the local markets was thus, quite naturally, the climate: following a good harvest, prices declined substantially, and vice versa. This is of course exactly what would be expected if the markets were able to respond to scarcities, such as a bad harvest, or surpluses such as a good harvest. In the coastal zone of the Gold Coast, precipitation was to a large extent determined by evaporation from the ocean just south of the coast,

*Table 6.1* Factors explaining the price variation in staple crops on the Gold Coast, 1730–60

| | *Corn* | *Palm oil* | *Yams* |
|---|---|---|---|
| Average temperature deviation in the previous (%) year (degrees Celsius deviation from norm) (%) | –32 | **–99** | **–21** |
| War (dummy variable) (%) | **+11** | **+21** | **+10** |
| Slaves exported (per 1,000 slaves) (%) | 0 | +1 | **0** |
| Season: First quarter (%) | –6 | **–7** | **–5** |
| Season: Second quarter (%) | –6 | **–10** | **–2** |
| Season: Third quarter (%) | –2 | –4 | –3 |
| Season: Fourth quarter (%) | [ref.] | [ref.] | [ref.] |
| Time-trend (per annum) (%) | 0 | +2 | –1 |
| N | 302 | 443 | 211 |

Note: statistically significant results (at the 5 per cent confidence level) in bold. For a number of robustness tests, see appendix in Rönnbäck, 'Climate, Conflicts'.

Source: based on Rönnbäck, 'Climate, Conflicts': Table 3.

and would therefore be positively associated with the temperature – in contrast to many other parts of Africa, where a higher temperature might imply drought instead. The impact from droughts varied considerably between the crops – more drought-sensitive crops would fare worse during a drought, which also was reflected in the prices: The price of drought-resistant crops, such as yams or millet, increased some 20 to 30 per cent if annual average temperatures decreased one degree Celsius relative to the norm for the region (and then also decreased regional precipitation), whereas the more drought-sensitive palm oil almost doubled in price from a similar drop in temperature (and precipitation). Whatever historical climate data has been reconstructed so far from West Africa by natural scientists is very crude – only temperature data on an annual basis. The annual average temperature according to these estimates in general did not deviate a whole degree Celsius from the norm (the standard deviation of the estimated temperature variable was only 0.15 degrees Celsius). If it becomes possible to reconstruct more detailed climate data in the future (for example including precipitation estimates, or a more detailed time-series of climate data), it might perhaps be possible to determine with greater certainty the effect of droughts during crucial periods of the growing season.

Another very central factor in the equation determining the prices was the occurrence of war: in years of war in the region, prices increased by some 10 to 20 per cent. Again, the data underlying this estimate is very crude, being simply a dichotomous variable indicating whether or not (European) written sources mention any war in the region during the year in which a particular transaction took place. The sources are all too often very unspecific about these wars: when they started and ended, what belligerents were involved, and how large and intensive the wars really were. These issues are certainly of the utmost importance for a more detailed analysis, since short and small conflicts most certainly had a much smaller effect upon the local market, and market prices, than protracted and intensive bouts of war. If more data becomes available on this topic, it might be possible to study in more depth what the impact was during a war, as opposed to the immediate period before, or after, the war. Still, the results indicate a substantial negative impact from wars, over quite a long period of time.

There were also some seasonal fluctuations in the pricing on the markets, particularly of palm oil which seem to have dropped somewhat in price during the first half of each year, presumably following harvest season. The price of yams experienced a slight drop in post-harvest prices, whereas there was no such clear effect upon the price of corn. The difference in seasonal fluctuations between the three crops might be explained by how easy it was to store and preserve each crop in question: among the crops, corn was possibly the easiest to store between the years, and many polities also made use of national grain storage. There was on the other hand little evidence of any trend in the prices over the period studied: the results were statistically significant only in the case of yams, and even in this case, the impact was small (a negative trend of around 1% per year).

## The demand for provisions to the slave ships

One of the factors that seem to have had *no* impact on the prices of foodstuffs on the local markets was the extent of the slave trade: the prices on the markets in general did not change, no matter how many slaves were exported from the coast (see Table 6.1 above). This might seem surprising to some readers, given that some previous research has claimed that the slave trade supposedly contributed to a positive boost in demand for foodstuffs. If this is true, it seems reasonable to assume that the slave trade ought to have had at least some effects on the prices for the foodstuffs on the local markets.

That many ships purchased provisions from local producers is evident from qualitative sources, such as European travel accounts. This is for example how Willem Bosman described the Fante on the Gold Coast: 'is very rich in Gold, Slaves, and all sorts of Necessaries of Life; but more especially Corn; which they sell in large Quantities to the English Ships'.[39] It could, however, sometimes be problematic to get the local population to actually supply what surplus they had, as the chief of the English fort at Sekondi, Thomas Bucknell, experienced. In early March of 1687, he wrote to the Cape Coast, in response to a request to purchase corn: 'Here is abundance of corn at the crooms, if I can perswade them to bring it down'.[40] The Danish company likewise faced many problems provisioning for their needs. One problem was local shortages in the area near the Danish Christiansborg castle at Accra, forcing the Danish company representatives to purchase foodstuffs in places quite far away.[41] Another problem was also an active trade boycott of the Danish initiated by the local *caboceers* in 1730, prohibiting the sale of any corn to the Danish company.[42]

In general, then, provisioning for the slave trade was a key concern for the European companies. So why did this demand not have any influence on the local price for foodstuffs? One possible explanation to this seeming paradox might be technical issues, such as multicollinearity, in the statistical analysis. If there was a close relationship between wars and the slave trade – as many previous scholars certainly have argued – this could perhaps explain this non-result: when including both variables in the estimated multivariate regression, any impact from the slave trade would perhaps be already captured by the war variable.

Another possible reason why an expanding slave trade had little or no impact upon the prices for foodstuffs is that the demand for provisions was simply of such limited importance to the slave trade on the local markets that the Company essentially was a price-taker on the local markets. As was noted previously in this chapter, the qualitative evidence seems to point in this direction. Using estimates from previous research of the population on the Gold Coast (discussed in Chapter 2), it is also possible to arrive at some very crude quantitative estimates of how important the demand for provisions might have been to the slave trade.

Patrick Manning has estimated that the local population in the Akan-speaking areas of the Gold Coast amounted to almost three million people around the year 1700, and decreasing over the following century.[43] Manning's population figures have however been criticized as being far too high.[44] Of this population, perhaps one-third lived in Asante, which most probably was too far from the coast to supply ships with any substantial amounts of provisions. Many of the people living on the Gold Coast south of Asante might also have lived too far from the coast to really experience any consequences of the coastal demand for foodstuffs: Ray Kea has argued that the area up to around 30–40 miles from the coast was a region of agricultural surplus, but that few producers probably transported their goods more than 5 to 10 miles over land to supply an urban centre.[45] The immediately impacted area might thus have amounted to around one-tenth of the Gold Coast south of Asante. The population densities were on the other hand possibly higher along the coastal area than further inland. Kea has finally also argued that the populations living in towns or villages might have amounted to around 10 to 20 per cent of the total population in the coastal region.[46] Under all these estimates and assumptions, the population in towns and villages in the immediate coastal zone of the Gold Coast might thus have amounted to around 25–30,000 people. This is thus the number of people living in towns and villages on the Gold Coast, and they must have required food throughout the year in order to stay alive. Since most of the rural population was probably self-sufficient in agricultural produce, the commercial demand for foodstuffs arose mainly among these urban populations. We do not know exactly how much food the local population on average consumed. For lack of any better data, it is here assumed that all of the local population consumed a very simple diet, similar to what was provided to the slaves on-board the slave ships. Most probably, a large fraction of the local inhabitants on the Gold Coast had the possibility to consume a richer diet. The assumption made therefore biases the results against the hypothesis proposed. It is, furthermore, noteworthy that the figure for the local population used in the estimates below is considerably lower than the population estimates of both Patrick Manning (for the Gold Coast in total) and Ray Kea (for coastal towns on the Gold Coast, around 60–75,000 people).[47] The lower figure will be used in the estimates below, in order to at least not overestimate the local demand for foodstuffs, thus again biasing the results against the hypothesis.

It is, furthermore, possible to arrive at an estimate of how large the commercial demand for foodstuffs ought to have been from the slave trade. The number of slaves exported can be gathered from the Transatlantic Slave Trade Database.[48] In order to not underestimate the demand from the slave trade, it is assumed that the slave ships on average bought provisions necessary for 200 days of consumption per slave. This is substantially longer than what they probably would have needed (the time of the Middle Passage was around 70 days, and average waiting time off the African coast for the ships was around 100 days, but the slave traders did not have to support a full load of slaves for the whole of this time). It is, furthermore, assumed that the ships demanded some provisions for the crewmen, to supplement the European provisions they brought along, and that the staff employed at the European castles and forts were provided for with locally produced foodstuffs.

Graph 6.4 then shows how large this demand for foodstuffs to supply the slave trade was, relative to a crude estimate of the possible demand from the local population on the Gold Coast. The graph shows the demand from slave traders purchasing slaves and provisions on the Gold Coast, relative both to just the urban population in the coastal region of the Gold Coast, as well as to the total (urban and rural) population in this part of the region. David Eltis has, furthermore, argued that the Gold Coast, in particular, provisioned many ships that traded for slaves elsewhere, including a number of ships which later purchased slaves in the Bight

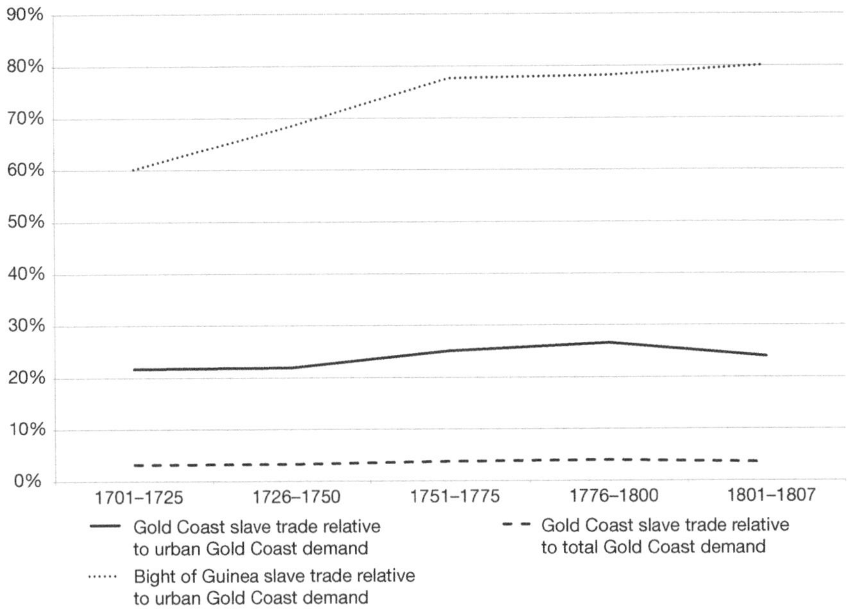


*Graph 6.4* Demand for provisions from slave ships as a share of local demand for foodstuffs on the Gold Coast, 1701–1807

Source: data on slaves traded from TSTD2, local population data based on Manning, 'African Population 1650–1950' and Frankema and Jerven, 'Writing History Backwards'.

Note: see text above for assumptions about daily rations needed annually for both populations.

of Benin or the Bight of Biafra.[49] How many of the ships acted in this way is unknown, but in order to account for this possibility, the graph also shows how large the external demand for foodstuffs might have been, under the assumption that *all* ships trading for slaves in the region from the Gold Coast to the Bight of Biafra purchased *all* their provisions on the Gold Coast. The assumption is most certainly highly unrealistic, but does at least provide an upper-bound estimate for how large the demand at most might have been.

As can be seen in the graph, the demand grew substantially in importance over the period, as the slave trade increased. In quantitative terms, however, the demand was not overwhelming, if considered relative to domestic demand. Relative to the demand from urban markets in the coastal part of the Gold Coast, the demand for provisions from slave traders actually trading slaves in this region contributed to an incremental demand of some 20 to 30 per cent relative to what was already demanded from the urban population. The pre-colonial Gold Coast was to a large extent an agricultural economy, with a large share of the population living in rural areas. Most farmers were without a doubt primarily subsistence farmers, who sold little or almost nothing of their produce on any market. The urban markets were therefore of quite limited size and importance relative to total agricultural output in the region. Graph 6.4 therefore also shows how large the demand from the slave trade might have been if considered relative to how large the domestic production of foodstuffs in the region must have been in order to feed the total population with a basic diet. Relative to this production, the demand from the slave trade must be considered very marginal: it might not have amounted to more than around 3 to 4 per cent of what must have been produced in order to feed the whole of the local population in the region.

These estimates are of course very crude, most importantly because the population estimates from the region are built on very slender evidence, as was discussed in Chapter 2. It is therefore important to keep in mind that the ambition has been to avoid underestimating the impact of the external demand: the figures for the size of the local urban population are therefore for example less than half of those estimated by some previous scholars, while the number of provisions purchased per slave exported could be substantially higher than what many slave traders probably purchased. The assumptions are therefore quite biased against the hypothesis suggested here.

The point of this exercise is of course not to deny that the demand was important for those farmers that in this way could contribute to a growing commercial economy. The figures in Graph 6.4 do however suggest that the farmers of the Gold Coast, on aggregate, probably faced few problems in meeting what incremental demand there was from the slave traders requiring foodstuffs. This incremental demand for foodstuffs might have enticed some individual farmers to increase their production to meet this demand, or enticed some subsistence farmers to switch (at least partly) to commercial production of foodcrops. What impact there was, was surely mostly concentrated in the immediate hinterland of the towns and cities, forts and castles involved in the slave trade. The *direct* impact from the slave trade per se on the development of a commercial agriculture on the Gold Coast – let alone the economies on the whole of the West African coast – must however have been quite limited. The most important growth in demand for commercial production of foodstuffs must instead have come from the population living in the towns and villages on the coast (which in itself possibly could be argued to be related to the slave trade). Given these results, it is not very surprising that the slave trade had no discernible effect on the prices of foodstuffs, even on the urban coastal markets, as was shown in Table 6.1 above.

As was noted previously, Eltis claimed that the demand for foodstuffs might have been reinforced on the Gold Coast in particular by slave traders who purchased provisions on the Gold Coast, but slaves further east along the coast. While this might be true, a very large share of all slave-trading ships must have acted in this way in order for the demand to reach truly decisive levels, as was shown in Graph 6.4. If that was the case, furthermore, it would primarily mean that any positive multiplier effects from provisioning the slave trade would have been concentrated geographically in a small part of the Gold Coast in particular, rather than being spread out along the West African coast.

## Conclusion

This chapter has shown how the testimonies from Europeans writing about markets on the pre-colonial Gold Cost provide evidence of vibrant and well-functioning markets. This was one area where the European travel accounts were comparatively positive: in contrast to many other areas, such as the work ethic of the population (see Chapter 4) or the material standards of the population (see Chapter 7), where negative European racial prejudices permeate much of what is written, many European observers seem to find quite a bit to praise when it comes to how the markets were functioning on the Gold Coast. To the extent that they find anything to criticize, it is primarily that the African agents they trade with were too skilled or too 'cunning' as merchants, thus not being easily fooled or exploited.

Traditionally, much of the trade in these markets had been through barter. This was also how much of the European trade with local agents was conducted in the eighteenth century. The barter trade then to a large extent reflected the use value that the parties to a transaction could find in the bartered goods. Europeans found that the arms primarily were demanded by those selling slaves, providing support for the so-called 'guns-for-slaves' hypothesis of an intimate relationship between the European arms sales and an intensification of the process of enslavement in West Africa. A status item such as foreign alcohol was on the other hand primarily demanded by the wealthy elite trading in gold, possibly as a means to transform material wealth into social status, whereas the African commoners bartered what goods they had for sale for more everyday respectability goods.

One of the most important markets was the one held at Cabo Corso, later to be renamed Cape Coast. This particular market seems to have experienced an important growth, judging from the fact that it developed into a daily held market during the course of the seventeenth century. Even though there existed no coinage on this market, there did exist a universal means of exchange in the form of gold dust. Prices of goods were therefore accounted for by their value in gold. As was shown in the chapter, price series constructed for three of the main staple crops (corn, palm oil and yams), using the accounts of the English Royal African Company, indicate that prices fluctuated quite drastically both within a single year, and between the years. Within a single year, the prices for African staple products could fluctuate up to ±50 per cent, and the variation between the years in average annual prices normally varied within a similar broad band. A multivariate regression trying to explain the price variations indicated that they primarily were attributable to two factors: the climate and wars. First, higher average temperatures and precipitation increased the yields, which drove down the price on the market throughout the next year, until the next harvest. How large the impact was depended on how drought-sensitive each crop was – more sensitive crops experienced more drastic fluctuations in price as an effect of a given deviation in climate. Second, wars created insecurities and chaos – destroying croplands, enslaving agricultural workers and/or forcing them to flee from their agriculture – which negatively impacted the markets for staple crops. In years of war in the region, prices increased substantially.

What does *not* seem to have impacted the prices to any discernible degree, was the demand for provisions from the slave trade. In the multivariate regression, the number of slaves exported had no effect at all upon the prices for the crops sold as provisions to the slave trade. This was most certainly explicable by the size of the demand for provisions to the slave trade, relative to the demand from local inhabitants in towns and cities on the Gold Coast – let alone to the whole population living in the region. It was shown in the chapter that the demand for provisions from the slave trade was simply too small, relative to the demand from local inhabitants living in urban areas on the Gold Coast, to have any major effect upon the local markets, or upon the market prices. The slave traders thus essentially acted as price-takers on the local markets.

## Notes

1 De Marees, *Description and Historical*, p. 62.
2 Van den Broecke, *Pieter van den Broecke's Journal of Voyages to Cape Verde, Guinea and Angola*, p. 50.
3 De Marees, *Description and Historical*, p. 63.
4 De Marees, *Description and Historical*, p. 63.
5 De Marees, *Description and Historical*, pp. 63–4.
6 De Marees, *Description and Historical*, p. 64.
7 De Marees, *Description and Historical*, p. 62.
8 Barbot, *Barbot on Guinea*, p. 547.
9 Jones, *German Sources*, p. 244.
10 Barbot, *Barbot on Guinea*, p. 547.
11 Villault, *A Relation of the Coasts*, p. 165.
12 Hopkins, *An Economic History*, p. 56.
13 Barbot, *Barbot on Guinea*, p. 547.
14 Jones, *German Sources*, p. 244.

15 Barbot, *Barbot on Guinea*, p. 547.
16 See for example Perbi, *A History of Indigenous*.
17 See for example Lovejoy, P., *Caravans of Kola: The Hausa Kola Trade, 1700–1900* (Nigeria: Ahmadu Bello University Press, 1980); Kriger, C., 'Mapping the History of Cotton Textile Production in Precolonial West Africa', *African Economic History*, 33 (2005), pp. 87–116; Garrard, T., *African Gold* (Munich: Prestel, 2011).
18 De Marees, *Description and Historical*, p. 65.
19 Polanyi, K., 'Sortings and "Ounce Trade" in the West African Slave Trade', *Journal of African History*, 5(3) (1964), pp. 381–93; Johnson, M., 'The Ounce in Eighteenth-Century West African Trade', *Journal of African History*, 7(2) (1966), pp. 197–214.
20 Barbot, *Barbot on Guinea*, p. 477.
21 Justesen, *Danish Sources*, pp. 152–3, 759.
22 Rømer, *A Reliable Account*, p. 196.
23 GCPPD.
24 Kea, *Settlements, Trade, and Polities*, table 8.2. For data on the weight of sorghum stalks, see Ruskin, *Lost Crops of Africa*, p. 134.
25 Law, *The English in West Africa 1*, Letter 287.
26 Law, *The English in West Africa 1*, Letters 65 and 68.
27 Law, *The English in West Africa 3*, Letter 797.
28 Law, *The English in West Africa 3*, Letter 842.
29 Law, *The English in West Africa 2*, Letter 229.
30 Law, *The English in West Africa 2*, Letter 233.
31 Law, *The English in West Africa 2*, Letter 494.
32 Law, *The English in West Africa 2*, Letter 508; see also Letters 505 and 676.
33 See for example Law, *The English in West Africa 1*, Letter 7; Justesen, *Danish Sources*, p. 272.
34 Law, *The English in West Africa 3*, Letters 997–8.
35 Law, *The English in West Africa 3*, Letter 67.
36 GCPPD.
37 Justesen, *Danish Sources*, pp. 343–4.
38 Law, *The English in West Africa 2*, Letter 87.
39 Bosman, *A New and Accurate*, pp. 49–50.
40 Law, *The English in West Africa 2*, Letter 72.
41 Justesen, *Danish Sources*, pp. 116, 152–3, 759.
42 Justesen, *Danish Sources*, p. 436.
43 Manning, 'African Population, 1650–1950'.
44 Frankema and Jerven, 'Writing History Backwards'. It is here assumed that Frankema and Jerven's assumptions are realistic, and that the higher population growth rates they assume could counteract any population drain by the slave trade, so that there was no population decrease prior to the 1850s, as Manning's assumptions imply.
45 Kea, *Settlements, Trade, and Polities*, p. 16 and map 1.2.
46 Kea, *Settlements, Trade, and Polities*, pp. 34–5.
47 Manning, 'African Population, 1650–1950'; Kea, *Settlements, Trade, and Polities*, p. 35.
48 TSTD2.
49 Eltis, 'The Slave Trade', p. 44.

# 7 Housing and material wealth

## Introduction

As was discussed earlier (Chapter 4), work can be assumed to be a means to an end – to enable consumption of goods and services, including the consumption of more durable goods of various sorts. One potential aspect of how to study the living standards on the Gold Coast is therefore to study patterns of consumption of goods and of material wealth in the region. While archaeological research has contributed with much important knowledge on the more durable aspects (objects and structures) of the material culture, written sources have previously not been used much for a study of this topic. This is going to be the focus of the present chapter, focusing upon how the material wealth of the people on the Gold Coast is described in these sources. The chapter will also discuss the material culture of some other societies along the West African coast described by the European observers, in order to put the evidence from the Gold Coast into regional perspective.

## Huts and houses

Previous scholars have to some extent emphasized how unique the Gold Coast seems to have been in that the houses in a couple of the coastal towns were made of stone. It is certainly true that stone houses can be found in the descriptions of some of the coastal cities and towns on the Gold Coast, most importantly in Elmina, at least from the late seventeenth century onwards. In Barbot's description from the late seventeenth century, 'most of the houses are of masonry', whereas some other descriptions from the early nineteenth century claimed that all houses in Elmina by this time were built of stone.[1] However, the most common description of the housing used by the common population on the Gold Coast, according to the European observers, was by the term 'hut'. Most of these houses, or 'huts', were described as being pretty small, one storey high only.[2] A number of these houses together made up a compound, shared by a family, so that the individual members of the family could live in separate houses, all according to their status in the family. A compound could also have one or more such houses for other purposes such as for storage. Wilhelm Müller thus concluded that the compounds on the Gold Coast normally were made up of six to seven houses in total.[3] In the compound, one could also, in many cases, find a garden or space for grazing animals.[4] The 'huts' were primarily made of mud or clay.[5] Pieter de Marees described in detail one specific technique – the wattle-and-daub – used for building such houses:

> First, they take four forked Posts or Trees, which they erect on the ground so as to make a square. Then they lay other Trees on top of the Posts and fasten them well. Between the posts they place many thin sticks, thus forming the house; and they bind them together with Laths so tightly that one can hardly squeeze one's hand in between. Then they take Mud out of yellow earth, which they take from the open country, and pound it till it is fine and thin like Potter's earth. They slap handfuls of this mud against the framework of the house, all around, from top to bottom, front and back, wherever they want it to be filled. They press the mud in between this wattle with their hands, so that it will stick to the supports. Once they have filled the walls of their House with this mud, nearly half a foot thick, they let it dry and become as hard as brick.[6]

Another detailed description of the wattle-and-daub-technique can be found in Edward Bowdich's account of his mission to Asante in the early nineteenth century. In his description, two rows of stakes and wattle-work were built at a short distance from each other, and the space between filled with 'a gravelly clay'.[7] In essence, these houses thus used clay as the main construction material, constructed around a frame of wooden poles and latticework.

In general, the European observers dismissed the general housing standards on the Gold Coast as very low, throughout the period studied in this book. One common strategy used by many European authors to illustrate just how simple they thought the local houses were, was then to compare the housing in the region to the shelters of domesticated animals in Europe. Pieter de Marees thus described the houses he encountered on the Gold Coast in the following terms: 'In general their dwellings or houses are nothing special, being of very poor quality and rather like Pig-Sties: indeed, I think that in many Countries even Pig-Sties are better than the houses and dwellings which some people have here'.[8] This particular comparison was echoed in later published secondary accounts. One example is to be found in the geographer John Ogilby's account of Africa, published in 1670, where he compared the houses to 'Hog-Styes'.[9] That Ogilby's account echoed de Marees' is no surprise, since Ogilby's account largely was a translation of Olfert Dapper's geographical overview of Africa, which in turn had been heavily influenced by de Marees' account (see Chapter 3). Another method to illustrate how low the Europeans thought the standards of West African housing were, was to compare it to the housing standards of some (presumably poor) group back home in Europe, which the reader was assumed to have at least some idea of. Wilhelm Johann Müller conveyed his thoughts about housing standards in Fetu on the Gold Coast in the following terms: 'All the houses or homes one finds in the Fetu country are of very poor quality. Many people might say that the peasant houses in Europe are far better built'.[10] Yet another strategy, exhibited for example by Jean Barbot, was to simply pour invectives into the description: 'Generally the houses are dirty, uncomfortable and for the most part stinking, particularly those which have privy-huts'.[11]

The pejorative judgements about the local housing standards were on the other hand not uncontested. Quite a few of the European observers had quite high thoughts about the housing standards of the population on the Gold Coast. Most contested was without a doubt the claim that the houses generally were dirty. A number of authors directly denied any such claims, and argued that the houses in general were kept neat and clean by the women in charge of the domestic work.[12] Many also argued that while the houses might be simple, they were not of low quality. By the early seventeenth century, the German explorer Samuel Brun wrote that houses on the Gold Coast 'are made very strangely and cleverly'.[13] Some of the authors particularly suggested a number of positive characteristics of the type of housing. The houses were essentially argued to be quick, easy and cheap to build, but could nonetheless withstand the elements to an extent that surprised many of the European observers. Wilhelm Johann Müller for example claimed that 'each native [on the Gold Coast] understands how to build his own house and does not need to call on specialist carpenters'.[14] Since construction material was sourced locally, and construction was easy and fast, the costs of the houses were also very low. Jean Barbot for example wrote that the cost of building a house was cheap, since the construction material could be gathered for free (exclusive of the cost of the labour time necessary to do so).[15] Constructing a house of clay or mud, furthermore, did not take a very long time, according to the European observers. Jean Barbot thought that the construction time of a house was around a week.[16] John Adams wrote about the reconstruction of the Cape Coast town on the Gold Coast after a fire:

> If Rome was not built in a day, Cape Coast town was nearly rebuilt in that time; for every man in it is a mechanic of sufficient ability to erect a dwelling for himself and family, and the materials necessary to be used on the occasion, are abundantly supplied by the woods in the vicinity.[17]

Similar statements can be found from H.C. Monrad, and C.H. Bonné.[18] All the testimonies thus agreed that it only took a few days, or at most a week, to build a house from scratch. The houses were nonetheless quite functional in the sense of protecting the inhabitants against the climate, at least. Most important was protection against the rain, especially during the rainy seasons when the amount of downpour could be very high. This was a task that the indigenous houses seem to have been able to meet much better than what many of the Europeans initially expected, given that quite a few took notice of this characteristic. Paul Erdmann Isert for example argued that 'the thatch of the roofs is so solidly woven that even in the strongest storm the huts remain dry'.[19] Unsurprisingly, the walls of the clay houses could not withstand every torrent, no matter how well the owner had tried to thatch the roof and plaster the walls, Pieter de Marees attested.[20]

The European observers also described a social stratification as to the quality of housing on the Gold Coast. There were a number of ways in which the housing was stratified socially. One way was in the technique used for its construction. In coastal towns such as Elmina, some houses were thus described as being built out of stone, as was noted previously. This was potentially a marker of social status and affluence, with only the most important and affluent people – such as local rulers or successful merchants – being able to build such a house of stone.[21] The number of storeys in a house could also be a signifier of social stratification. Multi-storeyed houses were primarily described in accounts of some of the ports on the Gold Coast, but also in Kumasi in Asante.[22] A third, and perhaps the most common way, that housing was socially stratified was simply by the size and dimension of the house (or houses, if a whole housing compound is considered). Many authors simply noted that the houses of the rich across the region were considerably larger than those of the commoners. Nicholas Villault for example argued that while the common population on the Gold Coast 'have their walls so low, they seldome exceed the height of a man', the great men build houses with 'high and lofty roofes'.[23] William Hutton for his part thought that the houses in Kumasi, the capital of Asante, north of the Gold Coast, resembled bee-hives, but added: 'This last observation, however, does not apply to the principal houses, some of which are very superior, and upon a larger scale than any we observed on our journey'.[24]

## Furniture and household utensils

If opinions were divided about the quality of the housing, virtually all Europeans agreed on one point: the limited amount of furniture and other household possessions that could be found in the normal home, and the quite simple nature of what furniture there was. By the end of the seventeenth century, Jean Barbot described what he thought the contents of a typical household on the Gold Coast looked like:

> These Africans hardly spend anything on furniture. They limit themselves to what is necessary, and the only things you see in their homes are a few wooden seats, a small chest, a few pots for cooking or drinking, and some weapons hung on the walls. Noblemen have tables and rush mattresses, on which they spread their mats to sleep. The mattresses are an inch thick. Others have simply mats, or a few cattle-hides, and skins of other animals, and as a head-rest a small piece of wood.[25]

Even the noblemen were thus described to own a rather limited amount of material possessions. The difference between the rich and the poor was, furthermore, not very large, judging from Barbot's description.

Mats and hammocks were clearly popular for sleeping on. These could be spread on a mattress, as described by Barbot above (possibly inspired by reading Pieter de Marees). An alternative way of designing a bed was to build a platform out of mud to lie upon, as Nathaniel Uring found examples of on the Gold Coast: 'they raise Places with Clay, about Two Foot higher than the Floor, and lay Mats or Carpets thereon, where they sleep'.[26] One particular feature of the beds, that some of the Europeans took note of, was also an absence of soft pillows. Instead, the people were described as either using logs, a rock, or a small stool devised specifically for that purpose.[27] Most of the European observers seem to have believed that there were few other household utensils in a typical commoner's households. Wilhelm Johann Müller described what he thought were typical households in Fetu on the Gold Coast around the middle of the seventeenth century in some detail:

> In the homes of common people one sees very few utensils. Seldom does one see more than perhaps a large calabash, or a copper kettle or basin, out of which they wash daily; a stool, on which they sit; a pot, in which they cook food; one or two calabashes, which they use as drinking vessels; an earthenware dish, from which they eat; one or two straw mats, besides several small animal-skins, on which they sleep. In daytime they roll these mats and skins up and hang them on the wall with two cords. Distinguished people, particularly those who have contact with the Whites, possess more utensils, far more precious. There are some among them who are in this respect not inferior, indeed far superior, to many of us.[28]

Similar descriptions, containing roughly the same list of material objects, can be found in some of the other contemporary accounts. These authors occasionally left out some of the items mentioned by Müller, and/or added other goods, as well as changed the number of items held in what they described as a typical household (for example the number of stools that could be found in a typical household). Some items added to the list of possessions that often could be found in a commoner's household included baskets, chests or boxes for storage, mortars and pestles for pounding corn, pottery for storing and cooling water, fans and prapras (brushes), tools for fishing as well as weapons and hunting equipment.[29] And while Müller described the number of utensils in the home of commoners as 'few', this was not necessarily the opinion of all observers. In one of her stories from the Gold Coast from the early nineteenth century, Sarah Lee described a household inhabited by an elderly couple and their only son, living by the river Volta. The family was indeed poor, she argued, but was nonetheless described as possessing all the furniture and household utensils described above – seemingly suggesting through her wording in the description that such a list of household possessions indeed signified that the family might not have been as void of possessions as some of the other, more sceptical European authors had argued previously.[30]

Further, one particular observation by Nicolas Villault does provide us with reason to interpret evidence on this account cautiously, since 'Among the common sort, there is nothing of household-stuff, or what is us'd commonly about the house to be seen; all is locked up in their Coffers, which they buy of the Whites'.[31] It is thus perfectly possible that many of the travel accounts simply did not get the chance to see much of the material possessions held by the common population, even if they were allowed to enter a home.

## Textiles and clothing

If the typical household was described as holding few durable household utensils and similar possessions, many observers noted the great care which many Africans had for their clothing. The primary sources are comparatively rich in their descriptions of the customs on the Gold Coast in particular. Judging from what descriptions there are, the style of clothing used seems to exhibit quite a large degree of continuity over the period studied in this book. One of the first to describe customary types of clothing on the Gold Coast was, again, Pieter de Marees. He described the male dress as

> they take two fathoms of Linen and put it between their legs and around their body, like a belt, letting it hang down below the knees, like Portuguese Trousers. When they go outside their houses they take another fathom of Linen, Silk or other cloth around their neck or over their shoulders and under their arms, as if it were a Mantle.[32]

The female dress was described in quite similar terms:

> They wrap 1 or 1½ fathoms of Linen around their bodies, letting it hang from below their Breasts or Navel down to their knees. Then they take a piece of red, blue or yellow Cloth, with which they make a Belt, and tie it around their bodies.[33]

Several illustrations in the contemporary travel accounts depicted people, intentionally or unintentionally providing evidence of the style of dress used. Figures 7.1 and 7.2 are illustrations from the manuscripts of Jean Barbot, thought to have been made by Jean Barbot himself during his stay in West Africa – and thus not necessarily distorted by the mediation of engravers or publishers, as some publications' illustrations might be. The illustrations show a style of dress very reminiscent of what Pieter de Marees was describing by the early seventeenth century.

Several later authors also described a highly similar custom, where the people on the Gold Coast – both men and women – would wrap long pieces of cloth around them as clothes.[34] Some of the European authors explicitly compared the style to the togas used in ancient Rome.[35] Many of the authors also noted that local population, of both genders, then primarily or only covered the lower half of the body with the cloth. This custom might however have been a practical solution for how to deal with this type of clothing when working, Henry Meredith suggested by the early nineteenth century:

*Figure 7.1* The style of dress for men on the Gold Coast. Person A, to the left, is described as 'a nobleman'.

Source: Illustration from the manuscripts of Jean Barbot, British National Archives ADM 7/830B. Reproduction by the author.

*Figure 7.2* The style of dress for women on the Gold Coast.

Source: Illustration from the manuscripts of Jean Barbot, British National Archives ADM 7/830B. Reproduction by the author.

> The men wear a piece of cloth, of about four yards long and two wide, wrapt loosely about them, when they are unemployed; when engaged in any occupation, part of it is folded round the loins, the remainder hangs down and covers the lower part of the body.[36]

Some of the authors also took note of the social stratification in clothing among the people on the Gold Coast. Wilhelm Johann Müller thus noted that the style of clothing varied according to 'rank and fortune': 'Distinguished men adorn themselves with splendid clothes and precious ornaments', he wrote, whereas men of 'very slender means' had to suffice with a piece of quite coarse linen used in the manner described by de Marees above. Those who were very poor, and were unable to afford even that, had to make do with only an ell of some very cheap textile – hardly enough, he claimed, to even cover their private parts.[37] The descriptions also suggest substantial social stratification in the styles of clothing used. Many authors thus agreed that one important class distinction was in the quality of the cloth used.[38] There was also a social stratification in exactly what type of textile was used for the clothes. Presumably, many of the textiles used by commoners were locally produced, even if the European authors rarely mentioned this. When the origin of the textiles was discussed, it was often particularly because they were imported. According to Jean Barbot, for example, many of the more plain varieties of textiles used by the commoners on the Gold Coast were of European origin – such as Leiden serge. On the other hand, he claimed, 'Nobles and merchants distinguish themselves from the common people by wearing larger and richer material, China satin, taffetas, or coloured Indian cloth'.[39] Willem Bosman added that the common habit was made either of 'velvet, silk, cloth, *perpetuana*, or some sort of stuff' but that some people had their dress made out of 'fifty sorts of stuff', possibly as a way to flaunt one's riches.[40]

Whereas the descriptions of household possessions might be quite short, even in the travel accounts where they are mentioned at all, different styles of clothing was certainly an issue that a lot of the European authors took notice of. The style of clothing may have seemed exotic to many of the European observers, but at least some of them would find reason to compare it to the antique European style of clothing. Many of the authors would also come to express an understanding of the social stratification in the local styles of clothing on the Gold Coast.

## Material wealth on the Gold Coast in regional perspective

The evidence of the material wealth of the population on the Gold Coast exhibits many similarities to the evidence from many other parts of coastal West Africa. The term hut is for example found over and over again in the European accounts of local housing standards, describing various African societies all along the West African coast throughout the period covered in this book. Many of these huts were described as small and round, without any windows, and having only a very low entrance. The descriptions of how one had to bend over in order to enter such a hut are therefore quite common.[41] Quite a few of the authors also compared the shape of the huts to bee-hives or dovecotes. This specific metaphor was particularly popular among some of the early French authors writing about Senegambia, in particular, suggesting that some early description might have become highly influential for many later authors who thought about and described the houses.[42]

The primary sources did however describe a somewhat greater variety in construction materials used for the housing in coastal West Africa than what can be found in the descriptions of the Gold Coast housing. For starters, descriptions of stone houses can be found in the written accounts of some particular other places along the West African coast, such as in Senegal or in Ouidah.[43] Mud or clay was, however, undoubtedly the most important construction material throughout much of coastal West Africa, just as it was on the Gold Coast, judging from the number of authors mentioning it.[44] Many of these descriptions do not specify how the clay was used, but it seems reasonable to assume that the wattle-and-daub technique described from the Gold Coast was in use in many places along the coast. A very different technique was the building of adobe houses, using sun-dried bricks for the building of the houses. This technique might have been rare or non-existent on the Gold Coast at this time, judging from the fact that no consulted account seems to mention that this construction technique was used there. Accounts of adobe houses, using 'burnt' or 'baked' brick, can however be found in accounts from a couple of other places in West Africa (including Senegambia, Sierra Leone and Benin).[45]

Other building materials were also important in some parts of coastal West Africa. European sources from the fifteenth and sixteenth centuries that mention houses in Senegambia primarily described them as being constructed out of reeds or straw only.[46] Occasional references to houses made of straw or reeds can still be found in accounts from the early eighteenth century.[47] From the seventeenth century onwards, most of the travel accounts describing the region of Senegambia described the houses there, too, as being made of mud or clay.[48] Another important material for constructing houses was wood. Unsurprisingly, the references to houses built primarily of wood come from the forest zone of Western Africa, primarily from the region of Sierra Leone.[49] Wooden houses could occasionally also be found elsewhere along the pre-colonial West African coast.[50] It is however highly unclear how big the difference really was between these wooden houses, and those described as being made of mud or clay: the supposedly wooden houses were occasionally described as being plastered with clay, and the mud or clay houses were generally described as having been constructed around a wooden frame of some sort. The difference might thus have been one of degrees, rather than a qualitative one.

Regardless of the construction technique and building material, the descriptions of the quality of the houses are pretty similar throughout much of the region in many other aspects. De Marees' comparison of West African huts to hog-sties for example seem to have had repercussions on how other people, visiting other parts of West Africa, came to think about the quality of the housing. Soon after de Marees published his account, William Finch, for example, compared houses in Sierra Leone to pig-sties.[51] Another example comes from Thomas Phillips who compared the houses he saw to dog-kennels, or to sheep-houses.[52] Comparing the West African huts to the housing of the poor in Europe was also common when describing housing in West Africa elsewhere than on the Gold Coast, too.[53] Other authors did as Jean Barbot, and simply dropped any comparisons, to instead let the descriptions abound in invectives, when describing the housing of the commoners: dirty, small, stinking, inconvenient, wretched, miserable hovels.[54] But just as was the case regarding the Gold Coast, some authors explicitly disagreed on this issue, claiming that the houses might have been simple but were at least nice and clean.[55] Anna Maria Falconbridge even made a particular point of this: 'I went into several of them – saw nothing that did not discover the occupiers to be very clean and neat'.[56] A few authors even argued that the housing standards could be quite high in some regions. Most explicit was Olfert Dapper, who in 1668 described houses in Benin as large and pleasantly made, with handsome fronts: 'In brief there are no houses anywhere in those parts as nicely built as these'.[57] The houses were also described as easy and cheap to build throughout the region. Otto Friedrich von der Groeben for example believed that it took no more than half a day to build a typical hut, and only cost very little to build.[58] Claude Jannequin claimed instead that it took about 48 hours to build a new house of wood and clay from scratch.[59] No wonder, then, that many people seem to have considered some types of housing as temporary constructions, to be abandoned and re-built on a regular basis.[60] The main problem with the common types of houses, emphasized by a couple of authors, was instead their flammability. Particularly the supportive structure of wood, as well as the roofs (generally made of thatched leaves or straw), remained highly flammable.[61] This remained a big problem, particularly in cities and towns where a fire, once started, easily could spread between houses.

Some of the European observers are certainly somewhat astonished by what they perceived of as a very low degree of social stratification in housing in some parts of coastal West Africa, and explicitly remarked that the kings lived in houses quite similar in style to those of the commoners.[62] There are, however, several examples from all along the West African coast that the affluent people in the society lived in more advanced and extravagant forms of housing. By the early seventeenth century, Richard Jobson for example related that houses of the poor in Senegambia were made of straw and reed, whereas the houses of the 'better sort' were built of clay and mud.[63] In other areas, where adobe houses could be found, this was seemingly a prerogative of the rich, while the poorer classes lived in the more common huts.[64] Multi-storeyed houses were also occasionally to be found in the region, as were houses of very different sizes, and they were all described as being owned by the more affluent in each respective society.[65]

The descriptions of what material possessions the common population on the Gold Coast owned did not differ very much from what other European travellers described of their experiences elsewhere along the coast. Many of the same types of household utensils can, for example, be found in descriptions from many different places along the coast.[66] A rare depiction of (parts of) the interior of a house can also be found in Phérotée de Lacroix's *Relation universelle de l'Afrique* from

1688 (see Figure 4.2), illustrating many of the items mentioned by other authors. The beds, or rather the absence of proper beds, as many of the Europeans saw it, also captured the imagination and attention of a long list of European observers, travelling in many different parts of West Africa, throughout the pre-colonial period.[67] What rare accounts there are of Africans remembering life in West Africa from this period of time all describe the same type of bed – based on a platform built of mud – as was described from the Gold Coast.[68] The absence of what the Europeans considered normal decencies in a commoner household, such as proper beds, would in some cases be explicitly interpreted as evidence of poverty.[69] The perceived low value of the household possessions was similarly interpreted as a sign of poverty.[70]

Throughout much of coastal Africa, the style of clothing was something the European observers took notice of. Certainly, some of the authors – particularly in some of the first accounts from the fifteenth and sixteenth centuries – claimed that the Africans that they encountered went about almost completely naked, with many adults from the poorer strata in society only using the most minor amount of clothing to cover their private parts.[71] This particular claim was then emphasized in much of the secondary literature to such an extent that it soon turned into a stereotype about Africans. Any caveats or exceptions that the primary sources might have added (for example that only children or young people went around almost naked, or that the presumed nakedness in reality only concerned parts of the body, for example the upper body) then tended to disappear, so that the Africans generally were described as being stark naked in many widely spread secondary publications of the time.[72] Most authors of the primary travel accounts would however be at least somewhat more nuanced in their descriptions of the local styles of clothing. The evidence then indicates that the style of the clothing differed somewhat between societies along the West African coast. Further to the west, stretching from Senegambia to Sierra Leone, many of the authors described the customary habits for males – at least from the upper strata in society – as being made up of shirts and breeches, while the dress of the women was described in quite varied terms.[73] Further to the east, on the other hand, the customary style of clothing was much more similar to how the dress on the Gold Coast was described.[74] While the particular style of clothing might have differed, the evidence does not seem to suggest that the people on the Gold Coast were either very much better or worse clothed than other people elsewhere along the West African coast. The evidence does not, therefore, indicate that this aspect of the material wealth on the Gold Coast was very unusual to that in other parts of coastal West Africa.

## The birth of a consumer culture

As was noted previously, the common African population were described by the European writers as owning few durable material possessions. Some authors would attempt to explain this supposed phenomenon. Some authors simply connected it to the stereotype of African idleness, discussed in Chapter 4: people did not want to work very hard in order to consume material goods, but preferred leisure at the price of a materially more simple life. There were however also important socio-cultural aspects to the equation, aside from the individual's personal pleasure. One was the social status attributed to being able to provide for a large group of people, instead of in possessing material goods of one's own; for example being able to provide for a large number of partners in societies which allowed for polygamy. Thus, wrote Willem Bosman, men on the Gold Coast 'content themselves with one, two, ten or twenty Wives'.[75] Another aspect was the ability to provide for a number of other retainers, aside from the immediate family, in order to increase one's social standing and reputation.[76] The status involved in being able to provide for other people would in some cases also translate into general hospitality towards strangers.[77]

For a long period of time, durable European trade goods seem to be non-existent in all European descriptions of West African commoners' households and the possessions held therein. This would however change over time. Exactly when this change occurred is unfortunately hard to pinpoint because of how vague most of the sources are on this topic. Prior to the nineteenth century, it seems as if virtually no durable European trade goods were to be found in commoners' households, judging from the European accounts consulted from all along the West African coast: to the extent that the possession of such European trade goods was noted by the Europeans at that time, it was only as possessions in more affluent households. The implication might be that the vast majority of the durable imported goods were purchased by members of the local elites.[78] The only imported goods that the European observers describe as being consumed by local commoners were various sorts of simple textiles, as was described above. Many commoners might thus have used most of what economic surplus they were able to earn (see Chapter 8) to purchase non-durable goods, such as foodstuffs, alcohol or cloth.

In the nineteenth century, the descriptions did however start to change on this issue. The change is obvious in two of the accounts from the Sierra Leone in particular. In 1802, Anna Maria Falconbridge did for example mention a novelty in the list of household possessions she found, in what she described as a typical commoner household in Sierra Leone: pewter basins.[79] Peter Leonard, for his part, noticed that some small mirrors could be found in some commoners' houses in Sierra Leone by the early nineteenth century.[80] J.P.L. Durand at the time called the process a spread of 'artificial wants', created by commerce (in contrast to the 'natural' wants which easily could be satisfied by the natural abundance in the region, see Chapter 4). [81]

This spread of a consumer culture seems to have occurred on the Gold Coast as well. Dating it seems hard because most sources describing the Gold Coast at this time refrain from discussing the issue, but perhaps it occurred there around the same time as in Sierra Leone, some time during the late eighteenth or early nineteenth centuries. By the middle of the nineteenth century, at least, Brodie Cruikshank claimed that there were few houses on the Gold Coast 'in which many of the comforts and luxuries of civilized life are not to be found'. This was not limited, he emphasized, to those who had close contacts with the Europeans.

On the contrary, 'among all classes there is a much more general diffusion of a moderate and competent means of subsistence than is to be perhaps found in any other country in the world'.[82]

## Conclusion

The descriptions in the primary sources are often quite vague, and it is for that reason not easy to determine when or to what extent the material culture changed over the time period studied in this book. The evidence from the European travel accounts in general gives the impression of quite low living standards for the common population on the Gold Coast throughout much of the period. Houses were described as quite simple huts, built with quite non-durable materials, and were often compared to the housing of very poor people in Europe. Only more affluent members of Gold Coast society were described as living in larger and more durable housing. Household possessions were furthermore described as very limited, and many of the European observers seem almost astonished by how few utensils the Africans they encountered seem to have made do with.

One type of import that did come into quite general use early on was imported textiles. This is hardly surprising given the fact that textiles were the most important type of imports into West Africa at the time. There was on the other hand a rather clear social stratification in this consumption, according to the European observers: while commoners had to make do with coarser and cheaper imports from Europe, the more affluent members of society could consume the finer textiles from Asia.

One key finding is, on the other hand, that more durable imported goods seem to have been a prerogative of the more affluent strata of society for a very long period of time. They were only rarely, if at all, to be found in the homes of the common African population during most of the period studied in this book. One important change over time was therefore that other durable consumer goods imported from Europe, such as mirrors or pewter basins, started to be found in the descriptions of commoners' homes in the region. It seems to have occurred in some countries along the West African coast by the early nineteenth century, but it is hard to determine from the evidence when it might have started to happen on the Gold Coast in particular. By the middle of the nineteenth century, at least, this type of consumption of imported goods had spread rather drastically among large groups of the population there.

Naturally, none of the evidence shown in this chapter necessarily implies that West Africans in general, or people on the Gold Coast in particular, were very poor compared to people elsewhere in the world. The evidence from the travel accounts might to a large extent reflect a class bias on behalf of the observers: many of the European authors did after all come from quite affluent backgrounds themselves, and might have had a rather limited knowledge about how commoners in their own countries lived. The issue of comparing living standards on the Gold Coast with living standards elsewhere in the world is therefore going to be the topic of the next chapter.

## Notes

1 Barbot, *Barbot on Guinea*, p. 373; Hutton, *A Voyage to Africa*, p. 54; Bennett, N. and Brooks, G. (eds), *New England Merchants in Africa. A History through Documents 1802 to 1865* (Boston: Boston University Press, 1965), p. 118.
2 Barbot, *Barbot on Guinea*, pp. 272, 511; Loyer, *Relation du Voyage*, pp. 166–8.
3 Jones, *German Sources*, p. 202.
4 Beecham, *Ashantee and the Gold Coast*, pp. 144–5.
5 De Marees, *Description and Historical*, p. 75; Jones, *German Sources*, pp. 86, 108; Uring, *A History of the Voyages*, p. 160; Atkins, J., *A Voyage to Guinea*, p. 99; Meredith, *An Account of*, p. 95; Bowdich, T.E., *Mission from Cape Coast*, pp. 304–6.
6 De Marees, *Description and Historical*, p. 75.
7 Bowdich, *Mission from Cape Coast*, pp. 304–6.
8 De Marees, *Description and Historical Account*, p. 75.
9 Ogilby, J., *Africa: Being an Accurate Description of the Regions* (London, 1670) at EEBO [accessed 1 February 2013], p. 453.
10 Jones, *German Sources*, p. 201.
11 Barbot, *Barbot on Guinea*, p. 511.
12 See for example Villault, *A Relation of the Coasts*, p. 156; Atkins, *A Voyage to Guinea*, p. 99; Meredith, *An Account of*, p. 227; Hutton, *A Voyage to Africa*, p. 198.
13 Jones, *German Sources*, p. 86.
14 Jones, *German Sources*, p. 254.
15 Barbot, *Barbot on Guinea*, p. 512.
16 Barbot, *Barbot on Guinea*, p. 512.
17 Adams, *Remarks on the Country*, p. 31.
18 Monrad, H.C., *A Description of the Guinea Coast and its Inhabitants. Two Views from Christiansborg Castle, vol. II,* translated by S.A. Winsnes (Accra: Sub-Saharan, 2008 [1822]), p. 196; Bonné, C.H., *Søreiser paa Europas kyster og kysten af Guinea* (Thisted: Forfatternes forlag, 1833), at Det Kongelige Bibliotek [accessed 6 June 2013], pp. 62–3.
19 Isert, *Letters on West Africa*, p. 37.
20 De Marees, *Description and Historical Account*, p. 228.
21 Barbot, *Barbot on Guinea*, p. 373; Hutton, *A Voyage to Africa*, p. 54; Bennett and Brooks, *New England Merchants*, p. 118.
22 Barbot, *Barbot on Guinea*, p. 373; Uring, *A History of*, p. 160; Adams, *Remarks on the Country*, p. 38; Hutton, *A Voyage to Africa*, p. 238; Irvine, G. (ed.), *Huydecoper's Diary* (Legon: University of Accra, Department of History, 1962), p. 21.
23 Villault, *A Relation of the Coasts*, pp. 154–5.
24 Hutton, *A Voyage to Africa*, p. 236.
25 Barbot, *Barbot on Guinea*, p. 512.
26 Uring, *A History of*, p. 139.
27 Barbot, *Barbot on Guinea*, p. 512; Uring, *A History of*, p. 139.
28 Jones, *German Sources*, p. 202.
29 See for example de Marees, *Description and Historical Account*, p. 76; Atkins, *A Voyage to Guinea*, p. 99; Monrad, *A Description of*, p. 197; Bonné, *Søreiser paa Europas kyster*, pp. 62–3; Lee, *Stories of Strange Lands*, pp. 152–3.
30 Lee, *Stories of Strange Lands*, pp. 152–3.
31 Villault, *A Relation of the Coasts*, p. 156.
32 De Marees, *Description and Historical Account*, p. 34.
33 De Marees, *Description and Historical Account*, p. 39.
34 See for example Jones, *German Sources*, pp. 34, 86; Villault, *A Relation of the Coasts*, pp. 137–8; Loyer, *Relation du Voyage*, pp. 61–3; Bosman, *A New and Accurate*, pp. 102–3; Meredith, *An Account of*, pp. 61–2; Hutton, *A Voyage to Africa*, p. 92.

35 Monrad, *A Description of*, p. 181; Lee, *Stories of Strange Lands*, p. 22.
36 Meredith, *An Account of*, pp. 109–10.
37 Jones, *German Sources*, pp. 203–4.
38 Jones, *German Sources*, pp. 203–4; Bosman, *A New and Accurate*, p. 103; Isert, *Letters on West Africa*, p. 113.
39 Barbot, *Barbot on Guinea*, pp. 493–4.
40 Bosman, *A New and Accurate*, p. 102.
41 Jones, *Brandenburg Sources*, pp. 191–2; Le Maire, J.-J., *A Voyage of the Sieur Le Maire* (London, 1696) at ECCO [accessed 1 February 2013], pp. 43–4; Phillips, T., 'A Journal of a Voyage made in the Hannibal of London', in *A Collection of Voyages and Travels, vol. VI* (London, 1732) at ECCO [accessed 3 June 2013], p. 192; Watt, *Journal of*, p. 12.
42 See for example Jannequin, C., *Voyage de Libye au royaume de Senegal, le long du Niger* (Paris, 1643) at Gallica [accessed 30 January 2013], p. 72; Jones, *Brandenburg Sources*, pp. 191–2; Loyer, *Relation du Voyage*, p. 51; Adanson, M., *A Voyage to Senegal, the Isle of Goree, and the River Gambia* (London, 1759) at ECCO [accessed 23 May 2012], p. 35; Saugnier, F., *Voyages to the Coast of Africa* (London 1792), at MOMW [accessed 1 February 2013], p. 181; Hutton, *A Voyage to Africa*, p. 236.
43 Hutton, *A Voyage to Africa*, p. 22; Bennett and Brooks, *New England Merchants*, pp. 65–6; Jones, *Brandenburg Sources*, pp. 191–2.
44 See for example Alvares, M., *Ethiopia Minor and a Geographical Account of the Province of Sierra Leone* (Liverpool University 1990 [c. 1615]), at the WISC African Studies Collection, http://uwdc.library.wisc.edu/collections/AfricanStudies/Africana, [accessed 13 June 2013], chapter 7, p. 9; Barbot, *Barbot on Guinea*, p. 88; Froger, *A Relation of*, p. 35; Moore, *Travels into the Inland*, pp. 76–7; Wyatt, J., *The Life and Surprizing Adventures of James Wyatt* (London, 1755) at ECCO [accessed 1 February 2013], p. 171; Adanson, *A Voyage to Senegal*, p. 162; Curtin, *Africa Remembered*, pp. 149, 177, 180, 267; Beaver, *African Memoranda*, p. 328; Durand, *A Voyage to Senegal*, p. 41; Phillips, 'A Journal of a Voyage', p. 192; Matthews, *A Voyage to*, p. 113; Spilsbury, F., *Account of a Voyage to the Western Coast of Africa* (London, 1807) at MOMW [accessed 13 February 2012], pp. 37–8; Pereira, D.P., *Esmeraldo de Situ Orbis*, translated by G. Kimble (London: Hakluyt Society, 1937 [1505–1508]), pp. 125–6; Dapper, *Olfert Dapper's Description*, p. 12; Phérotée de La Croix, A., *Relation universelle de l'Afrique ancienne et moderne* (Lyon, 1688) at Gallica [accessed 6 June 2013], p. 154; Jones, *Brandenburg Sources*, pp. 191–2; Bosman, *A New and Accurate Description*, p. 429; Smith, *A New Voyage to Guinea*, p. 234; Hawkins, J., *A History of a Voyage to the Coast of Africa* (Troy (1797) at ECCO [accessed 23 May 2012], pp. 73–5; Adams, *Remarks on the Country*, pp. 77, 128; Park, *Travels in the Interior*, p. 199; Monrad, *A Description of*, p. 258.
45 Alvares, *Ethiopia Minor*, chapter 4, p. 2; Jobson, *The Discovery of*, p. 288; Curtin, *Africa Remembered*, p. 149; Beaver, *African Memoranda*, p. 328; Adams, *Remarks on the Country*, p. 128.
46 Cadamosto, *The Voyages of*, pp. 29–30. See also Diogo Gomes in Cadamosto, *The Voyages of*, p. 97; de Almada, A.Á., *Brief Treatise on the Rivers of Guinea* (Madison: WISC, 1984 [c. 1594]), p. 43; Jobson, *The Discovery of*, p. 107.
47 See for example Le Maire, *A Voyage of*, pp. 43–4; Jones, *Brandenburg Sources*, pp. 191–2; Loyer, *Relation du Voyage*, pp. 92–3.
48 See for example de Almada, *Brief Treatise*, pp. 43, 73, 76, 111; Alvares, *Ethiopia Minor*, chapter 7, p. 8; Jobson, *The Discovery of*, p. 288; Barbot, *Barbot on Guinea*, p. 88; Froger, *A Relation of*, p. 35; Moore, *Travels into the Inland*, pp. 76–7; Wyatt, *The Life and Surprizing Adventures*, p. 171; Adanson, *A Voyage to Senegal*, p. 162; Curtin, *Africa Remembered*, p. 149; Beaver, *African Memoranda*, p. 328; Durand, *A Voyage to Senegal*, p. 41.

49 Afzelius, A., *Sierra Leone Journal*, ed. A.P. Kup (Uppsala: Uppsala University, 1967 [1795–1796]), p. 111.; Atkins, *A Voyage to Guinea*, p. 50; Padenheim, D.P., *Bref til en vän i Sverige, innehållande historisk och geographisk beskrifning öfver Colonien Sierra Leona i Afrika* (Stockholm, 1801), pp. 95–6; Falconbridge, *Narrative of Two Voyages*, p. 27; Winterbottom, *An Account of*, pp. 81–2; Hutton, *A Voyage to Africa*, pp. 29–30.

50 Curtin, *Africa Remembered*, pp. 74–5; Williamson, D., *A True Narrative of the Sufferings of David Williamson, Mariner* (London, 1772), at ECCO [accessed 28 January 2013], pp. 10–11; Hawkins, *A History of a Voyage*, p. 55; Falconbridge, *An Account of*, p. 51; Crow, H., *Memoirs of the Late Captain Hugh Crow of Liverpool* (London, 1830) at MOMW [accessed 6 June 2013], pp. 195–6; Meredith, *An Account of*, p. 62; Irvine, *Huydecoper's Diary*, p. 21.

51 Hair, P.E.H., *Sierra Leone and the English in 1607* (Institute of African Studies, University of Sierra Leone, 1981), p. 55.

52 Phillips, 'A Journal of a Voyage', pp. 192, 216.

53 See for example Uring, *A History of*, pp. 129–30; Falconbridge, *Narrative of Two Voyages*, p. 27; Leonard, P., *Records of a Voyage to the Western Coast of Africa* (Edinburgh, 1833) at MOMW [accessed 13 February 2012], p. 41.

54 See for example Hair, P.E.H., *André de Faro's Missionary Journey to Sierra Leone in 1663–64* (Institute of African Studies, University of Sierra Leone, 1982), p. 29; Jones, *Brandenburg Sources*, p. 183; Watt, *Journal of*, p. 12; Afzelius, *Sierra Leone Journal*, p. 136; Durand, *A Voyage to Senegal*, p. 41; Adams, *Remarks on the Country*, pp. 136–7; Leonard, *Records of a Voyage*, p. 184.

55 See for example Moore, *Travels into the Inland*, p. 77; Falconbridge, *An Account of*, p. 53; Durand, *A Voyage to Senegal*, p. 153.

56 Falconbridge, *Narrative of Two Voyages*, p. 27, see also p. 79.

57 Dapper, *Olfert Dapper's Description*, p. 12.

58 Jones, *Brandenburg Sources*, p. 26.

59 Jannequin, *Voyage de Libye*, p. 88; see also Adanson, *A Voyage to Senegal*, pp. 255–6.

60 See for example da Mota, A.T. and Hair, P.E.H. (eds), *Jesuit Documents on the Guinea of Cape Verde and the Cape Verde Islands 1585–1617* (Madison: WISC African Studies Collection, 1989), Document 13, p. 13; Corry, J., *Observations upon the Windward Coast* (London, 1807) at MOMW [accessed 6 June 2013], p. 64.

61 See for example Barbot, *Barbot on Guinea*, p. 272; Moore, *Travels into the Inland*, p. 109; Winterbottom, *An Account of*, p. 81.

62 Le Maire, *A Voyage of*, pp. 43–4. See also Ritchie, 'Impressions of Senegal', p. 86; Park, *Travels in the Interior*, p. 36; Durand, *A Voyage to Senegal*, p. 41.

63 Jobson, *The Discovery of*, p. 107.

64 Curtin, *Africa Remembered*, pp. 149, 180.

65 Curtin, *Africa Remembered*, pp. 149, 180, 186, 267; Park, *Travels in the Interior*, p. 199; Donelha in Jobson, *The Discovery of*, p. 288; Leonard, *Records of a Voyage*, p. 256; Dapper, *Olfert Dapper's Description*, p. 12.

66 See for example Hair, *Sierra Leone*, pp. 55–6; Ritchie, 'Impressions of Senegal', p. 86; Moore, *Travels into the Inland*, p. 75; Adanson, *A Voyage to Senegal*, p. 36; Park, *Travels in the Interior*, p. 36; Beaver, *African Memoranda*, p. 328; Durand, *A Voyage to Senegal*, p. 41; Curtin, *Africa Remembered*, p. 268.

67 Jones, *German Sources*, pp. 76, 202; Alvares, *Ethiopia Minor*, chapter 1, p. 7; Ritchie, 'Impressions of Senegal', p. 86; Le Maire, *A Voyage of*, pp. 44–5; Adanson, *A Voyage to Senegal*, p. 36; Jones, *Brandenburg Sources*, p. 24; Phillips, 'A Journal of', pp. 192, 216; Moore, *Travels into the Inland*, p. 75; Williamson, *A True Narrative*, p. 23; Saugnier, *Voyages to the Coast*, p. 181; Park, *Travels in the Interior*, p. 36; Padenheim, *Bref til en vän*, p. 98; Durand, *A Voyage to Senegal*, p. 41; Bonné, *Søreiser paa Europas kyster*, pp. 62–3; Leonard, *Records of a Voyage*, pp. 89–90.

68 See for example Curtin, *Africa Remembered*, pp. 74–5, 149, 267–8.
69 See for example Jones, *German Sources*, p. 70; Matthews, *A Voyage to*, p. 115; Durand, *A Voyage to Senegal*, p. 104.
70 See for example Jones, *Brandenburg Sources*, p. 26.
71 Cadamosto, *The Voyages of*, pp. 31–2; Pereira, *Esmeraldo de Situ Orbis*, pp. 80, 98; Madox, R., *An Elizabethan in 1582. The Diary of Richard Madox, Fellow of All Souls* (London: Hakluyt Society, 1976 [1582]), p. 170; Jones, *German Sources*, p. 13; Hair, *Sierra Leone*, p. 55; Barbot, *Barbot on Guinea*, p. 85.
72 See for example LeBlanc, V., *The World Surveyed or the Famous Voyages & Travailes of Vincent LeBlanc* (London, 1660) at EEBO [accessed 1 February 2013], p. 322; Anonymous, *The Golden Coast or a Description of Guinney*, (London, 1665) at EEBO [accessed 1 February 2013], p. 42; Blome, R., *A Geographical Description* (London, 1670), at EEBO [accessed 30 May 2013], pp. 48–9; Ogilby, *Africa*, pp. 319, 325, 360, 373; Clarke, S., *A New Description of the World*, (London 1689) at EEBO [accessed 27 April 2012], p. 177; Curson, H., *A New Description of the World* (London, 1704) at EEBO [accessed 29 January 2013], p. 363; Anonymous, *The Compleat Geographer* (London, 1723) at ECCO [accessed 29 January 2013], p. 173; Hadding, J., *A Description of the Four Parts of the World* (unknown place of publication, 1760), at ECCO [accessed 29 January 2013], pp. 17–8.
73 For Senegambia, see Jobson, *The Discovery of*, p. 113; Jannequin, *Voyage de Libye*, p. 96; Ritchie, 'Impressions of Senegal', p. 78; Barbot, *Barbot on Guinea*, p. 85; Le Maire, *A Voyage of*, pp. 84–5; Park, *Travels in the Interior*, p. 35; Durand, *A Voyage to Senegal*, pp. 40–1; Spilsbury, *Account of a Voyage*, p. 16. For Sierra Leone, see Alvares, *Ethiopia Minor*, Part 2, p. 3; Hair, *Sierra Leone*, p. 55; Barbot, *Barbot on Guinea*, p. 186; Matthews, *A Voyage to*, pp. 108–10; Winterbottom, *An Account of*, p. 98.
74 See for example Dapper, *Olfert Dapper's Description*, pp. 13–14; Bosman, *A New and Accurate*, pp. 326, 410.
75 Bosman, *A New and Accurate*, p. 320.
76 Bosman, *A New and Accurate*, p. 409.
77 Durand, *A Voyage to Senegal*, pp. 175–6.
78 See for exampel Crow, *Memoirs*, p. 196.
79 Falconbridge, *Narrative of Two Voyages*, p. 27.
80 Leonard, *Records of a Voyage*, pp. 89–90.
81 Durand, *A Voyage to Senegal*, p. 175.
82 Cruickshank, *Eighteen Years*, pp. 293–5.

# 8 Living standards in a comparative perspective

## Introduction

Chapter 5 discussed the conditions of labour for people employed by the English Royal African Company in particular. One question that was left unanswered in that chapter is what the wages paid to these employees meant in the form of purchasing power. This chapter will utilize the evidence from wages and prices presented in previous chapters, in order to arrive at an estimate of what the real wages of the people working for the European Company were. The chapter will also discuss what this evidence can tell us about material living standards in the region; what determined the wage levels; how it might have changed over time; and what the evidence tells us about living standards on the pre-colonial Gold Coast, compared to living standards elsewhere in the world at that time.

## Labour in the European enclaves

The quantitative evidence assembled in this research is based on a rather limited number of workers primarily at the Cape Coast Castle. One question is therefore if the conditions that these workers toiled under were representative of the conditions for any larger group of workers, or whether these particular workers were rather unique for their time? Ray Kea has previously argued that there was a quite large pool of free labourers in towns and villages on the Gold Coast, and that the people working for the European companies probably were 'broadly representative' of these urban commoners.[1] The qualitative primary sources consulted for this book also suggest that there lived a substantial group of people in the port towns on the Gold Coast, who could be engaged as labourers. Certainly, Pieter de Marees argued by the early seventeenth century in passing that 'one does not find here any Servants who serve people for payment or a salary: all of them are Slaves or Captives who have to spend their life in slavery'.[2] Later European observers would, however, paint a slightly different picture, something which seems to suggest that the market for labour on the Gold Coast transformed over time. In his description of the Gold Coast in the 1660s, Nicolas Villault for example stated that people who did not grow their own food were forced to purchase it on the local markets with what they earned 'by fishing, by making Palm-Wine, by building or repairing of houses, carrying home what the Merchants have bought on Ship-board, and such other servile imployments'.[3] While some of these (for example the fishermen) might have been self-employed, and traded goods on local markets, it seems reasonable to assume that many of the other people Villault described indeed were paid employees. All of these people in 'servile employments' were, on the other hand, not necessarily paid a wage in cash, but could occasionally be paid in kind: Villault later described that, in the harbours of the port cities, 'several boyes' who helped the fishermen out with carrying the fish were always to be found, and they made up lines and nets for them 'for which pains, they usually gratifie them with some little present of fish'.[4] The economic accounts and correspondence of the European companies provide much further evidence of free labourers being employed at least from the late seventeenth century (see Chapter 5). By the early nineteenth century, Henry Meredith also argued that labourers 'can be procured with facility, and in considerable numbers' on the Gold Coast. He suggested, however, that people who wanted labourers for example for a plantation ought to make use of pawns instead of free labourers, since they were 'more attached to the interest of the planter'.[5] The evidence thus suggests that labourers indeed could be hired in the European enclaves on the Gold Coast.

## Labour mobility on the Gold Coast

A more complex issue is the relationship between the people employed at the Cape Coast Castle and other people living on the Gold Coast, outside the immediate European enclaves. As was noted in Chapter 3, how good proxy urban real wages (and thus subsistence ratios) are for the general living standards in a country will depend upon the socio-economic context. No town or city exists completely separated from a rural hinterland. There are reasons to assume that urban labourers' wages interacted with living standards at least in the nearby region surrounding the town or city in question. It would, for example, be quite irrational to work for a low wage in the urban sector, if it was possible to get access to land that would make it possible to earn a better living from subsistence farming in the countryside. How integrated the urban and rural sectors were economically, therefore, depended upon a number of factors, including cultural, institutional and geographical factors determining the urban–rural mobility of labour.

Previous research on labour mobility in nineteenth-century West Africa has in particular singled out the Kru, a people from a region in modern-day Liberia, as particularly mobile. Evidence supporting this can certainly be found in quite a few of the primary sources, at least from the early nineteenth century. Many of the European authors of travel accounts stated that the Kru-men were engaged as sailors and traders for months at a time on European vessels sailing along the West African coast.[6] Since the Kru-men could be employed to work along a large part of the West African coast, this created a quite flexible labour market, according to G.A. Robertson: 'Labour can be obtained at a low rate, as the Cooro people can be hired at all times, if the native inhabitants should be found unwilling to work'.[7] Samuel Swan also emphasized the great flexibility that employing free

Kru labourers entailed: 'As they [the Kru] were hired on wages there was no obligation to keep them'.[8] Having made some money from their labour, Peter Leonard argued, they 'return home again, and are succeeded by some more of their fortune-pushing countrymen'.[9] The Kru were thus often emphasized in the primary sources, at least from the early nineteenth century onwards, as being particularly willing not only to work for wages, but also to move quite long distances in order to do so.

Many travel accounts also indicate a quite high level of labour mobility among the peoples living on the Gold Coast. Robert Norris for example argued by the late eighteenth century that it was wise to hire Fante canoemen on the Gold Coast before proceeding eastwards to Ouidah, since the Fante canoemen were 'hardy, active men, who undertake this business, and return in their canoe to their own country, when the captain, in whose employ they serve, has finished his trade'.[10] John McLeod, too, claimed by the early nineteenth century that this procedure was necessary, both because the Fante were 'more expert in crossing the bar than any other people' and because other peoples along the coast were less prone to accept working as canoemen for cultural or religious reasons.[11] Some of the people, who were engaged on the Gold Coast to work on European ships heading for Ouidah, did however quit working for the Europeans once they reached Ouidah.[12] The process of labour mobility was on the other hand not unidirectional, away from the Gold Coast. The Dutch governor Willem Bosman argued that, by the late seventeenth and early eighteenth centuries, the population of Accra on the Gold Coast included people who 'came from other places hither to live'.[13] The statement shows that people might have migrated to the town of Accra in order to make a living, but Bosman does not elaborate on the reasons for doing so or where the people came from. The governor of the British fort at Winneba on a similar note complained in a letter of a lack of craftsmen, but at the same time stated that skilled such people could be tempted to move to Winneba 'with proper encouragement'.[14] Exactly what this 'encouragement' meant was unfortunately not specified in the letter.

People could also be hired for services which in themselves implied considerable geographical mobility, such as long-distance porters. Many porters were employed by the Europeans in coastal towns on the Gold Coast, in order to carry goods quite far inland. They were also employed by African agents, as was shown in the travel accounts of Jean Barbot:

> Those inland Blacks, who come down without slaves of their own to carry back the commodities purchased, hire either free-men or slaves, who commonly live under the forts, at such rates as they can agree upon, according to the distance of the places the goods are to be carried to.[15]

Another important aspect of the social mobility of the labour force was the involuntary mobility induced by wars or other similar disruptive push-factors. When wars raged this could create streams of refugees. Many people then took refuge in towns close to or by the Europeans forts and castles, and thereby created a link between the urban and the rural economies in the region. This was for example what Willem Bosman argued in his account from the Gold Coast:

> the last fatal War betwixt the *Anteans* and *Adomians* hath reduced it [the land] to a miserable condition, and stript it of most of its Inhabitants: Besides which, the miserable few left behind are so dispirited, that they shelter themselves under our Fort near *Boutry*, leaving the greatest part of the Land wild and uncultivated.[16]

Refugees could be found in other places along the West African coast, too. This is for example shown in William Snelgrave's account from Ouidah. After Ouidah had been conquered by Dahomey, the king of Ouidah, together with 'many Thousands of People', had taken refuge in a barren island near Great Popoe, and therefore 'lived in a miserable manner'.[17] Presumably, the refugees could in this case not find refuge in any less desolate place, but had to make do on the unnamed, barren island.

What the evidence presented so far shows is then, first, a seemingly high mobility of urban labourers (e.g. between towns and villages along the coast), and second, some factors leading to a rural to urban mobility (as refugees or due to employment opportunities).

## Land tenure on the Gold Coast

One of the most important aspects influencing urban–rural mobility was, however, the institutional access to land. While population density might have been low on the Gold Coast in global comparison, this does not necessarily mean that the population could easily access land for cultivation. For lack of better sources, the statements by the Europeans can perhaps give us some insight into the forms of land tenure in the region. A comparatively detailed early description of land tenure on the Gold Coast has come down to us in de Marees' account of the Gold Coast in the early seventeenth century. In the account, de Marees described the absence of private ownership over land:

> Nobody here has his own land which he may use for his own purposes, because the King has all the Forests, Fields and Lands under him, and the people are not allowed to plant or sow in them without his consent.[18]

De Marees seemed in this case to be generalizing about various polities on the Gold Coast. According to the statement, the kings on the Gold Coast thus owned all the agricultural land in the region, and permission had to be asked in order for an individual to sow the land. Nicolas Villault, too, described how commoners regularly (in the month of April every year) were required to ask the king's representative for permission to cultivate a particular piece of land.[19]

As a compensation for the right to cultivate a specific plot of land for themselves, the farmers were required to 'help' (in de Marees' words) the king to till his land.

The king in turn had to repay those who worked his land by bringing them palm-wine and food during the time that these people 'helped' him. De Marees, furthermore, described that the farmers after the harvest had to provide the king with a certain amount of land rent in the form of gold. The gold was earned, it was claimed in the account, from selling part of the surplus production on local markets. In de Marees' eyes, the latter custom was, however, somewhat strange, since 'each brings as much as he thinks proper, as there is no fixed sum stipulated, but they give according to their wealth'.[20] Again, the king had to retribute the farmers for this 'gift', by providing them with 'food and drink to fill their bellies'.[21] That the kings on the Gold Coast required land rent from the peasants is also confirmed by the travel account of Erick Tilleman, an agent of the Danish slave-trading company, by the end of the seventeenth century. Among the rights a king of Accra had, Tilleman wrote, was 'that he enjoys a portion of the country's produce after the annual harvest, from all who live everywhere in the country, not so much for the sake of the value of the produce as for the proof that they owe submission to him'.[22]

How high the land rents charged were is, unfortunately, not revealed in the sources consulted for this book. The statements claiming that the rent to be paid in gold was unfixed a priori do however seem to suggest that this part of the rents might not have been exorbitantly high. More important was perhaps the requirement that farmers had to put in a number of days' work to cultivate the king's land, in exchange for the right to cultivate a plot of land of their own. De Marees explicitly mentions three tasks they were required to do: clearing the land of shrubs, tilling the land and planting it (with corn, according to de Marees' account). It is unclear if other work also was required (for example harvesting the crop on the king's land) and de Marees just mentioned these three tasks as examples of the duties of the farmers, or if these other tasks were solved in some other way than through mandatory labour. Further, exactly how many days these tasks required is unclear from the description – de Marees only notes that the people started to work for the king on a Sunday, but reveals nothing on when they stopped doing this and continued to work on some other farmers' land. The tasks that they were supposed to 'help' the king with were, however, some of the most time-consuming tasks in the agricultural cycle: according to Ivor Wilks' research from the region, clearing and preparing the land, and planting crops on it, could require some several weeks of work per year per acre of land.[23]

Some specific pieces of evidence reveal how large a share of the realized surplus was expropriated in other sectors of the economy. The fishermen of the Gold Coast were for example expected to hand over a certain share of their catch in tax to the local king. Pieter de Marees claimed that the fishermen had to hand over every fifth fish over a certain size.[24] According to Nicolas Villault, writing half a century later, the king's representative would 'carry with him a full third of what they [the fishermen] bring on shore'.[25] Traders were on the other hand according to de Marees charged a duty of 'not less than a quarter of what he has brought', at least when trading for larger amounts of gold.[26] Further, passages by both de Marees and Villault show how much the free gold-diggers were taxed: 'One half of what they find is for the labourers, and of the other half the King or proprietor of the Mine is to benefit'.[27] These taxes can perhaps provide a rough idea of the share of the surplus expropriated by the local rulers more generally, as Ray Kea has suggested.[28] It is however highly uncertain if the rate of taxation or surplus extraction necessarily was equivalent between different sectors of an economy. It is certainly possible that kings held certain economic activities in a much firmer grip, and thereby found it possible to tax these activities substantially more highly, than other sectors.

The unsatisfactory situation is, therefore, that there seems to exist no direct empirical evidence of the level of the land rents on the Gold Coast in the period studied. In essence, however, given that there evidently existed institutional barriers to individuals' access to land, if nothing else in the form of farmers having to pay for the land in the form of day labour and/or land rent as described by de Marees and others, it does not seem reasonable to describe the resource of land as completely 'open'. Propertyless labourers thus faced some important social constraints when trying to get access to land on which they could support themselves. On the other hand, the forms of land tenure do not seem to have formed a completely impenetrable barrier for mobility. There was therefore a potential for interaction between the earnings of the urban labourers and the rural peasants. While the interaction most certainly was far from perfect, it seems reasonable to treat the living standards of the urban labourers as a crude proxy of living standards of the working classes more broadly in the region.

## Social stratification on the Gold Coast

Living standards on the Gold Coast were on the other hand not homogeneous across strata in society. Many human societies have been stratified socially, for example along class or estate lines. Pre-colonial West Africa was indeed no exception to this rule. Exactly how this class or estate stratification looked is, unfortunately, not perfectly clear from the sources.

The most detailed description of the social stratification on the Gold Coast can perhaps be found in Willem Bosman's description from the early eighteenth-century Gold Coast. In the English translation of the account, the Gold Coast society was described as being stratified along five 'degrees': the king, the *caboceers* ('chief men'), merchants, commoners and slaves. The *caboceers* were, according to Bosman, supposed to 'take care of the welfare of the City or Village'. They were supposedly chosen from among the common people in parts of the Gold Coast (but he added that this was not the practice everywhere along the coast, and never elaborated in detail on who were included in the electorate). The newly elected *caboceer* would – after having been elected – also have to present his elders with presents in the form of a cow and some liquor.[29] The merchants had, according to Bosman, in some previous European travel accounts been described as noblemen. They were however nothing of the sort, according to his description. Some of these people could certainly have inherited their riches, but others had earned them by their own trade. Once enough money had been earned to afford it, an initiation ceremony enabled a person to be included in this 'degree' of men. The ceremony included presenting seven blowing-horns made of ivory before the public, and hosting a very lavish feast (which could become very expensive). Once this ceremony was over, Bosman stated, 'they are free to blow upon their Horns at pleasure', thereby suggesting that this entailed a considerable honour or social status.[30] The Norwegian priest Johannes Rask, who worked for the Danish slave-trading company on the Gold Coast in the early eighteenth century, described the merchant class somewhat further, arguing that they primarily acted as brokers 'since they accompany the inland Negroes to the fortresses, arrange and conclude sales for them, and interpret their language, since those from inland do not understand the Portuguese language, and the Europeans do not understand them'.[31] Other authors described seemingly quite similar social stratification elsewhere along the West African coast, such as in Benin.[32]

The sources from the eighteenth century thus describe a distinct social stratification, both on the Gold Coast and elsewhere along the West African coast. It is certainly possible that the European observers miss many cultural, political or religious aspects of the social stratification that they describe. The descriptions do, however, provide an idea of the socio-economic stratification of societies in the region. In contrast with Rask, who compares the *caboceers* with European nobility, Bosman made a point of *not* drawing such a parallel, for the simple reason that any person from the commonalty could be included among them, as long as they had earned enough money to finance the initiation ceremony. Rask furthermore made no mention of the slaves, possibly because he found them unworthy of mention in this context, but only found it worthwhile to discuss the stratification of the free population. The level of detail was very low in these descriptions, yet these descriptions of the social stratification of pre-colonial African societies are not very different from the very crude account given, for example, by Brodie Cruickshank, published in the nineteenth century: by the middle of the nineteenth century, Cruickshank could simply dismiss the issue of stratification as a simple dichotomy, when claiming that Gold Coast society was made up of 'master and slave' only.[33]

## Changing living standards over time

The late seventeenth and early eighteenth centuries were a period of quite drastic changes on the Gold Coast: conflicts between different polities saw the emergence of new important polities – most importantly the Asante Empire – while other polities succumbed and disappeared. It was also a period of very rapidly growing slave trading from the region; the external slave trade reached a first peak around the first decades of the eighteenth century (see Graph 2.1). It is plausible to assume that many of these factors had an impact upon the living standards of the population. In which direction this impact would drive the living standards is, on the other hand, not certain a priori, and the impact might also have been socially stratified. Take, for example, the case of the slave trade in particular: on the one hand, the growth of this trade, horrendous as it was for those who became its victims, might potentially have enriched some people lucky enough to escape enslavement. This is obviously the case for those agents selling the slaves, as has been argued in previous research.[34] Other agents might also have gained from participating in the slave trade. If the trade created a growing demand for labourers or craftsmen in the trading ports, this could contribute to improving the bargaining position of those free labourers who had managed to avoid being enslaved themselves. On the other hand, it is well-established that the slave trade created a lot of social disruption including, not least, increasing the number and intensity of conflicts in the region. This could work in the opposite direction when it comes to living standards of the non-slave population, by driving up the cost of living (if wars for example increased the cost of basic foodstuffs, as was shown in Chapter 6 that they did), by creating flows of refugees to cities and towns, seeking protection from enslavement (increasing the supply on local labour markets, and competing with the urban proletarians for any job opportunities available), or by increasing the prevalence of domestic slavery on the coast (potentially increasing the supply on the local labour market further). Theoretically, the slave trade might thus have had opposing effects upon the living standards of the (non-enslaved) population in African societies. The issue of which effect(s) dominated must therefore be settled by empirical evidence.

Gold Coast societies were quite distinctly stratified, both along various classes or estates, as described previously in this chapter, and along a crude division of labour into a number of different occupations, as was described in Chapters 4 and 5. The living standards of people of different occupations were, unsurprisingly, also highly differentiated. Whereas some labourers barely earned enough for their subsistence from their employment for a European company, others were considerably better off. This is shown quantitatively in Graph 8.1, using the method of subsistence ratios discussed in Chapter 3.

The interpreters no doubt often belonged to the most well-paid among all the Africans employed by the RAC. These interpreters employed by the Company could often earn an income many times higher than basic subsistence costs. It must be noted, as was mentioned in Chapter 3, that the samples underlying the estimates for the more skilled labourers are very small – ranging from a single individual in some years (for the linguists in particular), to at most a handful of carpenters or other craftsmen in any single year. The large fluctuations in real wages over time for the linguists is to some extent misleading, since they largely seem to be attributable to quite different skill levels of the particular individuals employed. Two of the linguists – Thomas Awishee (employed in 1707) and Cudjoe (employed in 1728) – were employed for a long period of time, and can therefore be followed in the accounts over several decades. As was noted in Chapter 5, Thomas Awishee clearly had a very steady ‘career’, as did Cudjoe, starting out with quite low wages when first employed, but receiving substantial wage increases over the course of their many years of working for the Company. Many other linguists only stayed with the Company for quite a short period of time and never experienced any such wage increases. The substantial drop of the linguist wages in the 1750s is thus the combined result of one of the old faithful servants of the

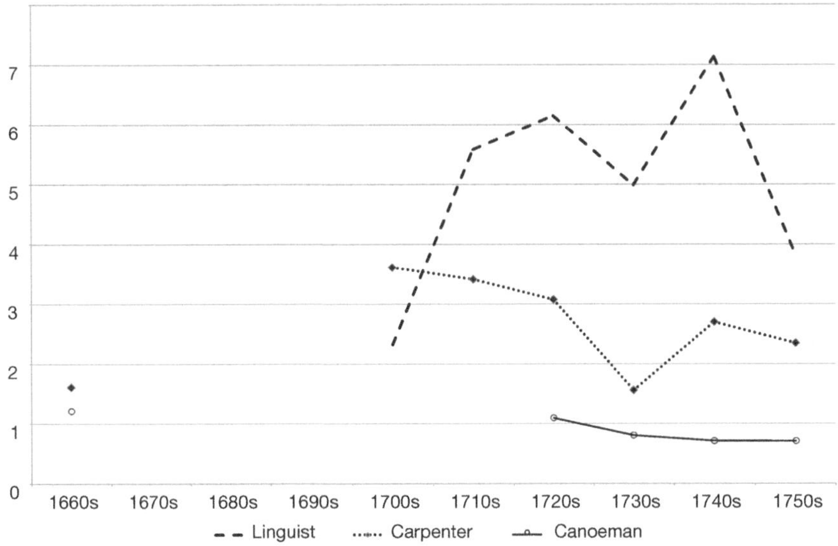


*Graph 8.1* Mean subsistence ratios for three categories of African labourers on the Gold Coast, 1660s–1750s

Note: The estimated ratios take into account the fact that the company was trying to cheat many of the labourers of part of their wages, when paying them in kind. It does, on the other hand, assume that the employees had to feed themselves on their wages, and that they received no provisions while working. Kea's data refers to 1659 for wages, and the 1650s and 1660s for prices. Data on prices are lacking from this period for a couple of goods; in these cases, I have added the same percentage to the total cost of the consumer basket as these goods were worth in the early eighteenth century (=20%).

Source: data for 1660s based on Kea, *Settlements, Trade, and Polities*, pp. 308–10. Data for later periods based on GCPLD and GCPPD.

Company, Thomas Awishee, who had stopped working for the Company around the middle of the 1740s (after thirty-seven years of service, by this time receiving a very high wage, which is reflected in the estimated subsistence ratio for this decade), being replaced by a couple of new (and much lower paid) linguists in the early 1750s. The wage levels for the skilled linguists did thus after a few years of service rise to the equivalent of a subsistence ratio of around six to seven times the cost of a subsistence basket of goods, whereas the recently employed (and presumably less skilled) linguists had to make do with a subsistence ratio not much higher than subsistence costs. The high subsistence ratio for the more skilled labourers thus indicates that the wages that these employees could earn from working for the Company left them quite some room either to indulge in material consumption – to purchase decencies and even some luxuries – or to use the economic surplus for other purposes, such as supporting a larger family, or investing any surplus in economic activities on the side.

The wages paid to skilled craftsmen, such as the African carpenters shown in Graph 8.1, would also seem to change quite drastically during the period. This does not seem to be related to the skill levels of the individuals in the same way as it was for the linguists: the carpenters were quite rarely employed over as long periods of time as the linguists were, and do not seem to make any similar 'career' (with a single individual experiencing rising wages over his life-course) as they did. It thus seems reasonable to assume that the carpenters' wages to a greater extent reflect prevailing wages for an average carpenter, and less the particular skills of the individuals employed. From what limited evidence there is available from Dutch archives in the seventeenth century, it seems as if the subsistence ratio for the carpenters at this time was quite low, with a wage not much higher than the cost of subsistence. Very little is known about how the supply of skilled craftsmen might have changed during the late seventeenth century. As for the demand, on the other hand, it seems reasonable to assume that the initial growth of the slave trade possibly also created some local linkage effects in the form a growing demand for various support services – building constructions or making canoes, repairing ships and so on. This increase in demand might explain the rising wages to the craftsmen employed during the late seventeenth century: when data on wages start to appear in the accounts of the RAC during the first decade of the eighteenth century, the real wages paid to craftsmen were three times what they had been a few decades earlier. Due to a lack of data, it is not possible to determine exactly when the real wages paid to the craftsmen peaked. From the first decade of the eighteenth century, at least, the real wage paid to craftsmen does, however, seem to have started to decrease. The decline in real wages paid to the craftsmen then continued during the first half of the eighteenth century, as could be seen in Graph 8.1.

As can be seen in the Graph 8.1, finally, the canoemen working at the fort were not paid very high wages at all. Indeed, the income earned from working for the Company was for many years lower than the annual cost of living for a whole family (leading to an estimated subsistence ratio below one). The canoemen would therefore generally have been unable to support a whole model family of six (two adults and four children) on this income alone. Such a big family would, therefore, have required supplementary incomes – either income on the side for the canoemen, or contributions by the female and/or children. As we have seen in a previous chapter (see Chapter 4), women certainly were responsible for many economic activities in pre-colonial West Africa including, not least, much of the agricultural work; so the female contribution to family income was most certainly substantial. Further, as was noted in Chapter 5, to the extent that the Company employed female workers, they were also paid a wage, even if it was lower than the wages paid to the men – equivalent to three-quarters of what a male worker was paid. Assuming that the gender income gap was quite similar by the early eighteenth century, household income would perhaps have to be adjusted upwards around 75 per cent in order to reflect real household income, if both adults in the assumed model family were working. In such a case, household income for the canoemen would have been somewhat higher than what would have been necessary for absolute subsistence needs. We will return to the issue of labour time, and the possibility of subsistence production to complement the

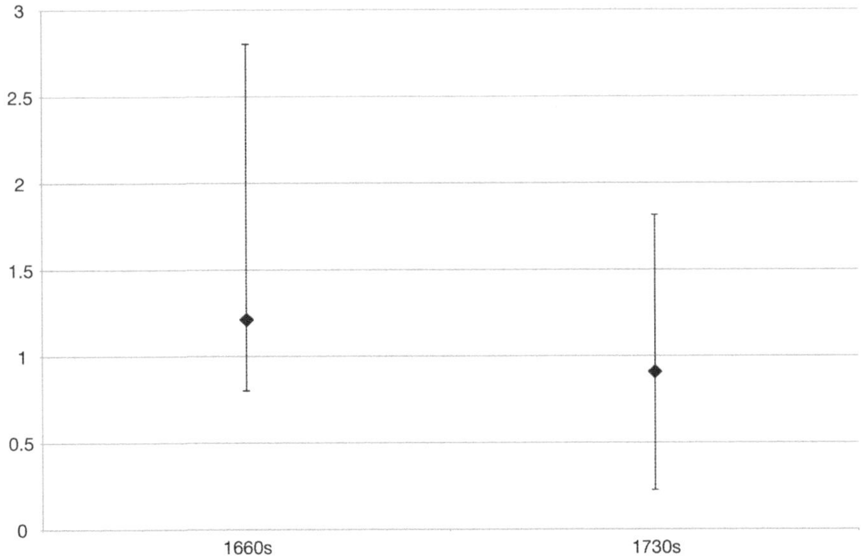


*Graph 8.2* Subsistence ratios for African canoemen on the Gold Coast, 1660s and 1730s

Note: Kea's data refers to 1659 for wages, and the 1650s and 1660s for prices. Data on prices are lacking from this period for a couple of goods; in these cases, I have added the same percentage to the total cost of the consumer basket as these goods were worth in the early eighteenth century (=20%). The wage ratio shown in the graph for the 1660s is what Kea claims 'most' canoemen working for the Dutch West India Company received at this time, whereas it shows the median wage paid to the sample of canoemen working for the British Royal African Company in the 1730s. The error bars show the wage span of the wages paid to the canoemen in each respective period.

Source: data for 1660s based on Kea, *Settlements, Trade, and Polities*, pp. 308–10. Data for 1730s based on GCPLD.

wage payments, below. Since the sample of canoemen is quite large, particularly from the 1730s onwards, it is also meaningful to study this sample of labourers in somewhat greater detail. Graph 8.2 details the wages paid to the canoemen at two benchmark periods, the 1660s and 1730s, respectively, including data on the maximum, median and minimum subsistence ratios.

According to the estimates from the real wage data presented in Graph 8.2, the median real wage, as measured by the subsistence ratio, decreased by 25 per cent between the two benchmark periods in this graph. The highest paid canoemen faced a more drastic drop in real wages, by 35 per cent. The most drastic drop was however for the lowest paid canoemen: the lowest wages paid to the canoemen dropped more than 70 per cent between the 1660s and the 1730s. The estimates must be interpreted with some caution, since the data is far from perfect. The figures do however remain practically the same even if the method of calculating the subsistence basket is changed (see below in Graph 8.3).[35] In total, the evidence suggests that the living standards for the canoemen deteriorated quite substantially during this period.

There is no reason to believe that the demand for canoemen was reduced during the period in question. On the contrary; with a growing external trade in slaves, the demand for canoemen who could transport slaves from the shore to the ships, and goods from the ships to the shore, ought if anything to have increased. Unfortunately, there is no evidence in the accounts of the RAC on wages paid to free canoemen during the early years of the eighteenth century. It is therefore not possible to determine whether the canoemen experienced a similar development as the craftsmen (i.e. rising real wages between the data from the 1660s and the 1700s, followed by a decline in the ensuing decades), or whether the wages to the canoemen essentially remained stagnant during this period of missing data. It is therefore not possible to determine exactly when wages to the canoemen started to decline; if this happened only from the 1730s onwards or if the decline started several decades earlier.

Regardless of exactly when the real wages peaked for people of a specific occupation, it seems plausible to assume that the deteriorating living standards for various labourers on the Gold Coast (here exemplified by canoemen and carpenters) at least partly was related to the twin processes of a growing external slave trade from and increasing levels of violence on the Gold Coast. As has been shown earlier in this chapter, European observers such as Willem Bosman gave witness to how many people sought refuge in coastal towns when fleeing from conflicts and/or slave raids. This ought to have had an impact upon the urban labour markets, perhaps particularly for more unskilled groups of labour such as canoemen, as the refugees would have increased the supply of labour available on the local market. These factors would then have contributed to a downward pressure on the wage levels, as the free workers might have had to accept a lower reservation wage in order to find a job where they could at least earn some income to sustain themselves. The development was possibly also related to the growth of the institution of castle slavery, discussed in Chapter 5. With a growing number of castle slaves labouring at the castle, the competitive situation for free labourers would have put a downward pressure on the wages paid to them, possibly contributing to explaining their declining real wages. This would not have an effect upon the market for unskilled labour alone. As was noted in Chapter 5, the RAC at this time seem to have put in place a system of training castle slaves to undertake ever more skilled tasks (see Chapter 5). This would have increased supply of skilled craftsmen, and increased competitive pressures on the market for skilled labour, too. Conflicts, and the resulting waves of refugees from the countryside, finally, could also – as was shown in Chapter 6 – have an impact upon the prices of many staple goods, thus driving up the cost of living (and consequently driving down the real wages) of the waged workers, unless they were able to achieve some form of compensation for more dear times.

## West African living standards in a global comparison

Having estimated how the living standards on the Gold Coast changed over time, we can now turn to the issue of comparing the living standards on the Gold Coast with living standards elsewhere in the world. This is shown in Graph 8.3. The graph shows the subsistence ratios of the Gold Coast canoemen in comparison with the same ratio for unskilled labourers at various other places around the world. It is assumed here that being a canoeman on the Gold Coast was an occupation requiring limited skills in general. The canoes used on the Gold Coast could be very large, up to several dozen men in the same canoe.[36] While it might be a risky business to try to cross the bar and the surf along the African coast, it most probably did not require very high skills from every individual canoeman, but primarily from the one steering the canoe. This would explain how some people could be blind but still be employed as a canoeman (see Chapter 5): working in a large team, what was required of most of the canoemen was probably bodily strength. Treating the canoemen as unskilled labour also fits in with how the occupation is classified in the Historical International Social Class Scheme: as largely unskilled.[37]

The graph shows estimates of the living standards for two periods of time – the end of the seventeenth and the beginning of the eighteenth centuries. There are

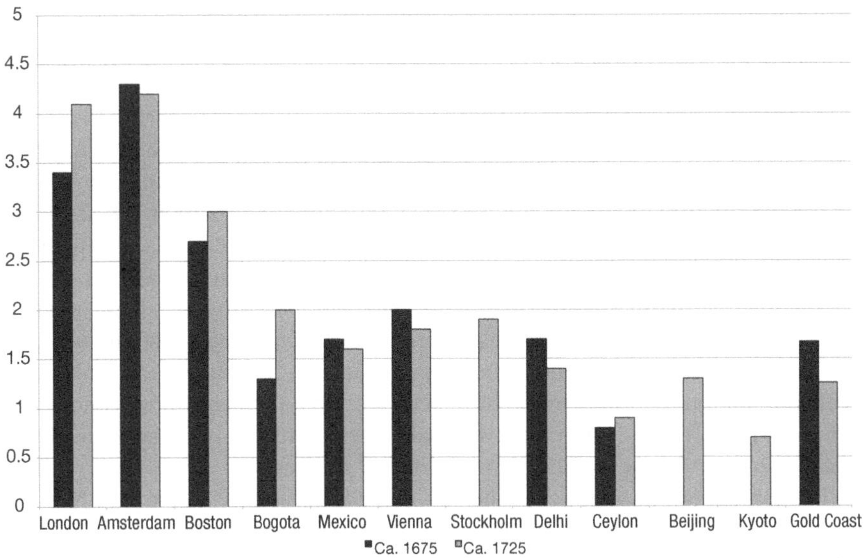


*Graph 8.3* Subsistence ratios for unskilled labour around the world, *c.* 1675 and 1725

Note: the subsistence ratios for the Gold Coast are in this graph calculated using the unrevised assumptions underlying many of the older subsistence ratio calculations (based on an assumption of a smaller family size, and requiring fewer calories per person per day), in order to enable a comparison with previous research. The figures for the subsistence ratios of the Gold Coast labourers are therefore higher than those estimated in Graphs 8.1–8.2. The data for the Gold Coast is from the 1660s and 1730s (see Graph 8.2), respectively, but here considered relative to data from 1675 and 1725 reported by Robert Allen. Data for Kyoto is similarly from the 1730s.

Source: data for London, Amsterdam, Vienna, Delhi and Beijing based on Allen, *The British Industrial Revolution*, fig. 2.3; Boston and Bogota from Allen et al., 'The Colonial Origins', fig. 5. Data on Ceylon and Kyoto based on de Zwart, 'Population, Labour', fig. 2. Data on Cape Coast based on GCPLD and GCPPD.

without a doubt a number of problems associated with comparing subsistence ratios internationally, as discussed in Chapter 3. The comparison ought however at least to be able to provide us with a rough idea of the comparative level of the West African living standards around this time. As can be seen in the graph, the living standards on the Gold Coast were undoubtedly far below that of north-western Europe, here represented by the subsistence ratios of labourers in London and Amsterdam. This is in no way surprising, since the previous research in the field generally has shown that north-western Europe at this time experienced very high living standards for the working population, seen in a global perspective.[38] What is more interesting is that the living standards on the Gold Coast were not very much lower than those found in some other parts of Europe, and even higher than those found in many parts of Asia. Again, the evidence from the 1660s must be interpreted with some caution, as mentioned above. The evidence does however clearly show that the Gold Coast at least cannot be said to have been outstandingly poor at all times.

## Labour time

In order for a comparison of the material living standards based on real wages around the world to be a measure of actual material welfare, it is also necessary to discuss the amount of labour time required to earn a particular real wage. In much of the previous research estimating welfare ratios, the welfare ratio has been calculated based on the daily wage of a day labourer, in combination with an assumption that the people work 250 days per year (see Chapter 3). The wage data from the Company on the Gold Coast is instead reported for a full month of work. As was noted in Chapter 5, there is no information in the sources on how much time the particular workers who were employed by the RAC actually worked for their monthly wages, except for the fact that wages were reduced if a person was absent for a part of the month. We can, for that reason, only work with assumptions that they might have been working quite customary amounts of time – but how much labour time was customary on the Gold Coast at this time? Some evidence can be found in the qualitative sources.

The labourers most probably did not work every single day of the year. In Europe, Sundays and Mondays were customarily respected as days of rest.[39] Similar practices, on different week-days, were seemingly respected in West Africa. Nicolas Villault argued in the 1660s that 'they observe a Sabbath (which is our *Tuesday*) very strictly: Every man rests that day from his labour'.[40] Around the same time the German Wilhelm Johann Müller expanded on this theme:

> Instead of Sunday, Tuesday is celebrated throughout the country. It is called *ohinne da*, the king's day, by them. The fishermen living on the coast hold this day so sacred that they believe a great disaster would befall them if they went to sea to fish with hooks on that day. [. . .] The Cabo Corso Blacks celebrate not only Tuesday but also Sunday, to the extent that no farmer may do any work in the field. They keep this rule so zealously that they refuse to

> permit even foreign slaves who live at Cabo Corso and below Friedrichs-Berg to do any work in the field.[41]

Several accounts also tell of special festivities where people also ceased working for one or several days. The evidence does therefore not provide any clear-cut evidence of how much people normally worked. If Müller's account is to be trusted, however, the labourers at Cape Coast Castle only worked five-day working weeks on average, thus roughly equivalent to the 250 days per year assumed in many other estimates of welfare ratios, and then not even counting any days of special festivities.

Another issue is the number of hours of work per day. The accounts of the RAC and successors do not seem to record any direct information of this from the Gold Coast. Joseph Adjaye has argued that traditionally, the Akan of the Gold Coast had no conception of dividing a day into distinct shorter spans of time (such as hours or minutes), but only 'general periods of time within the course of the day', suggesting that agreeing on working an exact amount of time for an employer might have been quite alien to the Akan workers at first.[42] The labour time that could be extracted from the labourers was however of the utmost importance to the Company, even if it might not have been so for the labourers (if Adjaye's claim is correct). As was shown in Chapter 5 the correspondence suggests that the free African workers employed on the Gold Coast normally worked around 7 hours per day. In Europe, the normal working day seems to have been considerably longer: Hans-Joachim Voth has shown that the normal working day in eighteenth century England amounted to around 12 to 13 hours per day.[43]

If the African employees of the European Company on the Gold Coast were expected to work some 7 hours per day for the wages that the European Company paid them, this left quite some time of daylight left every day (given that the sun in this part of the world is up around 12 hours per day throughout the year). The exhausting climate might certainly have prohibited many people from working very much more every day. If used as leisure time, this would, naturally, be another important aspect of their subjective living standards, in combination with the real wages they earned. Some people might however have been industrious enough to want to earn a higher income aside from the income they might earn from working for the Company, for example, through subsistence production of foodstuffs (reducing the cost of the subsistence basket), or through some other economic activity that might provide an income. Working for the Company might, for example, have been possible to combine with fishing. Many fishermen would, according to Pieter de Marees, sell part of their catch on the local markets.[44] Fishing was also undertaken on the Gold Coast primarily in the mornings, because of prevailing wind patterns.[45] If many of the people employed by the Company combined this waged employment with other economic activities on the side, the relative level of the living standards on the Gold Coast shown in the graphs above would be underestimated when compared to living standards elsewhere in the world.

The difference between the hours worked in Europe (12 to 13 hours per day), and the hours presumably worked by the African labourers employed by the

European Company (7 hours per day), might thus have amounted to five or six whole hours per day. We can unfortunately only assume what the labourers might have earned during that time, if they indeed chose to work during those hours, for example, as traders, hunters, farmers, fishermen or in some other trade. An upper-bound assumption is that the workers did work with some other economic activity those hours, and that they then could earn approximately the same net income as they could when working for the Company. Under such an assumption, it would be necessary to revise the estimated subsistence ratio upwards by some seventy to ninety per cent. The resulting upper bound for the Gold Coast subsistence ratio would then amount to approximately 2.6 around the year 1660 and 2.0 around the year 1730 (using the same unrevised method of calculating the ratio as in Graph 8.3). This would mean that the real wages of the Gold Coast canoemen, measured per unit of time actually worked, might have been on a par with or even higher than those of many North or Central European labourers.

## Free labourers in a slave society

One aspect of the subsistence ratios of the Gold Coast labourers is striking: the living standards on the Gold Coast (unadjusted for possible differences in labour time) were seemingly on a par primarily with parts of the world with a much higher population density, such as Asia. A high population density could be expected to put a downward pressure on wages, for example if population densities reached such a level as to force many people to farm increasingly marginal lands of low productivity, or was high enough to completely prohibit access to land for large groups of people. This could, as was argued above, also contribute to a downward pressure on urban wages, through urban–rural mobility. One might therefore wonder why the working class on the relatively sparsely populated Gold Coast was able to achieve *only* living standards on a par with those of substantially more densely populated Asia?

It seems plausible that this is at least partly explainable by the Nieboer–Domar hypothesis, discussed in Chapter 1. According to the hypothesis, a high population density (or ‘closed resources’, as some would have it) might drive down the reservation wage of the population, since alternative means of earning one’s subsistence are few, leading to a competitive pressure on what employed opportunities there are. Vice versa, the general reservation wage might be high if population density is low (or access to resources was ‘open’), since competition for scarce resources such as land then is so much lower. Landowners might in the latter case be tempted to try to coerce people into working for them, in order to reduce labour costs, instead of paying the high reservation wage necessary to get labourers to work voluntarily.

The Nieboer–Domar hypothesis, in its most basic form, talks about coercive labour practices as if they apply equally to all labourers in a given society: A land-rich society would be a slave society, whereas a land-scarce society would not. This is not always the case. Slavery and other labour practices could and did in some cases co-exist within the same society. This was certainly true in many early modern American societies, but it was also true for the pre-colonial Gold Coast. The existence of slavery could in such a case have repercussions on the free labour force: putting a pressure on the wages of the free labourers, since they would have had to compete for any positions not just with each other, but also with slaves. How large these repercussions were depended upon the context that the coercive labour institutions operated in. In a setting of completely 'open' resources and low costs of mobility, the existence of slavery within a society might have had very limited impact upon those people who managed to avoid enslavement, since any propertyless person then could move on quite easily to settle somewhere else, and work the land themselves. In reality, truly 'open' resources must have been a quite rare phenomenon once societies became more populated and people started to settle on the land.

As was described earlier in this chapter, resources in rural Gold Coast were probably not completely 'open', but the kings required land rent and work days in exchange for the right to cultivate land. The existence of slavery could then have had quite important negative repercussions for the living standards of the non-slave population on the Gold Coast. The impact that this competitive pressure had was most certainly not homogeneous for all types of labourers. It seems plausible that the competitive pressure was felt most severely for occupations requiring quite unskilled labourers. This could contribute to explaining why the real wages for the unskilled labourers on the Gold Coast were comparatively low, and approached those in much more densely populated parts of the world: with a limited number of employment positions available in urban areas, and limits to commoners' ability to get access to land or other resources, unskilled labourers such as many of the canoemen might have had a weak bargaining position, since they could be (and no doubt often were) replaced by slaves if they required too high a wage. The wages of the free labourers could therefore approach subsistence costs, even if population density in the region was very low. Skilled craftsmen, as the qualitative evidence presented earlier suggests (see Chapter 4), on the other hand, might have been much more scarce, and also less substitutable by slaves. This could then explain why so many of the craftsmen initially were earning much higher wages than the unskilled slaves. Once the Company systematically started to train some slaves in craftsmanship, however, the need to hire craftsmen might also have dropped, thereby contributing to the fall in subsistence ratios for these labourers as shown in Graph 8.1.

## Conclusion

As was mentioned at the outset of this chapter, there is a widespread idea that Africa historically was very poor. This does not necessarily seem to have applied to the pre-colonial Gold Coast, if measured by the subsistence ratio, as has been done in the present chapter. The free labourers on the Gold Coast on the contrary seem to have been considerably better off than received wisdom would suggest.

The wages paid to the African labourers, such as the canoemen, working for the English RAC on the Gold Coast were certainly lower in nominal terms than the wages paid to the day labourers in most parts of Europe at the time, but the African workers do on the other hand seem to have worked considerably shorter hours per day in order to earn that wage. If we include the hours worked into the equation, the real wages per hours worked for the Africans on the Gold Coast thus seem to approach those paid in many parts of Europe at the time, and considerably higher than those paid in many parts of Asia.

The evidence from travel accounts and other sources indicate that labour mobility on the Gold Coast was quite high: there seem to have been many flows of migrants, both to and from the Gold Coast. These flows included people who moved for economic reasons, such as getting a waged employment in a European company on the coast, and those who moved involuntarily, such as refugees from conflicts and wars, as well as the forced migration of slaves. The wages paid to those in the European enclaves might thus give a crude indication of the general living standards of the common population in the region beyond the European enclaves that the data originate from.

It might be asked why the African workers did not demand even higher wages than what was estimated in this chapter. There was, after all, most probably a quite low population density in the region. This implies that labour would have been scarce relative to other factors of production, such as land, and which, with all else being equal, ought to have enabled a high reservation wage. One aspect of this is certainly the productivity of agricultural land, which in the previous literature often has been argued to have been quite low in many parts of West Africa, for various reasons (see Chapter 2). Forms of land tenure might also have limited the real availability of land for the common population: What little evidence there is in the European travel accounts from the Gold Coast suggests that ownership over the land enabled the local rulers to expropriate part of the agricultural surplus from the farmers. This would have reduced the living standards for the rural working class, possibly making waged work in the coastal towns more appealing, even if the nominal wages were not always that high. The widespread – and most probably growing – existence of domestic slavery on the Gold Coast would finally also contribute to keeping the reservation wage down: if free labourers were to request too high wages, it could be cheaper for a potential employer to instead purchase a slave on the local market, and coerce the slave to undertake the work required.

The living standards might, furthermore, have changed over time. The sources are far from ideal, but what data there is suggests that living standards for the urban working class might perhaps have deteriorated, especially during the early decades of the eighteenth century. It is not possible in a case study such as this to establish any causality between the slave trade (or the increasing levels of violence that most scholars argue were associated with it) and the possibly deteriorating living standards. They do however coincide well in time to fit in with such an interpretation of the development.

## Notes

1 Kea, *Settlements, Trade, and Polities*, p. 308.
2 De Marees, *Description and Historical Account*, p. 177.
3 Villault, *A Relation of the Coasts*, p. 162.
4 Villault, *A Relation of the Coasts*, pp. 220–1.
5 Meredith, *An Account of*, p. 212.
6 Winterbottom, *An Account of*, p. 9. See also Hutton, *A Voyage to Africa*, p. 34; Leonard, *Records of a Voyage*, p. 55.
7 Robertson, G.A., *Notes on Africa: Particularly those Parts which are Situated between Cape Verde and the River Congo* (London, 1819), p. 38.
8 Brooks, 'A View of Sierra Leone', p. 28.
9 Leonard, *Records of a Voyage*, p. 55.
10 Norris, R., *Memoirs of the Reign of Bossa Ahádee, King of Dahomy, an Inland Country of Guiney* (London, 1789) at Gallica [accessed 1 February 2013], p. 62. See also Smith, 'The Canoe', p. 517.
11 McLeod, J., *A Voyage to Africa* (London: John Murray, 1820) at Google Books [accessed 24 March 2014], pp. 7–8.
12 Dickson, *A Historical Geography*, p. 67.
13 Bosman quoted in Feinberg, 'Africans and Europeans', p. 13.
14 Quoted in Hagan, G.P., *Divided We Stand – A Study of Social Change among the Effutu of Coastal Ghana* (Trondheim: Norwegian University of Science and Technology, African Series no. 2, 2000), p. 25.
15 Barbot, *Barbot on Guinea*, pp. 518–19.
16 Bosman, *A New and Accurate*, p. 15.
17 Snelgrave, W., *A New Account of Some Parts of Guinea* (London, 1734) at MOMW [accessed 13 February 2012], pp. 112–13.
18 De Marees, *Description and Historical Account*, pp. 110–11.
19 Villault, *A Relation of the Coasts*, p. 262.
20 De Marees, *Description and Historical Account*, p. 112. See Villault, *A Relation of the Coasts*, p. 263 for a very similar description.
21 De Marees, *Description and Historical Account*, p. 112.
22 Tilleman, E., *A Short and Simple Account of the Country Guinea and its Nature [En Kort og Enfoldig Beretning om det Landskab Guinea og dets Beskaffenhed]*, translated and edited by S.A. Winsnes (Madison: University of Wisconsin, African Studies Program, 1994 [1697]), p. 29.
23 Wilks, *Forests of Gold*, p. 60.
24 De Marees, *Description and Historical Account*, p. 58.
25 Villault, *A Relation of the Coasts*, p. 221.
26 De Marees, *Description and Historical Account*, p. 58.
27 De Marees, *Description and Historical Account*, p. 190. See also Villault, *A Relation of the Coasts*, p. 266;
28 Kea, *Settlements, Trade, and Polities*, pp. 46–7, 312.
29 Bosman, *A New and Accurate*, pp. 112–14.
30 Bosman, *A New and Accurate*, pp. 112, 115.
31 Rask, *A Brief and Truthful Description*, p. 110.
32 Bosman, *A New and Accurate*, pp. 408–9.
33 Cruickshank, *Eighteen Years*, p. 18.
34 Evans and Richardson, 'Hunting for Rents'.
35 The calculations are however slightly sensitive to the assumption of how large the average corn- or *millie*-stalk was at the time, since this is how the prices were accounted for in the 1660s, according to Ray Kea, whereas the prices from the Royal African Company (reported in Chapter 6) primarily were accounted for by a chest of corn.

Smaller *millie*-stalks would bias the results when comparing the prices between the two periods, since it would mean that it would have been more expensive to purchase the equivalent of a whole chest of corn in the 1660s (a conversion necessary in order to compare the prices to the 1730s prices from the Royal African Company). As was noted in Chapter 6, the literature on traditional African crops claims that an average sorghum-stalk weighed around 100 grams. The estimates in the graph are based on an assumption that the stalks on average were of this size. Assuming a smaller size of the average stalk would reduce the difference between the estimated benchmark subsistence ratios. If the stalks were as small as 50 grams each on average, the mean subsistence ratios for the canoemen would be approximately the same in the 1660s as in the 1730s.

36 Barbot, *Barbot on Guinea*, p. 529.

37 Leeuwen and Maas, *HISCLASS*: Category 98190, Barge crews and other boatmen.

38 Allen, *The British Industrial Revolution*.

39 Voth, H.-J., *Time and Work in England 1750–1830* (Oxford: Clarendon Press, 2000), pp. 85–93.

40 Villault, *A Relation of the Coasts*, pp. 166–7.

41 Jones, *German Sources*, p. 167.

42 Adjaye, J., 'Time, Identity, and Historical Consciousness in Akan', in J. Adjaye (ed.), *Time in the Black Experience* (Westport: Greenwood, 1994) pp. 55–78, quote on p. 58.

43 Voth, *Time and Work*, pp. 72–6.

44 De Marees, *Description and Historical Account*, p. 27.

45 De Marees, *Description and Historical Account*, pp. 80, 118; Barbot, *Barbot on Guinea*, p. 519.

# 9 Concluding discussion

The aim of this book has been to study living standards on the pre-colonial Gold Coast, as a historical case study of living standards in West Africa in the time before formal colonization of the continent. The book has been inspired, on the one hand, by the school of dependency theory, of those such as Walter Rodney, and, on the other hand, by much new research on African economic history grounded in the neo-institutionalist theory. What unites these different strands of literature is that they emphasize the important interplay between domestic factors in the region, and the external transatlantic slave trade, for disrupting economic development in – or, in the terminology of dependency theory, the underdevelopment of – Africa. To study this issue requires an analysis of the actual levels of development in Africa prior to when the slave trade started as well as a historical analysis of change in reaction to the dynamics of the late seventeenth and early eighteenth century. One aspect of this economic development is to study the historical living standards of the common population. The Gold Coast is particularly suitable for such a study, given the fact that the transatlantic slave trade started comparatively late in this particular part of Africa – not until the late seventeenth century were there any substantial amounts of slaves exported from the region. There are thus comparatively many historical sources that can provide quite unique sorts of evidence of the level of development both prior to, and following, the start of the transatlantic slave trade. The Gold Coast can therefore be seen as a revelatory case study.

## The factor market for labour

One important theoretical debate in the previous literature has been concerned with the development of a factor market for labour, in particular to what extent African societies were slave societies and to what extent there existed any free labour that could be employed, should a potential employer so wish. As was noted in the introductory discussion, Gareth Austin has argued that free labour probably was vanishingly rare outside a few European enclaves. One key problem of this hypothesis is the great challenge of finding sources that actually could provide any evidence on the topic, given the general scarcity of sources for pre-colonial African history outside the European enclaves. In his own research on Asante,

Austin has not been able to find proof of any free labour prior to the late nineteenth century. Akosua Perbi has similarly found that free labour was rare or non-existent on Gold Coast, too, around the same time, since slaves by then were purchased to perform all the tasks that waged labourers would do in many other places.

This dependence on slavery was, at least on the Gold Coast, in itself the outcome of a historical process, and not the result of a lack of development of a factor market for free labour in this region. As has been shown in this book, free, hired labourers do not seem to have been rare on the Gold Coast from the late seventeenth to the early nineteenth centuries. Certainly, the case studied could be argued to have been a European enclave, and might thus say little about realities elsewhere in Africa, outside the enclave, if Austin is correct. The actual employees of the English Company studied in detail in this book were most certainly a part of such an enclave. On the other hand, the qualitative evidence, for example, from the correspondence of the Company agents suggests that it often was quite easy for the Company to hire people to work for wages in many of the coastal towns along the Gold Coast in the late seventeenth and early eighteenth centuries. The evidence also indicates that the European companies were not the only ones to employ free labourers, but sometimes had to compete with African agents wanting to employ them, for example, as porters.

African workers – both on the Gold Coast in particular, and in many other parts of Africa – were certainly often accused by Europeans of being lazy and indolent, and also described by a range of other racist stereotypes. One possible interpretation of this particular stereotype is that of a generally rather high reservation wage, so that many people refrained from working for the Europeans unless the pay offered met their requirements. Pejorative moralizing about the supposed laziness of the local population might thus have been the European response when realizing that they could not maximize the extraction of surplus value from the free labour force.

The existence of a market for free labour was, however, dependent upon the socio-economic context. Along with the growth of the external slave trade from the Gold Coast, domestic slavery has been argued to have expanded. The increased violence and conflicts that followed in the wake of the growth of the slave trade also induced increased migration to urban areas. Evidence presented in this book shows that the real wages seem to have decreased for unskilled labourers around the time that the slave trade from the region first expanded. It seems reasonable to conclude that these phenomena were related, so that the increase in violence in the region, the growth of domestic slavery and the influx of refugees into urban areas along the coast all put a downward pressure upon the wages paid to the free labourers on the Gold Coast. Over time, it might thus have become much less attractive to work for wages, if one had the opportunity to choose.

This suggests that the development of a factor market for labour in West Africa was far from a straightforward and unidirectional process, from a stage based on slave labour to a stage based on wage labour. On the contrary, the evidence suggests that the development of a factor market for labour was characterized by a rather complex interplay of different forces. It thus makes sense to think of the process as similar to what Tom Brass has described as a process of 'deproletarianization'. The term is here used hesitantly for the simple reason that it is uncertain whether the free labourers studied in this book really were completely proletarianized: while Ray Kea has argued that many of the urban workers indeed might have been propertyless labourers, some of them – not least, for example, many of the canoemen – might have at least co-owned some means of production. The waged employment might also have been combined with other economic activities, such as fishing or agriculture. The most essential aspect of the 'deproletarianization' thesis, from the perspective of this book is, however, that the development of a factor market for labour never was unidirectional. Free labour, whether completely proletarianized or not, could be replaced by slaves, if this turned out to be profitable and feasible for the employer/slaveholder. If free labour was rare on the Gold Coast by the late nineteenth century, as Akosua Perbi has argued, it might thus have been the outcome of a process where free labour became less attractive over time, both for the employers and the workers: for the employers, since the alternative of exploiting slaves indeed might have become more feasible and profitable with the growth of domestic slavery; and for the workers, since alternative economic activities, not the least various forms of subsistence production or self-employment, might have been more attractive, once the competition from slave labour started to push down the real wages paid to hired labourers.

## Living standards on the Gold Coast

Another important debate that this book has tried to engage with is the issue of living standards in pre-colonial Africa. Some authors – ranging from Paul Lovejoy to Daron Acemoglu and James Robinson – have argued that pre-colonial Africa in general was very poor, whereas others – for example John Thornton – on the contrary have argued that this depiction of Africa largely has been misleading. In this book, I have attempted to triangulate various pieces of evidence from several different sources. Taken together, the evidence suggests, on the one hand, that the living standards, at least on the Gold Coast, might indeed have been quite high in an international comparison: The subsistence ratio for unskilled labourers was higher than, or on a par with, those found in some other parts of the world around the same time, such as Asia or Latin America. If one takes into account the fact that the workers at the European enclaves on the Gold Coast probably worked comparatively fewer hours per day in order to earn the wages paid to them, the real wages paid to the Gold Coast workers (per hour worked) were perhaps even on a par with those in many parts of eastern, central or northern Europe.

At the same time, the qualitative evidence suggests that many commoners' households held relatively few material possessions. This evidence must certainly be interpreted with caution because of the potential for ethnicity-, gender- and class-biased observations. Nonetheless, the evidence suggests that most commoners consumed quite limited amounts at least of durable, imported goods. Certainly, the subsistence ratios estimated quantitatively in this study do not imply a very large economic surplus for the labourers, so the real wages earned from working for the company would not necessarily allow for much consumption above subsistence needs. It is at the same time important to keep in mind that the estimated ratios were based on a male breadwinner model family, and thus underestimate the real subsistence ratios of families, since it is certain that women made enormously important contributions to the household economy throughout West Africa – not least through being in charge of much of the subsistence agriculture. Even if one were to include female economic activity, however, commoner households would not have been able to afford much luxury consumption. The qualitative evidence suggests that, prior to the nineteenth century, one of a few imported consumer goods to reach a socially broader market of consumers was cheap, European textiles. More durable consumer goods would perhaps not spread into broader groups of commoners until late eighteenth or early nineteenth century. The qualitative evidence presented does also suggest that some of the economic surplus was turned to various uses other than the consumption of material goods, for example, to support a large family, including various dependents.

## The impact of the slave trade

Finally, the book has also attempted to discuss the issue of the impact of the slave trade. This is in no way intended to deny African 'agency', or that many domestic factors contributed to the socio-economic development in the region. There was undoubtedly a complex interplay between internal and external determining factors to the slave trade. Needless to say the expansion of the transatlantic slave trade was devastating for those poor souls who became enslaved, for those who died while resisting slavery and for the families of the dead or enslaved. Much previous research has also been devoted to the horrors of the slave trade.

The contribution of this book has been to study what impact the slave trade had for the working classes on the Gold Coast. The evidence from the RAC suggests that there indeed was a particular 'guns-for-slaves' pattern to the trade: when the Company had arms to sell, these were primarily demanded as payment for slaves, rather than for other commodities (such as for gold, ivory, provisions or other African exports). The evidence presented in this book also shows that the twin processes of increasing violence and external slave trade seem to have had quite large repercussions for many people on the Gold Coast, aside from the individuals enslaved, but that the impact was highly stratified socially. On the one end of the spectrum were the small elites that made fortunes from enslaving and selling other human beings into slavery. Some of these elites have been the focus of previous research. In this book, evidence has been shown that some of the key local collaborators in the trade, such as the interpreters working for the European companies, certainly could earn very high incomes from their participation in the slave trade, enabling them to lead a rather comfortable life. The interpreters studied here were, furthermore, most probably not among the people most well off from the trade, but merchant princes and local rulers probably earned considerably higher income.

At the other end of the spectrum were the unskilled labourers on the Gold Coast. As was noted above, the real wages paid to this group of labourers declined quite substantially as the slave trade expanded. This, it was argued, was probably the result of a downward pressure on their wages arising from an influx of refugees as a consequence of increasing levels of violence throughout the region, from a rising cost of living during years of intense warfare associated with the slave trade, as well as from growing competitive pressure from domestic slaves. The latter process was certainly something that the European companies seem to have made use of themselves: the population of so-called castle slaves grew substantially from the early eighteenth century.

The Companies also attempted to train the castle slaves, so that they could replace even skilled labourers. This in turn had repercussions even for a middle layer of free labourers: the skilled craftsmen. Wages paid to the skilled craftsmen on the Gold Coast were quite low by the middle of the seventeenth century, prior to the growth of the transatlantic slave trade. By the early eighteenth century, their real wages had increased substantially. The interpretation suggested in this book is that the growth of the external slave trade initially drove up demand for skilled labourers who could be employed to help with the construction of buildings, as well as other goods necessary to conduct the trade. The increasing demand was thus reflected in the higher wages found in the empirical evidence. When the Company started to reduce their dependence on freely employed skilled labourers, by training castle slaves to replace them, this would reduce the demand for free, skilled labourers. From the early eighteenth century, the wages paid to free craftsmen also started to deteriorate substantially, a process that continued for as long as data was available in the primary sources from the eighteenth century.

Finally, some scholars, for example David Eltis, have argued that the slave trade – horrible as it was – at least had the effect of contributing to the development of a commercial agriculture in some parts of Africa, due to the demand from the slave-trading ships for provisions. The evidence presented in this book suggests that this demand must have been rather marginal relative to the estimated size of the local demand – both from the urban population, and from the total population in the region. While the demand for provisions to the slave ships thus might have driven up the demand in some very small enclaves close to the exporting ports, it cannot have had a very substantial impact upon the aggregate commercialization of the Gold Coast economy, let alone the economy of West Africa in general. This would also fit well with the result that a growing slave trade had no substantial impact upon the prices for staple crops on the Gold Coast.

## Lessons from the case of the Gold Coast

This book has been based on a case study of the Gold Coast in particular, occasionally putting the Gold Coast into a regional perspective. Some previous research has suggested that the economy of the Gold Coast might have been particularly advanced relative to that in many other parts of West Africa, for example by being more commercialized after having many centuries of contact with Europeans trading for gold. Other African societies – in various areas ranging from the savannahs to the rainforest – certainly experienced very different circumstances than the population on the Gold Coast did. We must, for that reason, not generalize about West African societies, let alone the whole of the African continent, from this case study alone.

Yet, the case study might reveal some important revelations, not least cautioning against too broad theoretical generalizations. First, it shows that the development of factor markets for labour probably experienced no unidirectional development from slavery to free labour, but that the process could be reversed. Whether a similar process might have occurred elsewhere in Africa, too, might be a topic for future careful empirical research. The results of this case study do, however, caution against generalizing about pre-colonial labour markets based on evidence from later periods. Second, they show quite clearly that some previous broad generalizations about African poverty must be qualified: the Gold Coast was an example where pre-colonial living standards might have been quite high, from the perspective of early modern economic development globally. The qualitative evidence provided from elsewhere along the West African coast is problematic to interpret, but at least does not seem to indicate that the Gold Coast was very unique. On the contrary, the evidence about, for example, the material wealth of the common population suggests that people on the Gold Coast might have had a material culture quite similar to that of many other African peoples along the West African coast. The study of historical living standards in Africa is so far not much more than in its infancy. Future research into other areas and time periods might shed further light on this aspect of the history of other parts of the African continent.

Third, the study also shows that the living standards might have deteriorated for large parts of the population on the Gold Coast over the time studied in this book. The Gold Coast was not always poor; it became poorer over the time period studied. This might partly have been the result of various internal dynamics on the Gold Coast, including a protracted period of warfare between various polities in the region. The transatlantic slave trade no doubt also played an important role in this process. The Gold Coast would not necessarily be assumed to be among the worst affected by the slave trade, but perhaps rather the opposite: the slave trade started quite late from this region in particular, and only a minor share of the slaves exported in total across the Atlantic were exported from this part of the coast. Many of the people exported from the ports along the Gold Coast might, furthermore, have originated in areas quite some distance away from the coast. Other areas including, not least, West Central Africa, were regions of considerably larger exports of slaves. One possible interpretation is therefore that if the slave trade contributed to deteriorating living standards even on the Gold Coast, the impact of the trade might have been even greater along many other parts of the African coast.

# References

## Primary sources

### *Accounts and correspondence of the European companies*

Justesen, O. (ed.), *Danish Sources for the History of Ghana 1657–1754* (Copenhagen: Royal Danish Academy of Sciences and Letters, 2005).

Law, R. (ed.), *Correspondence of the Royal African Company's Chief Merchants at Cabo Corso Castle with William's Fort, Whydah, and the Little Popo Factory, 1727–1728* (Madison: University of Wisconsin-Madison, African Studies Program, 1991).

Law, R. (ed.), *The English in West Africa 1681–1683. The Local Correspondence of the Royal African Company of England 1681–1699. Part 1* (Oxford: Oxford University Press, 1997).

Law, R. (ed.), *The English in West Africa 1685–1688. The Local Correspondence of the Royal African Company of England 1681–1699. Part 2* (Oxford: Oxford University Press, 2001).

Law, R. (ed.), *The English in West Africa 1691–1699. The Local Correspondence of the Royal African Company of England 1681–1699. Part 3* (Oxford: Oxford University Press, 2006).

National Archives, Kew, Surrey, Royal African Company, T70 (NA T70), volumes 376–486, 1007–15 and 1450–3.

From these accounts, two databases have been constructed (see Chapter 3):

Gold Coast Pre-Colonial Labour Database (GCPLD), database based on National Archives, Kew, Surrey, Royal African Company, T70 (NA T70), volumes 376–486, 1007–1015 and 1450–1453.

Gold Coast Pre-Colonial Price Database (GCPPD) , database based on National Archives, Kew, Surrey, Royal African Company, T70 (NA T70), volumes 376–486, 1007–1015 and 1450–1453.

### *Travel accounts*

Adams, J., *Remarks on the Country Extending from Cape Palmas to the River Congo* (London: Whittaker, 1823).

Adanson, M., *A Voyage to Senegal, the Isle of Goree, and the River Gambia* (London, 1759) at ECCO http://gdc.gale.com/products/eighteenth-century-collections-online/ [accessed 23 May 2012].

Afzelius, A., *Sierra Leone Journal*, ed. A.P. Kup (Uppsala: Uppsala University, 1967 [1795–1796]).
Alvares, M., *Ethiopia Minor and a Geographical Account of the Province of Sierra Leone* (Liverpool University, 1990 [c. 1615]), at WISC African Studies Collection, http://uwdc.library.wisc.edu/collections/AfricanStudies/Africana [accessed 13 June 2013].
Anonymous, *The Golden Coast or a Description of Guinney* (London, 1665) at EEBO http://eebo.chadwyck.com/home [accessed 1 February 2013].
Anonymous, *The Compleat Geographer* (London, 1723) at ECCO http://gdc.gale.com/products/eighteenth-century-collections-online/ [accessed 29 January 2013].
Atkins, J., *A Voyage to Guinea, Brazil & the West Indies* (London: Frank Cass, 1970 [1735]).
Barbot, J., *Barbot on Guinea*, ed. P.E.H. Hair, A. Jones and R. Law (London: Hakluyt Society, 1992 [1678–1712]).
Beaver, P., *African Memoranda: Relative to an Attempt to Establish a British Settlement on the Island of Bulama* (London, 1805) at MOMW http://gdc.gale.com/products/the-making-of-the-modern-world-the-goldsmiths-kress-library-of-economic-literature-1450–1850/ [accessed 6 June 2013].
Beecham, J., *Ashantee and the Gold Coast* (London: John Mason, 1970 [1841]).
Benezet, A., *A Short Account of the Part of Africa, Inhabited by the Negroes* (Philadelphia, 1762) at MOMW http://gdc.gale.com/products/the-making-of-the-modern-world-the-goldsmiths-kress-library-of-economic-literature-1450–1850/ [accessed 28 January 2013].
Bennett, N. and Brooks, G. (eds), *New England Merchants in Africa. A History through Documents 1802 to 1865* (Boston: Boston University Press, 1965).
Blome, R., *A Geographical Description* (London, 1670) at EEBO http://eebo.chadwyck.com/home [accessed 30 May 2013].
Bonné, C.H., *Søreiser paa Europas kyster og kysten af Guinea* (Thisted: Forfatternes forlag, 1833) at Det Kongelige Bibliotek http://www.kb.dk/e-mat/dod/112808017972.pdf [accessed 6 June 2013].
Bosman, W., *A New and Accurate Description of the Coast of Guinea,* 2nd edn (London, 1721) at MOMW http://gdc.gale.com/products/the-making-of-the-modern-world-the-goldsmiths-kress-library-of-economic-literature-1450–1850/ [accessed 13 February 2012].
Bowdich, T.E., *Mission from Cape Coast Castle to Ashantee* (London: Frank Cass, 1966 [1819]).
Brooks, G., 'A View of Sierra Leone ca. 1815', *Sierra Leone Studies*, 13 (1960), pp. 24–31.
Cadamosto, *The Voyages of Cadamosto* (London: Hakluyt Society, 1937).
Clarke, S., *A New Description of the World* (London, 1689) at EEBO http://eebo.chadwyck.com/home [accessed 27 April 2012].
Condorcet, *Réflexions sur l'esclavage des Nègres* (Neufchatel, 1781) at Classiques des Sciences Sociales, http://classiques.uqac.ca [accessed 30 January 2014].
Corry, J., *Observations upon the Windward Coast* (London, 1807) at MOMW http://gdc.gale.com/products/the-making-of-the-modern-world-the-goldsmiths-kress-library-of-economic-literature-1450–1850/ [accessed 6 June 2013].
Crow, H., *Memoirs of the Late Captain Hugh Crow of Liverpool* (London, 1830) at MOMW http://gdc.gale.com/products/the-making-of-the-modern-world-the-goldsmiths-kress-library-of-economic-literature-1450–1850/ [accessed 6 June 2013].
Cruickshank, B., *Eighteen Years on the Gold Coast of Africa* (London: Frank Cass, 1966 [1853]).
Curson, H., *A New Description of the World* (London, 1704) at EEBO http://eebo.chadwyck.com/home [accessed 29 January 2013].

Curtin, P. (ed.), *Africa Remembered. Narratives by West Africans from the Era of the Slave Trade* (Madison: University of Wisconsin Press, 1967).

da Mota, A.T. and Hair, P.E.H. (eds), *East of Mina: Afro-European Relations on the Gold Coast in the 1550s and 1560s. An Essay with Supporting Documents* (Madison: WISC, 1988).

da Mota, A.T. and Hair, P.E.H. (eds), *Jesuit Documents on the Guinea of Cape Verde and the Cape Verde Islands 1585–1617* (Madison: WISC African Studies Collection, 1989).

Dapper, O., *Olfert Dapper's Description of Benin,* ed. A. Jones (Madison: University of Wisconsin-Madison, 1998).

de Almada, A.Á., *Brief Treatise on the Rivers of Guinea* (Madison: WISC, 1984 [c. 1594]).

De La Croix, P., *Relation universelle de l'Afrique ancienne et moderne* (Lyon, 1688) at Gallica http://gallica.bnf.fr [accessed 30 January 2013].

de Marees, P., *Description and Historical Account of the Gold Kingdom of Guinea (1602)*, ed. A. van Dantzig and A. Jones (Oxford: Oxford University Press 1987 [1602]).

de Zurara, G.E., *The Chronicle of the Discovery and Conquest of Guinea*, vol. I (Cambridge: Cambridge University Press, 2010 [1453]).

Durand, J.P.L., *A voyage to Senegal* (London, 1806) at MOMW http://gdc.gale.com/products/the-making-of-the-modern-world-the-goldsmiths-kress-library-of-economic-literature-1450–1850/ [accessed 13 February 2012]

Falconbridge, A., *An Account of the Slave Trade on the Coast of Africa* (London, 1788) at MOMW http://gdc.gale.com/products/the-making-of-the-modern-world-the-goldsmiths-kress-library-of-economic-literature-1450–1850/ [accessed 13 February 2012].

Falconbridge, A.M., *Narrative of Two Voyages to the River Sierra Leone* (London, 1802) at MOMW http://gdc.gale.com/products/the-making-of-the-modern-world-the-goldsmiths-kress-library-of-economic-literature-1450–1850/ [accessed 13 February 2012].

Froger, F., *A Relation of a Voyage. . .* (London, 1698) at EEBO http://eebo.chadwyck.com/home [accessed 27 April 2012].

Hadding, J., *A Description of the Four Parts of the World* (unknown place of publication, 1760) at ECCO http://gdc.gale.com/products/eighteenth-century-collections-online/ [accessed 29 January 2013].

Hair, P.E.H., *Sierra Leone and the English in 1607* (Institute of African Studies, University of Sierra Leone, 1981).

Hair, P.E.H., *André de Faro's Missionary Journey to Sierra Leone in 1663–64* (Institute of African Studies, University of Sierra Leone, 1982).

Hawkins, J., *A History of a Voyage to the Coast of Africa* (Troy, 1797) at ECCO http://gdc.gale.com/products/eighteenth-century-collections-online/ [accessed 23 May 2012].

Hutton, W., *A Voyage to Africa: Including a Narrative of an Embassy to One of the Interior Kingdoms in the Year 1820* (London: Longman, Hurst, Rees, Orme and Brown, 1821).

Irvine, G. (ed.), *Huydecoper's Diary* (Legon: University of Accra, Department of History, 1962).

Isert, P.E., *Letters on West Africa and the Slave Trade*, translated and edited by S.A. Winsnes (Oxford: Oxford University Press, 1992 [1788]).

Jannequin, C., V*oyage de Libye au royaume de Senegal, le long du Niger* (Paris, 1643) at Gallica http://gallica.bnf.fr [accessed 30 January 2013].

Jobson, R., *The Discovery of River Gambra*, ed. R. Gamble and P.E.H. Hair (London: Hakluyt Society, 1999 [1623]).

Jones, A., *German Sources for West African History 1599–1669* (Wiesbaden: Franz Steiner Verlag, 1983).

Jones, A., *Brandenburg Sources for West African History* (Stuttgart: Franz Steiner Verlag, 1985).

LeBlanc, V., *The World Surveyed or the Famous Voyages & Travailes of Vincent LeBlanc* (London, 1660) at EEBO http://eebo.chadwyck.com/home [accessed 1 February 2013].

Lee, S., *Stories of Strange Lands; and Fragments from the Notes of a Traveller* (London, 1835) at Google Books https://books.google.se/books?id=Mw0GAAAAQAAJ&lpg=PR3&ots=JNzA-xisiJ&dq=lee%20stories%20of%20strange%20lands&hl=sv&pg=PR3#v=onepage&q=lee%20stories%20of%20strange%20lands&f=false [accessed 18 August 2014].

Le Maire, J.-J., *A Voyage of the Sieur Le Maire. . .* (London, 1696) at ECCO http://gdc.gale.com/products/eighteenth-century-collections-online/ [accessed 1 February 2013].

Leonard, P., *Records of a Voyage to the Western Coast of Africa* (Edinburgh, 1833) at MOMW http://gdc.gale.com/products/the-making-of-the-modern-world-the-goldsmiths-kress-library-of-economic-literature-1450–1850/ [accessed 13 February 2012].

Linnaeus, C., *Systema Naturae per Regna Tria Naturae* (Vindobonae, 1766) at Biodiversity Heritage Library Online http://www.biodiversitylibrary.org/item/137337 [accessed 19 June 2013].

Loyer, G., *Relation du voyage du royaume d'Issyny* (Paris: Seneuze & Morel, 1714).

Madox, R., *An Elizabethan in 1582. The Diary of Richard Madox, Fellow of All Souls* (London: Hakluyt Society, 1976 [1582]).

Matthews, J., *A Voyage to the River Sierra Leone* (London: B. White and Son, 1788) at ECCO http://gdc.gale.com/products/eighteenth-century-collections-online/ [accessed 23 May 2012].

McLeod, J., *A Voyage to Africa* (London: John Murray, 1820) at Google Books Internet Archive https://archive.org/details/avoyagetoafrica00mantgoog [accessed 24 March 2014].

Meredith, H., *An Account of the Gold Coast of Africa* (London, 1812) at MOMW http://gdc.gale.com/products/the-making-of-the-modern-world-the-goldsmiths-kress-library-of-economic-literature-1450–1850/ [accessed 13 February 2012].

Metcalfe, G.E., *Great Britain and Ghana. Documents of Ghana History 1807–1957* (Accra: University of Ghana, 1964).

Monrad, H.C., *A Description of the Guinea Coast and its Inhabitants. Two Views from Christiansborg Castle,* vol. II, translated by S.A. Winsnes (Accra: Sub-Saharan, 2008 [1822]).

Moore, F., *Travels into the Inland Parts of Africa* (London, 1738) at MOMW http://gdc.gale.com/products/the-making-of-the-modern-world-the-goldsmiths-kress-library-of-economic-literature-1450–1850/ [accessed 13 February 2012].

Norris, R., *Memoirs of the Reign of Bossa Ahádee, King of Dahomy, an Inland Country of Guiney. . .* (London, 1789) at Gallica http://gallica.bnf.fr [accessed 1 February 2013].

Ogilby, J., *Africa: Being an Accurate Description of the Regions . . .* (London, 1670) at EEBO http://eebo.chadwyck.com/home [accessed 1 February 2013].

Oldendorp, C., *Tillförlåtlig underrättelse om negrerne på Guineakusten* (Uppsala, 1784).

Padenheim, D.P., *Bref til en vän i Sverige, innehållande historisk och geographisk beskrifning öfver Colonien Sierra Leona i Afrika* (Stockholm: Kumblinska tryckeriet,, 1801).

Park, M., *Travels in the Interior Districts of Africa* (New York, 1800) at MOMW http://gdc.gale.com/products/the-making-of-the-modern-world-the-goldsmiths-kress-library-of-economic-literature-1450–1850/ [accessed 6 June 2013].

Pereira, D.P., *Esmeraldo de Situ Orbis*, translated by G. Kimble (London: Hakluyt Society, 1937 [1505–1508]).

Phérotée de La Croix, A., *Relation universelle de l'Afrique ancienne et moderne* (Lyon, 1688) at Gallica http://gallica.bnf.fr [accessed 6 June 2013].

Phillips, T., 'A Journal of a Voyage made in the Hannibal of London' in *A Collection of Voyages and Travels*, vol. VI (London, 1732) at ECCO http://gdc.gale.com/products/eighteenth-century-collections-online/ [accessed 3 June 2013].

Rask, J., *A Brief and Truthful Description of a Journey to and from Guinea. Two Views from Christiansborg Castle*, vol. I, translated by S.A. Winsnes (Accra: Sub-Saharan, 2008 [1754]).

Ritchie, C.I.A., 'Impressions of Senegal in the Seventeenth Century', *African Studies*, 26(2) (1967), pp. 59–93.

Robertson, G.A., *Notes on Africa: Particularly those Parts which are Situated between Cape Verde and the River Congo* (London: Sherwood, Neely and Jones, 1819).

Rømer, L.F., *A Reliable Account of the Coast of Guinea*, ed. S.A. Winsnes (Oxford: Oxford University Press, 2000 [1760]).

Saugnier, F., *Voyages to the Coast of Africa* (London, 1792) at MOMW http://gdc.gale.com/products/the-making-of-the-modern-world-the-goldsmiths-kress-library-of-economic-literature-1450–1850/ [accessed 28 January 2013].

Smith, W., *A New Voyage to Guinea* (London, 1744) at ECCO http://gdc.gale.com/products/eighteenth-century-collections-online/ [accessed 28 January 2013].

Snelgrave, W., *A New Account of Some Parts of Guinea* (London, 1734) at MOMW http://gdc.gale.com/products/the-making-of-the-modern-world-the-goldsmiths-kress-library-of-economic-literature-1450–1850/ [accessed 13 February 2012].

Spilsbury, F., *Account of a Voyage to the Western Coast of Africa* (London, 1807) at MOMW http://gdc.gale.com/products/the-making-of-the-modern-world-the-goldsmiths-kress-library-of-economic-literature-1450–1850/[accessed 13 February 2012].

Struys, J.J., *The Voiages and Travels of Jan Janszoon Struys* (London, 1684) at EEBO http://eebo.chadwyck.com/home [accessed 27 April 2012].

Tilleman, E., *A Short and Simple Account of the Country Guinea and its Nature [En Kort og Enfoldig Beretning om det Landskab Guinea og dets Beskaffenhed]*, translated and edited by S.A. Winsnes (Madison: University of Wisconsin, African Studies Program, 1994 [1697]).

Uring, N., *A History of the Voyages and Travels of Capt. Nathaniel Uring* (London, 1726) at ECCO http://gdc.gale.com/products/eighteenth-century-collections-online/ [accessed 1 February 2013].

Van den Broecke, P., *Pieter van den Broecke's Journal of Voyages to Cape Verde, Guinea and Angola (1605–1612)*, translated and edited by J.D. La Fleur (London: Hakluyt Society, 2000).

Villault, N., *A Relation of the Coasts of Africk called Guinee* (London, 1670) at MOMW http://gdc.gale.com/products/the-making-of-the-modern-world-the-goldsmiths-kress-library-of-economic-literature-1450–1850/ [accessed 13 February 2012].

Watt, J., *Journal of James Watt: Expedition to Timbo Capital of the Fula Empire in 1794*, ed. B. Mouser (Madison: University of Wisconsin-Madison, African Studies Program, 1994 [1794]).

Williamson, D., *A True Narrative of the Sufferings of David Williamson, Mariner* (London, 1772) at ECCO http://gdc.gale.com/products/eighteenth-century-collections-online/ [accessed 28 January 2013].

Winterbottom, T., *An Account of the Native Africans of Sierra Leone,* vol. I (London, 1803) at MOMW http://gdc.gale.com/products/the-making-of-the-modern-world-the-goldsmiths-kress-library-of-economic-literature-1450–1850/ [accessed 13 February 2012].

Wyatt, J., *The Life and Surprizing Adventures of James Wyatt* (London, 1755) at ECCO http://gdc.gale.com/products/eighteenth-century-collections-online/ [accessed 28 January 2013].

## Literature

Acemoglu, D. and Robinson, J., 'Why is Africa Poor?', *Economic History of Developing Regions,* 25(1) (2010), pp. 21–50.

Ade-Ajayi, J.F., 'Remembering the Slave Trade' in J.K. Anquandah (ed.), *The Transatlantic Slave Trade: Landmarks, Legacies, Expectations* (Accra: Sub-Saharan, 2007), pp. 365–70.

Adjaye, J., 'Time, Identity, and Historical Consciousness in Akan' in J. Adjaye (ed.), *Time in the Black Experience* (Westport: Greenwood, 1994), pp. 55–78.

Akinjogbin, I.A., 'Archibald Dalzel: Slave Trader and Historian of Dahomey', *Journal of African History,* 7(1) (1966), pp. 67–78.

Akyeampong, E., 'Alcoholism in Ghana – A Socio-cultural Exploration', *Culture, Medicine and Psychiatry,* 19(2) (1995), pp. 261–80.

Akyeampong, E., *Drink, Power, and Cultural Change: A Social History of Alcohol in Ghana, c. 1800 to Recent Times* (Oxford: James Currey, 1996).

Alatas, S.H., *The Myth of the Lazy Native. A Study of the Image of the Malays, Filipinos and Javanese from the 16th to the 20th Century and its Function in the Ideology of Colonial Capitalism* (London: Frank Cass, 1977).

Allen, R., 'The Great Divergence in European Wages and Prices from the Middle Ages to the First World War', *Explorations in Economic History*, 38(4) (2001), pp. 411–47.

Allen, R., 'India in the Great Divergence' in T. Hatton, K. O'Rourke and A. Taylor (eds), *The New Comparative Economic History: Essays in Honor of Jeffrey G. Williamson* (Cambridge: MIT Press, 2007), pp. 9–32.

Allen, R., *The British Industrial Revolution in Global Perspective* (Cambridge: Cambridge University Press, 2009).

Allen, R., 'The High Wage Economy and the Industrial Revolution: A Restatement', *Economic History Review Early View Online*, 68(1) (2014), pp. 1–22.

Allen, R., Bassino, J.-P., Ma, D., Moll-Murata, C. and van Zanden, J.L., 'Wages, Prices, and Living Standards in China, 1738–1925: In Comparison with Europe, Japan and India', *Economic History Review*, 64(1) (2011), pp. 8–38.

Allen, R., Murphy, T. and Schneider, E., 'The Colonial Origins of the Divergence in the Americas: A Labour Market Approach', *Journal of Economic History*, 72(4) (2012), pp. 863–94.

Alpern, S., 'The European Introduction of Crops into West Africa in Precolonial Times', *History in Africa*, 19 (1992), pp. 13–43.

Alpern, S., *Original Sources for Precolonial Western Africa. An Updated and Expanded Supplement to Fage (1994)* (Madison: University of Wisconsin-Madison, African Studies Program, 2006).

Amin, S., *Unequal Development: An Essay on the Social Formations of Peripheral Capitalism* (Hassocks: Harvester Press, 1976).

Andah, B.W. and Anquandah, J.R., 'The Guinean Belt: The Peoples between Mount Cameroon and Côte d'Ivoire' in I. Hrbek (ed.), *General History of Africa, vol. III: Africa from the Seventh to the Eleventh Century* (Paris: UNESCO, 1992), pp. 240–57.

Anquandah, J.K., 'Researching the Historic Slave Trade in Ghana – An Overview' in J.K. Anquandah (ed.), *The Transatlantic Slave Trade: Landmarks, Legacies, Expectations* (Accra: Sub-Saharan, 2007), pp. 23–56.

Applebaum, H., *The Concept of Work: Ancient, Medieval, and Modern* (Albany: State University of New York Press, 1992).

Arhin, K., 'Peasants in 19th century Asante', *Current Anthropology*, 24 (1983), pp. 471–80.

Atkins, K., *The Moon is Dead! Give us our Money! The Cultural Origins of an African Work Ethic, Natal, South Africa, 1843–1900* (Portsmouth: Heinemann, 1993).

Austen, R., *African Economic History: Internal Development and External Dependency* (Oxford: James Currey, 1987).

Austen, R. and Headrick, D., 'The Role of Technology in the African Past', *African Studies Review*, 26(3/4) (1983), pp. 163–84.

Austin, G., '"No Elders were Present": Commoners and Private Ownership in Asante, 1807–1896', *Journal of African History*, 37(1) (1996), pp. 1–30.

Austin, G., 'Human Pawning in Asante, 1820–1950: Markets and Coercion, Gender and Cocoa' in P. Lovejoy and T. Falola (eds), *Pawnship, Slavery, and Colonialism in Africa* (Trenton: Africa World Press, 2003), pp. 187–224.

Austin, G., 'Sub-Saharan Africa: Land Rights and Ethno-National Consciousness in Historically Land-Abundant Economies' in S. Engerman and J. Metzer (eds), *Land Rights, Ethno-Nationality, and Sovereignty in History* (London: Routledge, 2004), pp. 276–93.

Austin, G., *Labour, Land and Capital in Ghana: From Slavery to Free Labour in Asante, 1807–1956* (Rochester: University of Rochester Press, 2005).

Austin, G., 'The Political Economy of the Natural Environment in West African History: Asante and its Savanna Neighbors in the Nineteenth and Twentieth Centuries' in R. Kuba and C. Lentz (eds), *Land and the Politics of Belonging in West Africa* (Leiden: Brill, 2006), pp. 187–212.

Austin, G., 'Labour and Land in Ghana, 1874–1939: A Shifting Ratio and an Institutional Revolution', *Australian Economic History Review*, 47(1) (2007), pp. 95–120.

Austin, G., 'The "Reversal of Fortune" Thesis and the Compression of History: Perspectives from African and Comparative Economic History', *Journal of International Development*, 20 (2008), pp. 996–1027.

Austin, G., 'Resources, Techniques, and Strategies South of the Sahara: Revisiting the Factor Endowments Perspective on African Economic Development, 1500–2000', *Economic History Review*, 61(3) (2008), pp. 587–624.

Austin, G., 'Factor Markets in Nieboer Conditions: Pre-Colonial West Africa, c.1500–c.1900'. *Continuity and Change*, 24 (2009), pp. 23–53.

Austin, G., 'Coercion and Markets: Integrating Economic and Social Explanations of Slavery in Precolonial West Africa, c1450–c1900' (paper presented at the Historical Economics Workshop, Paris, 2009).

Austin, G., 'Reconsidering Markets in Precolonial West Africa, c1450–c1890: Structure, Function and Process' (paper presented at the African Economic History Workshop, LSE, London, 2009), forthcoming as a chapter in the book *Markets, Slaves and States in West Africa*.

Austin, G., Baten, J. and Van Leeuwen, B., 'The Biological Standard of Living in Early Nineteenth-Century West Africa: New Anthropometric Evidence for Northern Ghana and Burkina Faso', *Economic History Review*, 64 (2011), pp. 1–23.

Barker, A., *The African Link: British Attitudes to the Negro in the Era of the Atlantic Slave Trade, 1550–1807* (London: Frank Cass, 1978).

Beaver, D., 'Writing Natural History for Survival – 1820–1856: The Case of Sarah Bowdich, later Sarah Lee', *Archives of Natural History*, 26(1) (1999), pp. 19–31.

Beckles, H.M., 'African Resistance to the Transatlantic Slave Trade' in J.K. Anquandah (ed.), *The Transatlantic Slave Trade: Landmarks, Legacies, Expectations* (Accra: Sub-Saharan, 2007), pp. 81–91.

Behrendt, S., 'Markets, Transaction Cycles, and Profits: Merchant Decision Making in the British Slave Trade', *William and Mary Quarterly*, 58(1) (2001), pp. 171–204.

Behrendt, S., Latham, A.J.H. and Northrup, D., *The Diary of Antera Duk, an Eighteenth-Century African Slave Trader* (New York: Oxford University Press, 2012).

Berger, I. and White, F., *Women in Sub-Saharan Africa: Restoring Women to History* (Bloomington: Indiana University Press, 1999).

Berry, S., *No Condition is Permanent: The Social Dynamics of Agrarian Change in Sub-Saharan Africa* (Madison: University of Wisconsin Press, 1993).

Berry, S., *Chiefs Know their Boundaries: Essays on Property, Power and the Past in Asante, 1896–1996* (Oxford: James Currey, 2001).

Boahen, A., 'Fante Diplomacy in the Eighteenth Century' (paper published in the *Proceedings of the Twenty-Fifth Symposium of the Colston Research Society*, London, 1973).

Boahen, A., 'The States and Cultures of the Lower Guinean Coast' in B.A. Ogot (ed.), *General History of Africa, vol. V: Africa from the Sixteenth to the Eighteenth Century* (Paris: UNESCO, 1999), pp. 204–20.

Bolland, O.N., 'Proto-Proletarians? Slaves Wages in the Americas: Between Slave Labour and Free Labour' in M. Turner (ed.), *From Chattel Slaves to Wage Slaves: The Dynamics of Labour Bargaining in the Americas* (Kingston: Ian Randle, 1995), pp. 123–47.

Boserup, E., *Woman's Role in Economic Development* (London: Allen & Unwin, 1970).

Brass, T., *Towards a Comparative Political Economy of Unfree Labour: Case Studies and Debates* (London: Routledge,1999).

Brooks, G., *The Kru Mariner in the Nineteenth Century: A Historical Compendium* (Newark: Liberian Studies Association in America, 1972).

Brooks, G., *Landlords and Strangers: Ecology, Society, and Trade in Western Africa, 1000–1630* (Boulder: Westview Press, 1993).

Bryceson, D.F. (ed.), *Women Wielding the Hoe: Lessons from Rural Africa for Feminist Theory and Development Practice* (Oxford: Berg, 1995).

Chouin, G., 'Seen, Said, or Deduced? Travel Accounts, Historical Criticism, and Discourse Theory: Towards an "Archaeology" of Dialogue in Seventeenth-Century Guinea', *History in Africa*, 28 (2001), pp. 53–70.

Clarence-Smith, W., 'The Dynamics of the African Slave Trade', *Africa*, 64(2) (1994), pp. 275–86.

Clark, G., 'Farm Wages and Living Standards in the Industrial Revolution: England, 1670–1869', *Economic History Review*, 54(3) (2001), pp. 477–505.

Coetzee, J.M., 'Idleness in South Africa', *Social Dynamics: A Journal of African Studies*, 8(1) (1982), pp. 1–13.

Cohen, W., *The French Encounter with Africans: White Response to Blacks, 1530–1880* (Bloomington: Indiana University Press, 1980).

Coleman, D., 'Sierra Leone, Slavery, and Sexual Politics: Anna Maria Falconbridge and the "Swarthy Daughter" of Late 18th Century Abolitionism', *Women's Writing*, 2(1) (1995), pp. 3–23.
Cooper, F., 'The Problem of Slavery in African Studies', *Journal of African History*, 20(1) (1979), pp. 103–25.
Cooper, F., 'Africa and the World Economy', *African Studies Review*, 24(2/3) (1981), pp. 1–86.
Coquery-Vidrovitch, C., *African Women: A Modern History* (Boulder: Westview Press, 1997).
Coquery-Vidrovitch, C., 'Research on an African Mode of Production' in R.R. Grinker, S. Lubkemann and C. Steiner (eds), *Perspectives on Africa: A Reader in Culture, History and Representation* (Malden: Wiley-Blackwell, 2010 [1969]), pp. 139–50.
Curtin, P., *The Image of Africa: British Ideas and Action, 1780–1850* (Madison: University of Wisconsin Press, 1973).
Curtin, P., *Economic Change in Precolonial Africa: Senegambia in the Era of the Slave Trade* (Madison: University of Wisconsin Press, 1975).
Curtin, P., 'The West African Coast in the Era of the Slave Trade' in P. Curtin, S. Feierman, L. Thompson and J. Vansin (eds), *African History from Earliest Times to Independence*, 2nd edn (London: Longman, 1995).
Curtin, P., *Disease and Empire: The Health of European Troops in the Conquest of Africa* (Cambridge: Cambridge University Press, 1998).
Daaku, K., *Trade and Politics on the Gold Coast 1600–1720: A Study of the African Reaction to European Trade* (Oxford: Clarendon Press, 1970).
Daaku, K., 'Trade and Trading Patterns of the Akan in the Seventeenth and Eighteenth Centuries' in C. Meillassoux (ed.), *The Development of Indigenous Trade and Markets in West Africa* (Oxford: Oxford University Press, 1971), pp. 168–81.
Daaku, K., 'Aspects of Precolonial Akan Economy', *International Journal of African Historical Studies*, 5(2) (1972), pp. 235–47.
Davidson, B., 'Slaves or Captives? Some Notes on Fantasy and Fact' in N. Huggins, M. Kilson and D. Fox (eds), *Key Issues in the Afro-American Experience* (New York: Harcourt Brace Jovanovich, 1971), pp. 54–73.
Davies, K.G., *The Royal African Company* (New York: Octagon Books, 1975).
Daykin, J., '"They Themselves Contribute to their Misery by their Sloth": The Justification of Slavery in Eighteenth-Century French Travel Narratives', *European Legacy*, 11 (2006), pp. 623–32.
DeCorse, C., 'Culture Contact, Continuity, and Change on the Gold Coast, AD 1400–1900', *African Archaeological Review*, 10 (1992), pp. 163–96.
DeCorse, C., *An Archaeology of Elmina: Africans and Europeans on the Gold Coast, 1400–1900* (Washington: Smithsonian Institution Press, 2001).
DeCorse, C. (ed.), *West Africa during the Atlantic Slave Trade – Archaeological Perspectives* (London: Leicester University Press, 2001).
De Vries, J., *The Industrious Revolution: Consumer Behavior and the Household Economy, 1650 to the Present* (Cambridge: Cambridge University Press, 2008).
de Zwart, P., 'Population, Labour and Living Standards in Early Modern Ceylon: An Empirical Contribution to the Convergence Debate', *Indian Economic Social History Review*, 49(3) (2012), pp. 365–98.
de Zwart, P., 'Real Wages at the Cape of Good Hope: A Long-Term Perspective, 1652–1912', *Low Countries Journal of Social and Economic History*, 10 (2013), pp. 28–58.

Diagne, P., 'African Political, Economic and Social Structures during this Period' in B.A. Ogot (ed.), *General History of Africa V: Africa from the Sixteenth to the Eighteenth Century* (Paris: UNESCO, 1992), pp. 23–45.

Dickson, K., *A Historical Geography of Ghana* (Cambridge: Cambridge University Press, 1971).

Diouf, S. (ed.), *Fighting the Slave Trade – West African Strategies* (Athens: Ohio University Press, 2003).

Domar, E., 'The Causes of Slavery and Serfdom: A Hypothesis', *Journal of Economic History*, 30(1) (1970), pp. 18–32.

Dumett, R., 'The Social Impact of the European Liquor Trade on the Akan of Ghana (Gold Coast and Asante), 1875–1910', *Journal of Interdisciplinary History*, 5(1) (1974), pp. 69–101.

Dumett, R., 'African Merchants of the Gold Coast, 1860–1905 – Dynamics of Indigenous Entrepreneurship', *Comparative Studies in Society and History*, 25(4) (1983), pp. 661–93.

Dumett, R., 'The Work of Slaves in the Akan and Adangme Regions of Ghana in the Nineteenth Century' in S. Beswick and J. Spaulding (eds), *African Systems of Slavery* (Trenton: Africa World Press, 2010), pp. 67–104.

Du Plessis, S. and Du Plessis, S. 'Happy in the Service of the Company: The Purchasing Power of VOC Salaries at the Cape in the 18th Century', *Economic History of Developing Regions*, 27(1) (2012), pp. 125–49.

Eltis, D., 'Welfare Trends among the Yoruba in the Early Nineteenth Century: the Anthropometric Evidence', *Journal of Economic History*, 50(3) (1990), pp. 521–40.

Eltis, D., 'The Slave Trade and Commercial Agriculture in an African Context' in R. Law, S. Schwarz and S. Strickrodt (eds), *Commercial Agriculture, the Slave Trade and Slavery in Atlantic Africa* (Woodbridge: James Currey, 2013), pp. 28–53.

Eltis, D. and Jennings, L., 'Trade between Western Africa and the Atlantic World in the Pre-Colonial Era', *American Historical Review*, 93(4) (1988), pp. 936–59.

Engerman, S., 'Some Considerations relating to Property Rights in Man', *Journal of Economic History*, 33(1) (1973), pp. 43–65.

Evans, E.W. and Richardson, D., 'Hunting for Rents: The Economics of Slaving in Pre-Colonial Africa', *Economic History Review*, 48(4) (1995), pp. 665–86.

Fage, J.D., *A History of West Africa*, 4th edn (Cambridge: Cambridge University Press, 1969).

Fage, J.D., 'A Commentary on Duarte Pacheco Pereira's Account of the Lower Guinea Coastlands in his "Esmeraldo de Situ Orbis", and on some other Early Accounts', *History in Africa*, 7 (1980), pp. 47–80.

Fage, J.D., 'Slaves and Society in Western Africa, c. 1445–c. 1700', *Journal of African History*, 21(3) (1980), pp. 289–310.

Fage, J.D., 'Seventeenth Century Gold Coast', *Journal of African History*, 29(2) (1988), pp. 326–8.

Fage, J.D., 'Hawkins' Hoax? A Sequel to "Drake's Fake"', *History in Africa,* 18 (1991), pp. 83–91.

Fage, J.D., 'Isert in English', *Journal of African History*, 33(3) (1992), pp. 489–91.

Fage, J.D., '"Good Red Herring": The Definitive Barbot', *Journal of African History*, 34(2) (1993), pp. 315–20.

Fage, J.D., *A Guide to Original Sources for Precolonial Western Africa Published in European Languages* (Madison: University of Wisconsin, African Studies Program, 1994).

Fall, B., *Social History in French West Africa: Forced Labour, Labour Market, Women and Politics* (Amsterdam: Sephis, 2002).

Falola, T. and Amponsah, N.A., *Women's Roles in Sub-Saharan African (Women's Roles through History)* (Santa Barbara: Greenwood, 2012).

Fapohunda, E., 'Female and Male Work Profiles' in C. Oppong (ed.), *Female and Male in West Africa* (London: George Allen & Unwin, 1983), pp. 32–53.

Farrar, T., *Building Technology and Settlement Planning in a West African Civilization: Precolonial Akan Cities and Towns* (Lewiston: Mellen University Press, 1996).

Feinberg, H., 'An Eighteenth-Century Case of Plagiarism: William Smith's "A New Voyage to Guinea" ', *History in Africa*, 6 (1979), pp. 45–50.

Feinberg, H., 'Africans and Europeans in West Africa: Elminans and Dutchmen on the Gold Coast during the Eighteenth Century', *Transactions of the American Philosophical Society*, 79(7) (1989), pp. 1–186.

Fenske, J., 'The Causal History of Africa: A Response to Hopkins', *Economic History of Developing Regions*, 25(2) (2010), pp. 177–212.

Fetter, B., 'Decoding and Interpreting African Census Data: Vital Evidence from an Unsavory Witness', *Cahiers d'études africaines*, 27 (105–6) (1987), pp. 83–105.

Firmin-Sellers, K., *The Transformation of Property Rights in the Gold Coast* (Cambridge: Cambridge University Press, 1996).

Fisher, H., *Slavery in the History of Muslim Black Africa* (London: Hurst & Company, 2001).

Fourie, J., 'The Remarkable Wealth of the Dutch Cape Colony: Measurements from Eighteenth-Century Probate Inventories', *Economic History Review,* 66(2) (2013), pp. 419–48.

Frank, A.G., *World Accumulation 1492–1789* (London: Macmillan, 1978).

Frankema, E. and Jerven, M., 'Writing History Backwards or Sideways: Towards a Consensus on African Population, 1850–2010', *Economic History Review*, 67(4) (2014), pp. 907–31.

Freund, B., 'Labor and Labor History in Africa: A Review of the Literature', *African Studies Review*, 27(2) (1984), pp. 1–58.

Freund, B., *The African Worker* (Cambridge: Cambridge University Press, 1988).

Freund, B., *The African City: A History* (Cambridge: Cambridge University Press, 2007).

Frost, D., *Work and Community among West African Migrant Workers since the Nineteenth Century* (Liverpool: Liverpool University Press, 1999).

Fynn, J.K., *Asante and its Neighbours 1700–1807* (Evanston: Northwestern University Press, 1971).

Garrard, T., *African Gold* (Munich: Prestel, 2011).

Gemery, H.A., Hogendorn, J. and Johnson, M., 'Evidence on English/African Terms of Trade in the Eighteenth Century', *Explorations in Economic History*, 27(2) (1990), pp. 157–77.

George, K., 'The Civilized West Looks at Primitive Africa: 1400–1800. A Study in Ethnocentrism', *Isis*, 49(1) (1958), pp. 62–72.

Getz, T., *Slavery and Reform in West Africa: Toward Emancipation in Nineteenth-Century Senegal and the Gold Coast* (Athens, OH: Ohio University Press, 2004).

Glickstein, J., 'Pressures from Below: Pauperism, Chattel Slavery, and the Ideological Construction of Free Market Labor Incentives in Antebellum America', *Radical History Review*, 1997(69) (1997), pp. 114–59.

Goody, J., 'Feudalism in Africa', *Journal of African History*, 4(1) (1963), pp. 1–18.

Green, T., 'The Export of Rice and Millet from Upper Guinea into the Sixteenth-Century Atlantic Trade' in R. Law, S. Schwarz and S. Strickrodt (eds), *Commercial Agriculture, the Slave Trade and Slavery in Atlantic Africa* (Woodbridge: James Currey, 2013), pp. 79–97.

Greene, S., *Gender, Ethnicity, and Social Change on the Upper Slave Coast: A History of the Anlo-Ewe* (London: James Currey, 1996).

Gutkind, P., 'Trade and Labor in Early Precolonial African History: The Canoemen of Southern Ghana' in C. Coquery-Vidrovitch and P. Lovejoy (eds), *The Workers of African Trade* (Beverly Hills: Sage Publications, 1985), pp. 25–50.

Gutkind, P., 'The Canoemen of the Gold Coast (Ghana): A Survey and an Exploration in Precolonial African Labour History', *Cahiers d'Études Africaines*, 29(115/116) (1989), pp. 339–76.

Hagan, G.P., *Divided We Stand – A Study of Social Change among the Effutu of Coastal Ghana* (Trondheim: Norwegian University of Science and Technology, African Series no. 2, 2000).

Hair, P.E.H., 'Barbot, Dapper, Davity: A Critique of Sources on Sierra Leone and Cape Mount', *History in Africa*, 1 (1974), pp. 25–54.

Hair, P.E.H., 'On Editing Barbot', *History in Africa*, 20 (1993), pp. 53–9.

Hair, P.E.H., 'The Early Sources on Guinea', *History in Africa*, 21 (1994), pp. 87–126.

Hair, P.E.H., 'Portuguese Documents on Africa and some Problems of Translation', *History in Africa*, 27 (2000), pp. 91–7.

Hatcher, J., 'Labour, Leisure and Economic Thought before the Nineteenth Century', *Past & Present*, 160 (1998), pp. 64–115.

Heintze, B., 'Translations as Sources for African History', *History in Africa*, 11 (1984), pp. 131–61.

Hernæs, P., 'Afro-Danish Trade on the 18th-Century Gold Coast. A Quantitative Assessment' in P. Hernæs (ed.), *The Danish Slave Trade from West Africa and Afro-Danish Relations on the 18th-Century Gold Coast* (Trondheim: University of Trondheim, 1992).

Hernæs, P., ' "Fort Slavery" at Christiansborg on the Gold Coast: Wage Labour in the Making?' in P. Hernæs and T. Iversen (eds), *Slavery across Time and Space: Studies in Slavery in Medieval Europe and Africa* (Trondheim: Norwegian University of Science and Technology, Department of History, 2002), pp. 197–230.

Hill, M., 'Towards a Chronology of the Publications of Francis Moore's "Travels into the Inland Parts of Africa" ', *History in Africa*, 19 (1992), pp. 353–68.

Hill, P., 'Notes on Traditional Market Authority and Market Periodicity in West Africa', *Journal of African History*, 7(2) (1966), pp. 295–311.

Hinchmann, M., 'House and Household on Gorée, Senegal, 1758–1837', *Journal of the Society of Architectural Historians*, 65(2) (2006), pp. 166–87.

Hofmeester, K., Lucassen, J. and Ribeiro da Silva, F., 'No Global Labor History without Africa: Reciprocal Comparison and Beond', *History in Africa*, 41 (2014), pp. 249–76.

Hogendorn, J.S. and Gemery, H.A., 'Assessing Productivity in Precolonial African Agriculture and Industry 1500–1800', *African Economic History*, 19 (1990/91), pp. 31–5.

Hogendorn, J. and Johnson, M., *The Shell Money of the Slave Trade* (Cambridge: Cambridge University Press, 1986).

Hopkins, A., *An Economic History of West Africa* (London: Longman, 1973).

Hopkins, A., 'On Importing André Gunder Frank into Africa', *African Economic History Review*, 2(1) (1975), pp. 13–21.

Hopkins, A., 'The New Economic History of Africa', *Journal of African History*, 50(2) (2009), pp 155–77.

Howard, R., *Colonialism and Underdevelopment in Ghana* (London: Croom Helm, 1978).

Hufton, O., *The Prospect Before Her: A History of Women in Western Europe, 1500–1800* (London: Fontana Press, 1995).

Hull, R., *African Cities and Towns before the European Conquest* (New York: W.W. Norton, 1976).

Humphries, J., 'The Lure of Aggregates and the Pitfalls of the Patriarchal Perspective: A Critique of the High Wage Economy Interpretation of the British Industrial Revolution', *Economic History Review*, 66(3) (2013), pp. 693–714.

Hymer, S., 'Economic Forms in Pre-Colonial Ghana', *Journal of Economic History*, 30(1) (1970), pp. 33–50.

Iliffe, J., *The Emergence of African Capitalism* (London: Macmillan, 1983).

Iliffe, J., *The African Poor: A History* (Cambridge: Cambridge University Press, 1987).

Inikori, J., 'The Import of Firearms into West Africa 1750–1807: A Quantitative Analysis', *Journal of African History*, 18(3) (1977), pp. 339–68.

Inikori, J., 'Africa in World History: The Export Slave Trade from Africa and the Emergence of the Atlantic Economic Order' in B.A. Ogot (ed.), *General History of Africa V: Africa from the Sixteenth to the Eighteenth Century* (Paris: UNESCO, 1999), pp. 39–55.

Inikori, J. 'Slaves or Serfs? A Comparative Study of Slavery and Serfdom in Europe and Africa' in I. Okpewho, C.B. Davies and A. Mazrui (eds), *The African Diaspora: African Origins and New World Identities* (Bloomington: Indiana University Press, 1999), pp. 49–75.

Inikori, J., 'Changing Commodity Composition of Imports into West Africa, 1650–1850: A Window into the Impact of the Transatlantic Slave Trade on African Societies' in J.K. Anquandah (ed.), *The Transatlantic Slave Trade: Landmarks, Legacies, Expectations* (Accra: Sub-Saharan, 2007), pp. 57–80.

Inikori, J., 'The Development of Commercial Agriculture in Pre-Colonial West Africa', *African Economic History Network Working Paper*, 9 (2013).

Irwin, G., 'Precolonial African Diplomacy: The Example of Asante', *International Journal of African Historical Studies*, 8(1) (1975), pp. 81–96.

Iselin, R., 'Reading Pictures: On the Value of the Copperplates in the "Beschryvinghe" of Pieter de Marees (1602) as Source Material for Ethnohistorical Research', *History in Africa*, 21 (1994), pp. 147–70.

Johnson, M., 'The Ounce in Eighteenth-Century West African Trade', *Journal of African History*, 7(2) (1966), pp. 197–214.

Jones, A., 'William Smith the Plagiarist: A Rejoinder', *History in Africa*, 7 (1980), pp. 329–32.

Jones, A., 'Double Dutch? A Survey of Seventeenth-Century German Sources for West African History', *History in Africa*, 9 (1982), pp. 141–53.

Jones, A., 'Semper Aliquid Veteris: Printed Sources for the History of the Ivory and Gold Coasts, 1500–1750', *Journal of African History*, 27(2) (1986), pp. 215–35.

Jones, A., *Raw, Medium, Well Done: A Critical Review of Editorial and Quasi-Editorial Work on Pre-1885 European Sources for Sub-Saharan Africa, 1960–1986* (Madison: University of Wisconsin, African Studies Program, 1987).

Jones, A., 'Decompiling Dapper: A Preliminary Search for Evidence', *History in Africa*, 17 (1990), pp. 171–209.

Jones, A., 'A Danish Record of the Coast', *Journal of African History*, 31(1) (1990), pp. 143–4.
Jones, A., 'Drink Deep, or Taste Not: Thoughts on the Use of Early European Records in the Study of African Material Culture', *History in Africa*, 21 (1994), pp. 349–70.
Jones, A., 'Written Sources for the Material Culture of the Gold Coast before 1800: A Provisional Checklist', *Journal des Africanistes*, 75(2) (2005), pp. 1–27.
Jordan, S., *The Anxieties of Idleness: Idleness in Eighteenth-Century British Literature and Culture* (Lewisburg: Bucknell University Press, 2003).
Kea, R., 'Firearms and Warfare on the Gold and Slave Coasts from the Sixteenth to the Nineteenth Centuries', *Journal of African History*, 12(2) (1971), pp. 185–213.
Kea, R., *Settlements, Trade, and Polities in the Seventeenth-Century Gold Coast* (Baltimore: Johns Hopkins University Press, 1982).
Kea, R., *A Cultural and Social History of Ghana from the Seventeenth to the Nineteenth Century*, vol. 2 (Lewiston: Edwin Mellen Press, 2012).
Kipre, P., 'From the Ivory Coast Lagoons to the Volta' in D.T. Niane (ed.), *General History of Africa, vol. IV: Africa from the Twelfth to the Sixteenth Century* (Paris: UNESCO, 1984), pp. 324–38.
Ki-Zerbo, J. (ed.), *General History of Africa, vol. I. Methodology and African Prehistory* (Paris: UNESCO, 1989).
Klein, H., *The Atlantic Slave Trade*, 2nd edn (Cambridge: Cambridge University Press, 2010).
Kolchin, P., 'In Defense of Servitude: American Proslavery and Russian Proserfdom Arguments, 1760–1860', *American Historical Review*, 85(4) (1980), pp. 809–27.
Kopytoff, I. and Miers, S., 'African "Slavery" as an Institution of Marginality' in S. Miers and I. Kopytoff (eds), *Slavery in Africa: Historical and Anthropological Perspectives* (Madison: University of Wisconsin Press, 1977), pp. 3–81.
Kriger, C., 'Looking for Labor and Markets in the Past'. *African Economic History*, 32, (2004), pp. 89–102.
Kriger, C., 'Mapping the History of Cotton Textile Production in Precolonial West Africa', *African Economic History*, 33 (2005), pp. 87–116.
La Fleur, J.D., *Fusion Foodways of Africa's Gold Coast in the Atlantic Era* (Leiden: Brill, 2012).
Lamousé-Smith, W.B., 'African Resistance to Slavery and Myths for Diasporan Disunity' in J.K. Anquandah (ed.), *The Transatlantic Slave Trade: Landmarks, Legacies, Expectations* (Accra: Sub-Saharan, 2007), pp. 225–40.
Latorre, J., 'Wealth Surpasses Everything: An Economic History of Asante, 1750–1874' (PhD dissertation, Berkeley: University of California, 1978).
Law, R., 'Jean Barbot as a Source for the Slave Coast of West Africa', *History in Africa*, 9 (1982), pp. 155–73.
Law, R., 'The Slave-Trader as Historian: Robert Norris and the History of Dahomey', *History in Africa*, 16 (1989), pp. 219–35.
Law, R., *The Slave Coast of West Africa 1550–1750: The Impact of the Atlantic Slave Trade on an African Society* (Oxford: Clarendon Press, 1991).
Law, R., 'Computing Domestic Prices in Precolonial West Africa: A Methodological Exercise from the Slave Coast', *History in Africa*, 18 (1991), pp. 239–57.
Law, R., 'Posthumous Questions for Karl Polanyi: Price Inflation in Pre-Colonial Dahomey', *Journal of African History*, 33(3) (1992), pp. 387–420.
Law, R., *Ouidah: The Social History of a West African Slaving 'Port' 1727–1892* (Athens: Ohio University Press, 2004).

Law, R., '"There's Nothing Grows in the West Indies but will Grow Here": Dutch and English Projects of Plantation Agriculture on the Gold Coast, 1650s–1780s' in R. Law, S. Schwarz and S. Strickrodt (eds), *Commercial Agriculture, the Slave Trade and Slavery in Atlantic Africa* (Woodbridge: James Currey, 2013), pp. 116–37.

Lawrence, A.W., *Trade Castles and Forts of West Africa* (London: Jonathan Cape, 1963).

Leeuwen, M. and Maas, I., *HISCLASS – A Historical International Social Class Scheme* (Leuven: Leuven University Press, 2011).

Leeuwen, M., Maas, I. and Miles, A., *HISCO – Historical International Standard Classifications of Occupations* (Leuven: Leuven University Press, 2002).

Lewicki, T., *West African Food in the Middle Ages according to Arabic Sources* (Cambridge: Cambridge University Press, 1974).

Loomba, A., *Colonialism/Postcolonialism* (London: Routledge, 1998).

Lovejoy, P., *Caravans of Kola: The Hausa Kola Trade, 1700–1900* (Nigeria: Ahmadu Bello University Press, 1980).

Lovejoy, P., 'The Impact of the Atlantic Slave Trade on Africa: A Review of the Literature', *Journal of African History*, 30(3) (1989), pp. 365–94.

Lovejoy, P., *Transformations in Slavery: A History of Slavery in Africa*, 2nd edn (Cambridge: Cambridge University Press, 2000).

Lovejoy, P., 'Pawnship, Debt, and "Freedom" in Atlantic Africa during the Era of the Slave Trade: A Reassessment', *Journal of African History*, 55(1) (2014), pp. 55–78.

Lovejoy, P. and Baier, S., 'The Desert-Side Economy of the Central Sudan', *International Journal of African Historical Studies*, 8(4) (1975), pp. 551–81.

Lovejoy, P. and Richardson, D., 'The Business of Slaving: Pawnship in Western Africa, c. 1600–1810', *Journal of African History*, 42(1) (2001), pp. 67–89.

Mackay, R., *'Lazy, Improvident People': Myth and Reality in the Writing of Spanish History* (Ithaca: Cornell University Press, 2006).

Magubane, Z., 'Labor Laws and Stereotypes: Images of the Khoikhoi in the Cape in the Age of Abolition' in M. Palmberg (ed.), *Encounter Images in the Meetings between Africa and Europe* (Uppsala: Nordic Africa Institute, 2001), pp. 76–95.

Maier, D., 'Precolonial Palm Oil Production and Gender Division of Labor in Nineteenth-Century Gold Coast and Togoland', *African Economic History*, 37 (2009), pp. 1–32.

Manchuelle, F., 'Slavery, Emancipation and Labour Migration in West Africa: The Case of the Soninke', *Journal of African History*, 30(1) (1989), pp. 89–106.

Mandala, E., 'The Making of Wage Laborers in Nineteenth Century Southern Africa: Magololo Porters and David Livingstone, 1853–1861', *International Labor and Working-Class History*, 86 (2014), pp. 15–35.

Manning, P., *Slavery and African Life: Occidental, Oriental, and African Slave Trades* (Cambridge: Cambridge University Press, 1990).

Manning, P., 'Replication Data for African Population Estimates, 1850–1960' (2009), at *World-Historical Dataverse, Catalog #2*, http://hdl.handle.net/1902.1/15281 [accessed 19 June 2014].

Manning, P., 'African Population, 1650–1950: Methods for New Estimates by Region' (paper presented at African Economic History Conference, Vancouver, 2013).

Manning, P., 'African Population, 1650–2000: Comparisons and Implications of New Estimates' in E. Akyeampong et al. (eds), *Africa's Development in Historical Perspective* (Cambridge: Cambridge University Press, 2014), pp. 131–50.

Mark, P., 'Constructing Identity: Sixteenth- and Seventeenth-Century Architecture in the Gambia-Geba Region and the Articulation of Luso-African Ethnicity', *History in Africa*, 22 (1995), pp. 307–27.

Mark, P., *Portuguese Style and Luso-African Identity* (Bloomington: Indiana University Press, 2002).

Marks, S. and Rathbone, R., 'The History of the Family in Africa: Introduction', *Journal of African History*, 24(2) (1983), pp. 145–61.

Martin, P., 'Power, Cloth and Currency on the Loango Coast', *African Economic History*, 15 (1986), pp. 1–12.

Massing, J.M., *The Image of the Black in Western Art. Vol. III, part 2: From the 'Age of Discovery' to the Age of Abolition. Europe and the World Beyond* (Cambridge: Belknap Press, 2011).

McCann, J., *Maize and Grace: Africa's Encounter with a New World Crop, 1500–2000* (Cambridge: Harvard University Press, 2005).

McCaskie, T.C., 'Drake's Fake: A Curiosity concerning a Spurious Visit to Asante in 1839', *History in Africa*, 11 (1984), pp. 223–36.

McCaskie, T.C., *State and Society in Pre-Colonial Asante* (Cambridge: Cambridge University Press, 1995).

McDougall, E.A., 'Production in Precolonial Africa', *African Economic History*, 19 (1990/91), pp. 37–43.

McGowan, W., 'African Resistance to the Atlantic Slave Trade in West Africa', *Slavery & Abolition*, 11(1) (1990), pp. 5–29.

McIntosh, R., 'Archaeology and Mud Wall Decay in a West African Village', *World Archaeology*, 6(2) (1974), pp. 154–71.

McNeill, J.R., *Mosquito Empires: Ecology and War in the Greater Caribbean, 1620–1914* (Cambridge: Cambridge University Press, 2010).

Meillassoux, C., 'Female Slavery' in C. Robertson and M. Klein (eds), *Women and Slavery in Africa* (Madison: University of Wisconsin Press, 1983), pp. 49–66.

Memmi, A., *The Colonizer and the Colonized* (London: Earthscan, 2003 [1965]).

Metcalf, G., 'A Microcosm of Why Africans Sold Slaves: Akan Consumption Patterns in the 1770s', *Journal of African History*, 28(3) (1987), pp. 377–94.

Meyerowitz, E., *The Early History of the Akan States of Ghana* (London: Red Candle Press, 1975).

Miller, J., *Way of Death: Merchant Capitalism and the Angolan Slave Trade 1730–1830* (Madison: University of Wisconsin Press, 1988).

Miracle, M., 'The Introduction and Spread of Maize in Africa', *Journal of African History*, 6(1) (1965), pp. 39–55.

Miracle, M. and Fetter, B., 'Backward-Sloping Labor-Supply Functions and African Economic Behavior', *Economic Development and Cultural Change*, 18(2) (1970), pp. 240–51.

Morgan, J., ' "Some Could Suckle over Their Shoulder": Male Travelers, Female Bodies, and the Gendering of Racial Ideology, 1500–1770', *William and Mary Quarterly*, 54(1) (1997), pp. 167–92.

Nieboer, H.J., *Slavery as an Industrial System*, 2nd rev. edn (Den Haag: Nijhoff, 1910).

North, D., *Institutions, Institutional Change and Economic Performance* (Cambridge: Cambridge University Press, 1990).

North, D., 'Institutions', *Journal of Economic Perspectives*, 5(1) (1991), pp. 97–112.

Northrup, D., *Africa's Discovery of Europe 1450–1850* (Oxford: Oxford University Press, 2009).

Nováky, G., *Handelskompanier och Kompanihandel. Svenska Afrikakompaniet 1649–1663. En studie i feodal handel* [Trading Companies and Company Trading. The Swedish Africa Company 1649–1663. A study in feudal trade] (Uppsala: Acta Universitatis Upsaliensis, 1990).

Nunn, N., 'The Long-Term Effects of Africa's Slave Trades'. *Quarterly Journal of Economics*, 123 (2008), pp. 139–76.

Nunn, N. and Wantchekon, L., 'The Slave Trade and the Origins of Mistrust in Africa', *American Economic Review*, 101 (2011), pp. 3221–52.

Nwokeji, G.U., 'African Conceptions of Gender and the Slave Traffic', *William and Mary Quarterly*, 58(1) (2001), pp. 47–68.

Obikili, N., 'The Trans-Atlantic Slave Trade and Local Political Fragmentation in Africa', *Economic Research Southern Africa Working Paper*, 406 (2014).

Okia, O., *Communal Labor in Colonial Kenya: The Legitimization of Coercion, 1912–1930* (New York: Palgrave Macmillan, 2012).

Olaniyan, B., *Economic History of West Africa* (Ibadan: Educational Research Institute, 1971).

Osberg, L., 'Leisure' in S. Durlauf and L. Blume (eds), *The New Palgrave Dictionary of Economics*, 2nd edn (Palgrave Macmillan, 2008) at www.dictionaryofeconomics.com [accessed 30 July 2014].

Palma, J.G., 'Dependency' in S. Durlauf and L. Blume (eds), *The New Palgrave Dictionary of Economics*, 2nd edn (Palgrave Macmillan, 2008) at www.dictionaryofeconomics.com [accessed 30 July 2014].

Peet, R. and Hartwick, E., *Theories of Development: Contentions, Arguments, Alternatives* (New York: Guilford Press, 2009).

Perbi, A., 'The Relationship between the Domestic Slave Trade and the External Slave Trade in Pre-Colonial Ghana', *Research Review (NS)*, 8(1–2) (1992), pp. 64–75.

Perbi, A., *A History of Indigenous Slavery in Ghana: From the 15th to the 19th Century* (Accra: Sub-Saharan, 2004).

Polanyi, K., 'Sortings and "Ounce Trade" in the West African Slave Trade', *Journal of African History*, 5(3) (1964), pp. 381–93.

Pomeranz, K., 'Ten Years After: Responses and Reconsiderations', *Historically Speaking*, 12(4) (2011), pp. 20–5.

Pratt, M.L., *Imperial Eyes: Travel Writing and Transculturation* (London: Routledge, 1992).

Priestley, M., 'An Early Strike in Ghana', *Ghana Notes and Queries*, 7 (1965), p. 25.

Priestley, M., *West African Trade and Coast Society: A Family Study* (London: Oxford University Press, 1969).

Prussin, L., 'An Introduction to Indigenous African Architecture', *Journal of the Society of Architectural Historians*, 33(3) (1974), pp. 182–205.

Rashid, I., '"Do Dady Nor Lef Me Make Dem Carry Me": Slave Resistance and Emancipation in Sierra Leone, 1894–1928', *Slavery & Abolition*, 19(2) (1998), pp. 208–31.

Rashid, I., 'Escape, Revolt, and Marronage in Eighteenth and Nineteenth Century Sierra Leone Hinterland', *Canadian Journal of African Studies*, 34(3) (2000), pp. 656–83.

Rathbone, R., 'Some Thoughts on Resistance to Enslavement in West Africa', *Slavery & Abolition*, 6(3) (1985), pp. 11–22.

Rawley, J., *The Transatlantic Slave Trade – A History*, rev. edn (Lincoln: University of Nebraska Press, 2005).

Reese, T., 'The Drudgery of the Slave Trade: Labor at Cape Coast Castle, 1750–1790' in P.A. Coclanis (ed.), *The Atlantic Economy during the Seventeenth and Eighteenth Century: Organization, Operation, Practice, and Personnel* (Columbia: University of South Carolina Press, 2005), pp. 277–96.

Reese, T.,'Facilitating the Slave Trade: Company Slaves at Cape Coast Castle, 1750–1807', *Slavery & Abolition*, 31 (2010), pp. 363–77.

Reese, T., 'Wives, Brokers, and Laborers: Women at Cape Coast, 1750–1807' in D. Catterall and J. Campbell (eds), *Women in Port: Gendering Communities, Economies, and Social Networks in Atlantic Port Cities, 1500–1800* (Leiden: Brill, 2012), pp. 291–314.

Reese, T., 'Controlling the Company: The Structures of Fante–British Relations on the Gold Coast, 1750–1821', *Journal of Imperial and Commonwealth History*, 41(1) (2013), pp. 104–19.

Reynolds, E., *Trade and Economic Change on the Gold Coast, 1807–1874* (New York: Longman, 1974).

Richards, W.A., 'The Import of Firearms into West Africa in the Eighteenth Century', *Journal of African History*, 21(1) (1980), pp. 43–59.

Richardson, D., 'Prices of Slaves in West and West-Central Africa: Towards an Annual Series, 1698–1807', *Bulletin of Economic Research*, 43(1) (1991), pp. 21–56.

Robertson, C., *Sharing the Same Bowl: A Socioeconomic History of Women and Class in Accra, Ghana* (Bloomington: Indiana University Press, 1984).

Rodney, W., 'Gold and Slaves on the Gold Coast', *Transactions of the Historical Society of Ghana,* 10 (1969), pp. 13–28.

Rodney, W., *How Europe Underdeveloped Africa* (Washington D.C.: Howard University Press, 1982 [1972]).

Rönnbäck, K., 'An Early Modern Consumer Revolution in the Baltic?', *Scandinavian Journal of History*, 35(2) (2010), pp. 177–97.

Rönnbäck, K., 'Enlightenment, Scientific Exploration and Abolitionism: Anders Sparrman's and Carl Bernhard Wadström's Colonial Encounters in Senegal, 1787–1788 and the British Abolitionist Movement', *Slavery & Abolition*, 34(3) (2013), pp. 425–45.

Rönnbäck, K., 'Climate, Conflicts, and Variations in Prices on Pre-Colonial West African Markets for Staple Crops', *Economic History Review*, 67(4) (2014), pp. 1065–88.

Rönnbäck, K., 'Living Standards on the Pre-Colonial Gold Coast: A Quantitative Estimate of African Laborers' Welfare Ratios', *European Review of Economic History*, 18 (2014), pp. 185–202.

Rönnbäck, K., 'The Idle and the Industrious: European Ideas about the African Work Ethic in Precolonial West Africa', *History in Africa*, 41 (2014), pp. 117–45.

Rönnbäck, K., '"The Men Seldom Suffer a Woman to Sit Down": The Historical Development of the Stereotype of the "Lazy African"', *African Studies*, 73(2) (2014), pp. 211–27.

Rönnbäck, K., 'Waged Slavery: Incentivizing Unfree Labour at the Cape Coast Castle in the Eighteenth Century' (forthcoming in *Slavery & Abolition*).

Rubiés, J.-P., *Travellers and Cosmographers: Studies in the History of Early Modern Travel and Ethnology* (Aldershot: Ashgate, 2007).

Ruskin, F.R., *Lost Crops of Africa, volume I: Grains* (Washington: National Academy Press, 1996).

Saidi, C., *Women's Authority and Society in Early East-Central Africa* (Rochester: University of Rochester Press, 2010).

Sanders, J., 'The Expansion of the Fante and the Emergence of Asante in the Eighteenth Century', *Journal of African History*, 20(3) (1979), pp. 349–64.

Sanders, J., 'The Political Development of the Fante in the Eighteenth and Nineteenth Centuries: A Study of a West African Merchant Society' (PhD dissertation, Evanston: Northwestern University 1980).

Schler, L., Bethlehem, L. and Sabar, G., 'Rethinking Labour in Africa, Past and Present', *African Identities*, 7(3) (2009), pp. 287–98.

Schmidt, A., 'Labour Ideologies and Women in Northern Netherlands, c. 1500–1800', *International Review of Social History*, 56(19) (2011), pp. 45–67.

Seddon, D. (ed.), *Relations of Production. Marxist Approaches to Economic Anthropology* (London: Frank Cass, 1978).

Shea, P., 'Big is sometimes Best: The Sokoto Caliphate and Economic Advantage of Size in the Textile Industry', *African Economic History*, 34 (2006), pp. 5–21.

Shumway, R., *The Fante and the Transatlantic Slave Trade* (Rochester: University of Rochester Press, 2011).

Shumway, R., 'Castle Slaves of the Eighteenth-Century Gold Coast (Ghana)', *Slavery & Abolition*, 35(1) (2014), pp. 84–98.

Smallwood, S., *Saltwater Slavery: A Middle Passage from Africa to American Diaspora* (Cambridge: Harvard University Press, 2007).

Smith, R., 'The Canoe in West African History', *Journal of African History*, 11(4) (1970), pp. 515–33.

Sparks, R., 'Two Princes of Calabar: An Atlantic Odyssey from Slavery to Freedom', *William and Mary Quarterly*, 59(3) (2002), pp. 555–84.

Sparks, R., *Two Princes of Calabar* (Cambridge: Harvard University Press, 2004).

Spicksley, J., 'Pawns on the Gold Coast: The Rise of Asante and Shifts in Security for Debt, 1680–1750', *Journal of African History*, 54(2) (2013), pp. 147–75.

St Clair, W., *The Door of No Return: The History of Cape Coast Castle and the Atlantic Slave Trade* (New York: Bluebridge, 2007).

Stewart, C.C., 'Emergent Classes and the Early State: The Southern Sahara' in D. Crummey and C.C. Stewart (eds), *Modes of Production in Africa – The Precolonial Era* (Beverly Hills: Sage Publications, 1981), pp. 69–92.

Stilwell, S., *Slavery and Slaving in African History* (Cambridge: Cambridge University Press, 2014).

Sutton, E., *Early Modern Dutch Prints of Africa* (Farnham: Ashgate, 2012).

Tarasov, A., 'The Religious Aspect of Labour Ethics in Medieval and Early Modern Russia', *International Review of Social History*, 56(19) (2011), pp. 125–40.

Thiaw, I., 'Slaves Without Shackles: An Archaeology of Everyday Life on Gorée Island, Senegal' in P. Lane and K. Macdonald (eds), *Slavery in Africa: Archaeology and Memory* (Oxford: Oxford University Press, 2011), pp. 147–66.

Thilmas, G. and de Moraes, N.I., 'Villault de Bellefond sur la Côte Occidentale d'Afrique: Les deux premières campagnes de l'*Europe* (1666–1671)', *Bulletin de l'I.F.A.N.*, 38(2) (1976), pp. 257–99.

Thornton, J., 'Precolonial African Industry and the Atlantic Trade, 1500–1800', *African Economic History*, 19 (1990/91), pp. 1–19.

Thornton, J., *Africa and Africans in the Making of the Atlantic World, 1400–1800* (Cambridge: Cambridge University Press, 1998).

TSTD2, *Transatlantic Slave Trade Database*, 2010 version, Estimates Spreadsheet, (2010) at www.slavevoyages.org/tast [accessed 11 January 2012].

van Dantzig, A., 'Willem Bosman's "New and Accurate Description of the Coast of Guinea": How Accurate is it?', *History in Africa*, 1 (1974), pp. 101–8.

van Dantzig, A., 'Effects of the Atlantic Slave Trade on some West African Societies', *Revue Francaise d'Histoire d'Outre-Mer*, 62 (226–7) (1975), pp. 252–69.

van Dantzig, A., 'English Bosman and Dutch Bosman: A Comparison of Texts', *History in Africa*, 2 (1975), pp. 185–216.

van der Linden, M., 'Studying Attitudes to Work Worldwide, 1500–1650: Concepts, Sources, and Problems of Interpretation', *International Review of Social History*, 56 (S19) (2011), pp. 25–43.

van der Linden, M., 'The Promise and Challenge of Global Labor History', *International Labor and Working-Class History*, 82 (2012), pp. 57–76.

Vansina, J., *Oral Tradition as History* (Madison: University of Wisconsin Press, 1985).

Vansina, J., 'Population Movements and Emergence of New Socio-Political Forms in Africa' in B.A. Ogot (ed.), *General History of Africa V: Africa from the Sixteenth to the Eighteenth Century* (Paris: UNESCO, 1992), pp. 46–73.

Voth, H.-J., *Time and Work in England 1750–1830* (Oxford: Clarendon Press, 2000).

Waldman, L., 'An Unnoticed Aspect of Archibald Dalzel's the History of Dahomey', *Journal of African History*, 6(2) (1965), pp. 185–92.

Walker Kilkenny, R., 'The Slave Mode of Production: Precolonial Dahomey' in D. Crummey and C.C. Stewart (eds), *Modes of Production in Africa – The Precolonial Era* (Beverly Hills: Sage Publications, 1981), pp. 157–74.

Wallerstein, I., 'The Three Stages of African Involvement in the World Economy' in P. Gutkind and I. Wallerstein (eds), *The Political Economy of Contemporary Africa* (Beverly Hills: Sage Publications, 1976), pp. 30–57.

Wallerstein, I., *The Modern World-System III: The Second Era of Great Expansion of the Capitalist World-Economy, 1730–1840s* (San Diego: Academic Press, 1989).

Warren, B., *Imperialism: Pioneer of Capitalism* (London: Verso, 1980).

Whatley, W., *The Gun–Slave Cycle in the 18th Century British Slave Trade in Africa* (Working paper, University of Michigan, 2012).

Whatley, W., 'The Transatlantic Slave Trade and the Evolution of Political Authority in West Africa' in E. Akyeampong et al. (eds), *Africa's Development in Historical Perspective* (Cambridge: Cambridge University Press, 2014), pp. 460–88.

Whatley, W. and Gillezeau, R., 'The Impact of the Transatlantic Slave Trade on Ethnic Stratification in Africa', *American Economic Review*, 101(3) (2011), pp. 571–6.

White, G., 'Firearms in Africa: An Introduction', *Journal of African History*, 12(2) (1971), pp. 173–84.

Whitehead, A., '"Lazy Men", Time-use, and Rural Development in Zambia', *Gender & Development*, 7(3) (1999), pp. 49–61.

Whitehead, A., 'Continuities and Discontinuities in Political Constructions of the Working Man in Rural Sub-Saharan Africa: The "Lazy Man" in African Agriculture', *European Journal of Development Research*, 12 (2000), pp. 23–52.

Wilks, I., *Asante in the Nineteenth Century. The Structure and Evolution of a Political Order* (Cambridge: Cambridge University Press, 1975).

Wilks, I., 'The State of the Akan and the Akan States: A Discursion', *Cahiers d'Études Africaines*, 22(87–88) (1982), pp. 231–49.

Wilks, I., *Forests of Gold: Essays on the Akan and the Kingdom of Asante* (Athens: Ohio University Press, 1993).

Wills, J.B. (ed.), *Agriculture and Land Use in Ghana* (London: Oxford University Press, 1962).

Winsnes, S.A., 'Voices from the Past: Remarks on the Translation and Editing of Published Danish Sources for West African History during the Eighteenth and Nineteenth Centuries', *History in Africa*, 14 (1987), pp. 275–85.

Yankah, K., *Speaking for the Chief: Kyeame and the Politics of Akan Royal Oratory* (Bloomington: Indiana University Press, 1995).

Yin, R.K., *Case Study Research – Design and Methods* (Los Angeles: Sage, 2014).

# Index

# A note on Anti-Slavery International

The author's royalties from the sales of this book are donated to Anti-Slavery International for their work.

Anti-Slavery International, founded in 1839, is the world's oldest human rights organization and has always been at the forefront of action against slavery. Slavery, servitude and forced labour are violations of individual freedoms that deny millions of people their basic dignity and fundamental human rights.

Slavery occurs when someone is forced to work with the threat of mental or physical punishment, is dehumanized and is treated as a commodity and denied freedom of movement. It is currently estimated that 20.9 million people across the world still have their rights abused in this way.

Anti-Slavery International's aim is to eradicate all forms of contemporary slavery including human trafficking, forced labour, bonded labour, the worst forms of child labour and forced marriage. Anti-Slavery International also runs projects to combat descent-based slavery in Niger, Mauritania and Mali, in West Africa. Anti-Slavery International does this by working with current and former victims of slavery, and working closely with local partners, benefiting from their experience and empowering them to combat slavery.

To find out more visit www.antislavery.org.

anti-slavery

**today's fight for tomorrow's freedom**

For Product Safety Concerns and Information please contact our EU representative GPSR@taylorandfrancis.com Taylor & Francis Verlag GmbH, Kaufingerstraße 24, 80331 München, Germany